THE WORKS OF JOHN MILTON

THE WORKS OF JOHN MILTON

VOLUME XVI

NEW YORK
Columbia University Press
1934

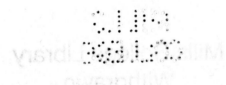

EDITORIAL BOARD

FRANK ALLEN PATTERSON
GENERAL EDITOR

ALLAN ABBOTT

HARRY MORGAN AYRES

DONALD LEMEN CLARK

JOHN ERSKINE

WILLIAM HALLER

GEORGE PHILIP KRAPP

W. P. TRENT

CONTENTS

De Doctrina Christiana
(*Continued*)

EDITED, WITH THE TRANSLATION OF
CHARLES R. SUMNER, D.D., BY JAMES HOLLY HANFORD
AND WALDO HILARY DUNN

DE DOCTRINA CHRISTIANA
[CONTINUED]

IOANNIS MILTONI

ANGLI

De Doctrina Christiana

EX SACRIS DUNTAXAT LIBRIS PETITA DISQUISITIONUM
LIBRI DUO POSTHUMI.

LIBER PRIMUS.

CAPUT XXI.

DE INSITIONE IN CHRISTUM, EIUSQUE EFFECTIS.

DICTUM est de REGENERATIONE EIUSQUE EFFECTIS, resipiscentia nimirum et fide: sequitur INSITIO IN CHRISTUM, qua Deus pater fideles Christo inserit, id est, Christi compotes reddit, porroque idoneos, qui in
5 unum corpus tandem cum Christo coalescant. Matt. xv. 13. *omnis planta quam non plantavit pater meus cœlestis, eradicabitur.* Ioan. xv. 1, 2. *ego sum vitis illa vera, et pater meus est agricola. omnem palmitem in me non ferentem fructum, tollit.* 1 Cor. i. 30. *ex ipso vos estis in Christo Iesu, qui factus*
10 *est nobis sapientia a Deo, iustitiaque et sanctificatio et redemptio.* et iii. 22, 23. *omnia vestra sunt. vos autem Christi, Christus vero Dei est.* Eph. i. 3. *qui benedixit nobis omni*

JOHN MILTON

AN ENGLISHMAN

His Christian Doctrine

COMPILED FROM THE HOLY SCRIPTURES ALONE
IN TWO POSTHUMOUS BOOKS.

BOOK ONE.

CHAPTER XXI.

OF BEING INGRAFTED IN CHRIST,
AND ITS EFFECTS.

REGENERATION AND ITS EFFECTS, repentance and
faith, have been considered. Next follows INGRAFT-
ING IN CHRIST.

Believers are said TO BE INGRAFTED IN CHRIST, when they are
5 planted in Christ by God the Father, that is, are made partakers of Christ, and meet for becoming one with him. Matt.
xv. 13. "every plant, which my heavenly Father hath not
planted, shall be rooted up." John xv. 1, 2. "I am the true
vine, and my Father is the husbandman: every branch in me
10 that beareth not fruit, he taketh away." 1 Cor. i. 30. "of him
are ye in Christ Jesus, who of God is made unto us wisdom,
and righteousness, and sanctification, and redemption." iii.
22, 23. "all are yours, and ye are Christ's, and Christ is

benedictione spirituali in cœlis in Christo. Heb. iii. 14. *Christi participes facti sumus.*

Regenerationis simul et insitionis huius effecta communia sunt VITA NOVA et AUCTIO. Quod enim in lapsu hominis erat
5 mors spiritualis eiusque progressus, ut de pœna peccati supra ostendimus, id nunc in restitutione hominis est vita nova spiritualis eiusque auctio.

VITA NOVA est qua dicimur Deo vivere. 2 Cor. iv. 10. *ut vita illa Iesu in corpore nostro manifesta fiat.* Rom. vi. 11. *ita*
10 *etiam vos colligite, vos tum mortuos esse peccato, tum vero vivere Deo per Iesum Christum Dominum nostrum.* et v. 4. *ita et nos nova vita ambulemus.* et cap. viii. 13. *si spiritu actiones corporis mortificetis, vivetis.* Gal. ii. 19. *ut vivam Deo.* et v. 20. *vixit in me Christus.* Col. iii. 3. *vita vestra*
15 *abscondita est cum Christo in Deo.* 1 Pet. iv. 6. *ut viverent secundum Deum,* id est, *spiritu.*

Vocatur et abnegatio sui. Luc. ix. 23. *si quis vult me sequi, abdicet seipsum, et attollat crucem suam quotidie, et sequatur me.*

20 Vitæ novæ prima munia sunt intelligentia rerum spiritualium, et charitas sive sanctitas vitæ. Quæ duo munia quemadmodum in morte spirituali labefactata et quasi extincta sunt, ita nunc in vita nova spirituali intellectus magna ex parte luci suæ, suæ voluntas libertati in Christo restituitur.

God's." Eph. i. 3. "who hath blessed us with all spiritual blessings in heavenly places in Christ." Heb. iii. 14. "we are made partakers of Christ."

Of this ingrafting, combined with regeneration, the effects are NEWNESS OF LIFE and INCREASE. For the new spiritual life and its increase bear the same relation to the restoration of man, which spiritual death and its progress (as described above, on the punishment of sin) bear to his fall.

NEWNESS OF LIFE is that by which we are said to live unto God. 2 Cor. iv. 10. "that the life also of Jesus might be made manifest in our body." Rom. vi. 11. "likewise reckon ye also yourselves to be dead indeed unto sin, but alive unto God through Jesus Christ our Lord." v. 4. "even so we also should walk in newness of life." viii. 13. "if ye through the Spirit do mortify the deeds of the body, ye shall live." Gal. ii. 19. "that I might live unto God." v. 20. "Christ liveth in me." Col. iii. 3. "your life is hid with Christ in God." 1 Pet. iv. 6. "that they might live according to God," that is, "in the Spirit."

This is also called self-denial. Luke ix. 23. "if any man will come after me, let him deny himself, and take up his cross daily, and follow me."

The primary functions of the new life are comprehension of spiritual things, and love of holiness. And as the power of exercising these functions was weakened and in a manner destroyed by the spiritual death, so is the understanding restored in great part to its primitive clearness, and the will to its primitive liberty, by the new spiritual life in Christ.

INTELLIGENTIA RERUM SPIRITUALIUM est INGENITUS A DEO HA-
BITUS QUO FIDELES CHRISTOQUE INSITI DISCUSSIS NATIVÆ IGNORAN-
TIÆ TENEBRIS ET ILLUMINATO AD CŒLESTIA PERCIPIENDA INTEL-
LECTU OMNIA AD SALUTEM ÆTERNAM VITAMQUE VERE BEATAM
5 NECESSARIA, EDOCTI A DEO, SCIUNT.

A DEO. Ier. xxxi. 33, 34. *indam legem meam menti eorum,
et cordi eorum inscribam eam: non autem docebunt amplius
quisque amicum suum, et quisque fratrem suum, dicendo,
cognoscite Iehovam; nam quotquot erunt cognoscent me a*
10 *minimo eorum usque ad maximum eorum, dictum Iehovæ,
me condonare iniquitatem ipsorum, et peccati ipsorum non
recordari amplius.* Isa. liv. 13. *et omnes filii tui edocti erunt
a Deo.* a patre nimirum; sic enim interpretatur Christus Ioan.
vi. 45. *scriptum est in prophetis, et erunt omnes docti a Deo.*
15 *quisquis ergo audivit a patre et didicit, venit ad me.* Matt. xvi.
17. *caro et sanguis hæc non retexit tibi sed pater meus.* Sic
1 Thess. iv. 9. *de fraterno amore non necesse habemus scribere vobis; ipsi namque divinitus docti estis ut diligatis alii
alios.*

20 Per filium. Matt. xi. 27. *omnia mihi tradita sunt a patre
meo; et nemo novit filium nisi pater, neque patrem quisquam
novit nisi filius, et cuicunque voluerit filius eum retegere.*
Col. iii. 16. *sermo Christi inhabitet in vobis copiose cum
omni sapientia.*

THE COMPREHENSION OF SPIRITUAL THINGS IS A HABIT OR CONDITION OF MIND PRODUCED BY GOD, WHEREBY THE NATURAL IGNORANCE OF THOSE WHO BELIEVE AND ARE INGRAFTED IN CHRIST IS REMOVED, AND THEIR UNDERSTANDINGS ENLIGHTENED FOR THE

5 PERCEPTION OF HEAVENLY THINGS, SO THAT, BY THE TEACHING OF GOD, THEY KNOW ALL THAT IS NECESSARY FOR ETERNAL SALVATION AND THE TRUE HAPPINESS OF LIFE.

BY THE TEACHING OF GOD. Jer. xxxi. 33, 34. "I will put my law in their inward parts, and write it in their hearts; and

10 will be their God, and they shall be my people: and they shall teach no more every man his neighbor, and every man his brother, saying, Know Jehovah: for they shall all know me, from the least of them unto the greatest of them, saith Jehovah: for I will forgive their iniquity, and I will remember

15 their sin no more." Isa. liv. 13. "all thy children shall be taught of God," namely, of God the Father, for so Christ explains it, John vi. 45. "it is written in the prophets, And they shall be all taught of God: every man therefore that hath heard, and hath learned of the Father, cometh unto me."

20 Matt. xvi. 17. "flesh and blood hath not revealed it unto thee, but my Father which is in heaven." 1 Thess. iv. 9. "as touching brotherly love ye need not that I write unto you; for ye yourselves are taught of God to love one another."

By the Son. Matt. xi. 27. "all things are delivered unto me

25 of my Father; and no man knoweth the Son but the Father, neither knoweth any man the Father, save the Son, and he to whomsoever the Son will reveal him." Col. iii. 16. "let the word of Christ dwell in you richly in all wisdom."

Et per spiritum sanctum. Ioan. xvi. 13. *spiritus ille veri-*
tatis dux viæ vobis erit in omnem veritatem, non enim loque-
tur a semetipso—. 1 Cor. ii. 10, &c. *nobis Deus ea revelavit*
per spiritum suum—. Animalis homo non est capax eorum
5 *quæ sunt spiritus Dei: sunt enim ei stultitia, nec potest ea*
cognoscere, quia spiritualiter diiudicantur. at spiritualis di-
iudicat quidem omnia, ipse vero a nemine diiudicatur. 1 Ioan.
ii. 20, 27. *vos unctionem habetis a sancto illo profectam, et*
nostis omnia; unctio quam vos accepistis ab eo, manet in vobis,
10 *nec necesse habetis a quoquam doceri vos: verum sicut eadem*
unctio docet vos de omnibus, quæ et verax est et non mendax;
et sicut docuit vos, manebitis in eo.

NECESSARIA AD SALUTEM. 1 Cor. ii. 12. *ut sciamus quæ Deus*
est nobis gratificatus. Tit i. 1, 2. *et agnitionem veritatis quæ*
15 *est secundum pietatem; ad spem vitæ æternæ—.*

Perfecta tamen in hac vita non est. 1 Cor. xiii. 9. *ex parte*
enim cognoscimus—.

Alterum effectum est CHARITAS EX SENSU DIVINI AMORIS IN
CORDA REGENITORUM PER SPIRITUM EFFUSI, QUA AFFECTI QUI IN
20 CHRISTUM INSERUNTUR, PECCATO MORTUI, DEO REDIVIVI, SUA
SPONTE AC LIBERE BONA OPERA PARTURIUNT. Eademque SANCTI-
TAS dicitur. Eph. i. 4. *ut simus sancti et inculpati in conspectu*
eius cum charitate.

Nam de charitate fraterna hic non agimus; cum hæc potius

And by the Holy Spirit. John xvi. 13. "when he, the Spirit of truth, is come, he will guide you into all truth, for he shall not speak of himself." 1 Cor. ii. 10, &c. "God hath revealed them unto us by his Spirit . . . the natural man receiveth
5 not the things of the Spirit of God; for they are foolishness unto him; neither can he know them, because they are spiritually discerned: but he that is spiritual judgeth all things, yet he himself is judged of no man." 1 John ii. 20, 27. "ye have an unction from the Holy One, and ye know all things
10 . . . the anointing which ye have received of him abideth in you, and ye need not that any man teach you; but as the same anointing teacheth you of all things, and is truth, and is no lie, and even as it hath taught you, ye shall abide in him."

NECESSARY TO SALVATION. 1 Cor. ii. 12. "that we might know
15 the things that are freely given to us of God." Tit. i. 1, 2. "the acknowledging of the truth which is after godliness, in hope of eternal life."

In the present life, however, we can only attain to an imperfect comprehension of spiritual things. 1 Cor. xiii. 9. "we
20 know in part."

The other effect is LOVE OR CHARITY, ARISING FROM A SENSE OF THE DIVINE LOVE SHED ABROAD IN THE HEARTS OF THE REGENERATE BY THE SPIRIT, WHEREBY THOSE WHO ARE INGRAFTED IN CHRIST BEING INFLUENCED, BECOME DEAD TO SIN, AND ALIVE
25 AGAIN UNTO GOD, AND BRING FORTH GOOD WORKS SPONTANEOUSLY AND FREELY. This is also called HOLINESS. Eph. i. 4. "that we should be holy and without blame before him in love."

The love here intended is not brotherly love, which belongs

dilectio Dei sit, neque ea solum qua nos Deum diligimus, sed ex eius dilectionis, qua is nos diligit, instinctu atque sensu, illa virtus quæ theologica nominatur post fidem et spem tertia: 1 Cor. xiii. 13. *nunc vero manet fides, spes, charitas, tria hæc;*
5 *maxima autem harum charitas:* et fidei quasi filia est, bonorumque operum quasi mater; Gal. v. 6. *fides per charitatem efficax.* Hæc describitur, 1 Cor. xiii. et 1 Ioan. iv. 16. *nos cognovimus et credidimus charitatem quam habet Deus erga nos: Deus charitas est; et qui manet in charitate in Deo*
10 *manet, et Deus in eo.*

PER SPIRITUM EFFUSI. Ezech. xxxvi. 27. *spiritum meum ponam in medio vestri, quo faciam ut in statutis meis ambuletis—.* Rom. v. 5. *spes non pudefacit eo quod charitas Dei effusa est in cordibus nostris per spiritum sanctum qui datus*
15 *est nobis.* Gal. v. 22. *fructus spiritus est charitas.*

QUI IN CHRISTUM INSERUNTUR. Ioan. xv. 4, 5. *manete in me, et ego in vobis manebo: sicut palmes non potest ferre fructum a semetipso, nisi manserit in vite; ita nec vos, nisi in me manseritis: ego sum vitis, vos palmites: is qui manet in me, et*
20 *in quo ego maneo, hic fert fructum multum: nam seorsim a me nihil potestis facere;* Eph. iii. 17, &c. *inhabitet Christus per fidem in cordibus vestris: ut in charitate radicati ac fundati* &c.

PECCATO MORTUI. Rom. vi. 22. *nunc vero liberati a peccato,*
25 *servi autem facti Deo, habetis fructum vestrum ad sanctimoniam.* 1 Pet. ii. 24. *ut peccato mortui, iustitiæ viveremus.*

to another place; nor even the ordinary affection which we bear to God, but one resulting from a consciousness and lively sense of the love wherewith he has loved us, and which in theology is reckoned the third after faith and hope. 1 Cor.
5 xiii. 13. "now abideth faith, hope, charity, these three; but the greatest of these is charity." This is the offspring, as it were, of faith, and the parent of good works. Gal. v. 6. "faith which worketh by love." It is described 1 Cor. xiii. and 1 John iv. 16. "we have known and believed the love that God hath
10 to us: God is love, and he that dwelleth in love dwelleth in God, and God in him."

SHED BY THE SPIRIT. Ezek. xxxvi. 27. "I will put my Spirit within you, and cause you to walk in my statutes." Rom. v. 5. "hope maketh not ashamed, because the love of God is shed
15 abroad in our hearts by the Holy Ghost which is given unto us." Gal. v. 22. "the fruit of the Spirit is love."

WHO ARE INGRAFTED IN CHRIST. John xv. 4, 5. "abide in me, and I in you: as the branch cannot bear fruit of itself, except it abide in the vine, no more can ye, except ye abide in me: I
20 am the vine, ye are the branches; he that abideth in me, and I in him, the same bringeth forth much fruit: for without me ye can do nothing." Eph. iii. 17, &c. "that Christ may dwell in your hearts by faith, that ye being rooted and grounded in love," &c.
25 DEAD UNTO SIN. Rom. vi. 22. "but now being made free from sin, and become servants to God, ye have your fruit unto holiness." 1 Pet. ii. 24. "that we, being dead to sins, should live unto righteousness."

DEO REDIVIVI. Rom. vi. 12, 13. *sistite vos Deo, ut ex mortuis vivos.*

SUA SPONTE AC LIBERE. nostra enim opera passim requiritur. Ezech. xviii. 31. *facite vobis cor novum et spiritum novum:*
5 *nam quare moreremini o domus Israelis.* Rom. vi. 12, 13. *ne regnato peccatum in mortali corpore vestro, ut auscultetis ei in cupiditatibus corporis; neque sistite membra vestra arma iniustitiæ peccato.* et xii. 2. *ne vos configurate sæculo isti; sed transformate vos per renovationem mentis vestræ ad hoc*
10 *ut probetis quæ sit voluntas Dei, bona illa, placens ac perfecta.* 2 Cor. vii. 1. *has igitur promissiones quum habeamus dilecti, purificemus nos ab omni inquinamento carnis ac spiritus, perficientes sanctitatem in timore Dei.* Gal. v. 16. *spiritu ambulate, et quod concupiscit caro ne perficite.* Eph. iv. 20, 21,
15 22, 23, 24. *si modo ipsum audivistis, et de eo edocti estis (sicut est veritas in Iesu) deponere quod ad pristinam conversationem attinet veterem illum hominem qui seductricibus cupiditatibus sese corrumpit; renovari vero spiritu mentis vestræ, et induere novum illum hominem, qui secundum*
20 *Deum conditus est ad iustitiam et sanctimoniam veram.* 2 Cor. vi. 1. *ne frustra gratiam Dei receperitis.* Col. iii. 5, 9, 10. *mortificate membra vestra terrestria, scortationem—: ne mentimini alius adversus alium, quum exuti sitis illo veteri homine cum factis ipsius, et induti sitis novo illo qui reno-*
25 *vatur in agnitionem congruentem imagini eius qui ipsum condidit.* 2 Tim. ii. 21. *si quis sese ab his expurgarit, erit vas ad decus sanctificatum et accommodum usibus Domini,*

ALIVE AGAIN UNTO GOD. Rom. vi. 12, 13. "yield yourselves unto God, as those that are alive from the dead."

SPONTANEOUSLY AND FREELY; for our own cooperation is uniformly required. Ezek. xviii. 31. "make you a new heart,
5 and a new spirit; for why will ye die, O house of Israel?" Rom. vi. 12, 13. "let not sin therefore reign in your mortal body, that ye should obey it in the lusts thereof, neither yield ye your members as instruments of unrighteousness unto sin." xii. 2. "be not conformed to this world, but be ye transformed by the
10 renewing of your mind, that ye may prove what is that good and acceptable and perfect will of God." 2 Cor. vii. 1. "having therefore these promises, dearly beloved, let us cleanse ourselves from all filthiness of the flesh and spirit, perfecting holiness in the fear of God." Gal. v. 16. "walk in the Spirit,
15 and ye shall not fulfil the lust of the flesh." Eph. iv. 20–24. "if so be that ye have heard him, and have been taught by him, as the truth is in Jesus: that ye put off concerning the former conversation the old man, which is corrupt according to the deceitful lusts, and be renewed in the spirit of your mind;
20 and that ye put on the new man, which after God is created in righteousness and true holiness." 2 Cor. vi. 1. "receive not the grace of God in vain." Col. iii. 5, 9, 10. "mortify therefore your members which are upon the earth; fornication," &c. "lie not one to another, seeing that ye have put off the old
25 man with his deeds, and have put on the new man, which is renewed in knowledge after the image of him that created him." 2 Tim. ii. 21. "if a man therefore purge himself from these, he shall be a vessel unto honor, sanctified and meet for

et ad omne opus bonum comparatum. 1 Ioan. ii. 3. *per hoc*
scimus nos Deum scire, si præcepta eius observemus. et iii. 3.
quisquis habet hanc spem in eo sitam, purum se conservat—.

Ex hac charitate seu sanctitate omnes fideles SANCTI nomi-
5 nantur. Philipp. iv. 21, 22. *salutate omnes sanctos in Christo*
Iesu—: et passim.

Sanctorum autem in hac vita sanctitas imperfecta utcunque
est. Psal. cxliii. 2. *at ne congrediaris iudicio cum servo tuo,*
nam non esset iustus coram te ullus vivens. et cxxx. 3. *iniqui-*
10 *tates observaveris, Iah, Domine, quis possit consistere.* Prov.
xx. 9. *quis dicere possit, purificavi animum meum, mundus*
sum a peccato meo? et xxiv. 16. *septies cadit iustus; exsurgit*
tamen. Rom. vii. 18, &c. *novi non habitare in me (id est*
in carne mea) bonum; nam velle adest mihi, sed ut quod
15 *bonum est perficiam, non assequor—.* Gal. v. 17. *caro con-*
cupiscit adversus spiritum; spiritus autem adversus carnem:
hæc autem inter se opposita sunt, ut non quæcunque volueritis
eadem faciatis. Iacob. iii. 2. *in multis impingimus omnes.*
si quis in sermone non impingit, hic perfectus est vir. 1 Ioan.
20 i. 8. *si dixerimus nos peccatum non habere, nos ipsos fallimus,*
et veritas in nobis non est.

Hactenus de vita nova eiusque effectis. Dicendum nunc
est de regenerati hominis AUCTIONE.

Estque ea vel absoluta sive interna vel relata sive externa.
25 Absoluta est A DEO PATRE eorum donorum auctio quæ per

the master's use, and prepared unto every good work."
1 John ii. 3. "hereby we do know that we know him, if we
keep his commandments." iii. 3. "every man that hath this
hope in him, purifieth himself, even as he is pure."

5   In consequence of this love or sanctity all believers are
called SAINTS. Philipp. iv. 21, 22. "salute every saint in Christ
Jesus"; and to the same effect in other passages.

    The holiness of the saints is nevertheless imperfect in this
life. Psal. cxliii. 2. "enter not into judgment with thy servant,
10 for in thy sight shall no man living be justified." cxxx. 3. "if
thou, Jah, shouldest mark iniquities, O Lord, who shall
stand?" Prov. xx. 9. "who can say, I have made my heart
clean, I am pure from my sin?" xxiv. 16. "a just man falleth
seven times, and riseth up again." Rom. vii. 18, &c. "I know
15 that in me, that is, in my flesh, dwelleth no good thing; for
to will is present with me; but how to perform that which is
good, I know not." Gal. v. 17. "the flesh lusteth against the
Spirit, and the Spirit against the flesh; and these are contrary
the one to the other: so that ye cannot do the things that ye
20 would." James iii. 2. "in many things we offend all: if any
man offend not in word, the same is a perfect man." 1 John
i. 8. "if we say that we have no sin, we deceive ourselves, and
the truth is not in us."

    Thus far of newness of life and its effects. It remains to
25 speak of THE INCREASE operated in the regenerate. This increase is either absolute, which is internal, or relative, which
is external.

    Absolute increase is an increase DERIVED FROM GOD THE

regenerationem et insitionem in Christum accepimus. 2 Cor.
x. 15. *augescente fide vestra.*

A DEO PATRE. Ioan. xv. 2. *et omnem palmitem qui fert*
fructum purgat, ut plus fructus adferat. Philipp. i. 3, 6.
5 *gratias ago Deo meo—, ut qui incepit in vobis opus bonum,*
perficiat illud usque ad diem Iesu Christi. 2 Thess. i. 3.
gratias agere debemus Deo semper de vobis, ut par est, quod
vehementer augescat fides vestra, et abundet mutua unius-
cuiusque omnium vestrum charitas. Heb. xiii. 20, 21. *Deus*
10 *vero pacis— compingat vos in omni opere bono, ad præ-*
standam ipsius voluntatem—.

Per filium. Heb. xiii. 21. *efficiens in vobis quod gratum*
sit in conspectu suo, per Iesum Christum. et cap. xii. 7. *intu-*
entes in fidei ducem ac consummatorem Iesum. hinc Luc.
15 xvii. 5. *dixerunt discipuli Domino, adauge nobis fidem.*

Spiritualis auctio, contra atque fit in auctione physica,
aliqua ex parte penes ipsos regeneratos esse videtur. 2 Cor.
iv. 16. *propterea non segnescimus, sed etiamsi externus homo*
noster corrumpitur, internus tamen renovatur indies. Eph.
20 iv. 15. *sincere nos gerentes cum charitate, prorsus augesca-*
mus in eum qui est caput Christus. Philipp. iii. 12. *non quod*
iam metam apprehenderim, aut iam sim consummatus; sed
persequor experiens an ipse quoque apprehendam—. Heb.
v. 13, 14. *cui cum lacte res est, is rudis est sermonis iustitiæ*

FATHER of those gifts which we have received by regeneration and ingrafting in Christ. 2 Cor. x. 15. "when your faith is increased."

DERIVED FROM GOD THE FATHER. John xv. 2. "every branch
5 that beareth fruit, he purgeth it, that it may bring forth more fruit." Philipp. i. 3, 6. "I thank my God . . . that he which hath begun a good work in you, will perform it until the day of Jesus Christ." 2 Thess. i. 3. "we are bound to thank God always for you, brethren, as it is meet, because that your faith
10 groweth exceedingly, and the charity of every one of you all toward each other aboundeth." Heb. xiii. 20, 21. "the God of peace . . . make you perfect in every good work, to do his will."

Through the Son. Heb. xiii. 21. "working in you that
15 which is well-pleasing in his sight, through Jesus Christ." xii. 2. "looking unto Jesus, the author and finisher of our faith." So also Luke xvii. 5. "the apostles said unto the Lord, Increase our faith."

Spiritual increase, unlike physical growth, appears to be
20 to a certain degree in the power of the regenerate themselves. 2 Cor. iv. 16. "for which cause we faint not; but though our outward man perish, yet the inward man is renewed day by day." Eph. iv. 15. "speaking the truth in love, may grow up into him in all things, which is the head, even Christ."
25 Philipp. iii. 12. "not as though I had already attained, either were already perfect; but I follow after, if that I may apprehend that for which also I am apprehended of Christ Jesus." Heb. v. 13, 14. "every one that useth milk is unskilful in the

(infans enim est) sed adultorum est solidus cibus, eorum vide-
licet, qui propter habitum sensus habent exercitatos ad discre-
tionem boni et mali. 1 Pet. ii. 2. *ut modo geniti infantes, lac*
illud sermonis sincerum expetite, ut per illud augescatis. et
5 2 Ep. iii. 18. *crescite in gratia et notitia Domini nostri, et*
servatoris Iesu Christi.

Et auctio quidem hactenus. Perfecto autem in hac vita
quamquam speranda non est, ad perfectionem tamen veluti ad
finem ultimum eniti et contendere debemus. Matt. v. 48.
10 *estote vos perfecti, ut pater vester qui est in cœlis perfectus est.*
2 Cor. xiii. 11. idem. Col. i. 28. *ut sistamus omnem homi-*
nem perfectum in Christo Iesu. et iv. 12. *ut stetis perfecti et*
completi in omni voluntate Dei. Iacob. i. 4. *ut sitis integri et*
toti, in nullo deficientes.

15 Unde illa lucta carnis et spiritus in homine regenerato.
Gal. v. 16. *spiritu ambulate, et quod concupiscit caro ne per-*
ficite. 1 Tim. vi. 12. *decerta præclarum illud certamen fidei.*
et 2 Ep. iv. 7. *certavi.* et contra mundum et Satanam. Ioan.
vii. 7. *mundus me odit, quoniam ego testor de eo, opera eius*
20 *mala esse.* et xv. 18, 19. *si mundus vos odit, scitis me prius-*
quam vos illis odio habitum. et xvii. 14. idem. Rom. xii. 2.
ne configurate vos sæculo isti—. Gal. vi. 14. *per quem*
mundus mihi crucifixus est, et ego mundo. Iacob. iv. 4. *adul-*
teri et adulteræ nescitis amicitiam mundi inimicitiam esse
25 *adversus Deum? quicunque ergo voluerit amicus esse mundi*

word of righteousness; for he is a babe: but strong meat belongeth to them that are of full age, even those who by reason of use have their senses exercised to discern both good and evil." 1 Pet. ii. 2. "as new born babes, desire the sincere milk
5 of the word, that ye may grow thereby." 2 Pet. iii. 18. "grow in grace and in the knowledge of our Lord and Savior Jesus Christ."

Thus much of increase. With regard to perfection, although not to be expected in the present life, it is our duty to strive
10 after it with earnestness, as the ultimate object of our existence. Matt. v. 48. "be ye therefore perfect, as your Father which is in heaven is perfect." See also 2 Cor. xiii. 11. Col. i. 28. "that we may present every man perfect in Christ Jesus." iv. 12. "that ye may stand perfect and complete in all the will
15 of God." James i. 4. "that ye may be perfect and entire, wanting nothing."

Hence the struggle between the flesh and the Spirit in the regenerate. Gal. v. 16. "walk in the Spirit, and ye shall not fulfil the lust of the flesh." 1 Tim. vi. 12. "fight the good
20 fight of faith." 2 Tim. iv. 7. "I have fought a good fight." A similar struggle is maintained against the world and Satan. John vii. 7. "the world hateth me, because I testify of it, that the works thereof are evil." xv. 18, 19. "if the world hate you, ye know that it hated me before it hated you." See also
25 xvii. 14. Rom. xii. 2. "be not conformed to this world." Gal. vi. 14. "by whom the world is crucified unto me, and I unto the world." James iv. 4. "ye adulterers and adulteresses, know ye not that the friendship of the world is enmity with God?

inimicus Dei constituitur. I Ioan. iii. 13. *ne miramini, fratres mei, si odit vos mundus.*

Et victoria. Apoc. ii. 7. *victori dabo edere——.* et v. 26. *auctoritatem inter gentes.* et cap. iii. 5. *amicietur vestibus* 5 *albis.* v. 12. *qui vicerit faciam ut is sit columna in templo Dei mei.* et 21. *qui vicerit tribuam ei ut sedeat mecum in throno meo, ut et ego vici, et sedeo cum patre meo in throno eius.* et cap. xxi. 7. *victor hæreditario iure obtinebit omnia et ero ei Deus, et ipse erit mihi filius.* Mundi. I Ioan. ii. 15. 10 et v. 4. *quicquid natum est ex Deo vincit mundum: et hæc est victoria quæ vicit mundum, nempe fides nostra.* Mortis. Prov. xii. 28. *in itinere iustitiæ est vita, et via semitæ eius immortalis est.* et xiv. 32. *recipit se in morte sua iustus.* Ioan. viii. 51. *si quis sermonem meum observaverit, mortem non* 15 *conspiciet in æternum.* Apoc. ii. 11. *qui vicerit, nequaquam lædetur a morte secunda.* et xiv. 13. *beati ab hoc tempore mortui ii, qui Domini causa moriuntur.——.* Satanæ. Eph. vi. 10, &c. *corroboramini in Domino—— ut possitis stare adversus artes diaboli——: contra quem* πανοπλία *induimur ibidem.* 20 Iacob. iv. 7. *obsistite diabolo, et fugiet a vobis.* I Ioan. ii. 14. *improbum illum vicistis.* Apoc. xii. 11. *sed ipsi vicerunt eum per sanguinem agni, et per sermonem testimonii sui.*

whosoever therefore will be a friend of the world is the enemy
of God." 1 John iii. 13. "marvel not, my brethren, if the
world hate you."

There is also a victory to be gained. Rev. ii. 7. "to him that
5 overcometh will I give to eat of the tree of life." v. 26. "he
that overcometh . . . to him will I give power over the
nations." iii. 5. "he that overcometh, the same shall be
clothed in white raiment." v. 12. "him that overcometh will
I make a pillar in the temple of my God." v. 21. "to him
10 that overcometh will I grant to sit with me in my throne, even
as I also overcame and am set down with my Father in his
throne." xxi. 7. "he that overcometh shall inherit all things,
and I will be his God, and he shall be my son." Over the
world; 1 John ii. 15. and v. 4. "whatsoever is born of God
15 overcometh the world, and this is the victory that overcometh the world, even our faith." Over death; Prov. xii. 28. "in
the way of righteousness is life, and in the pathway thereof
there is no death." xiv. 32. "the righteous hath hope in his
death." John viii. 51. "if a man keep my saying, he shall
20 never see death." Rev. ii. 11. "he that overcometh shall not
be hurt of the second death." xiv. 13. "blessed are the dead
which die in the Lord from henceforth." Over Satan; Eph.
vi. 10, &c. "be strong in the Lord . . . that ye may be able
to stand against the wiles of the devil": being clothed with
25 "the whole armor of God" to oppose him. James iv. 7. "resist
the devil, and he will flee from you." 1 John ii. 14. "ye have
overcome the wicked one." Rev. xii. 11. "they overcame him
by the blood of the Lamb, and by the word of their testimony."

Qua ratione qui in ista lucta strenue agunt, et ad perfectionem in Christo consequendam serio atque assidue nituntur,
imperfecti revera ut sint, imputatione tamen et misericordia
Dei, *perfecti* sæpe in scripturis, et *inculpati,* et *non peccare*
5 dicuntur; quia peccatum in iis ut hæreat non regnat tamen.
Gen. vi. 9. *Noach, vir iustus, integer erat in ætatibus suis.* et
xvii. 1. *indesinenter ambula coram me, et esto integer.* 1 Reg.
xv. 14. *excelsa quidem non amota sunt; sed animus Asæ fuit
integer erga Iehovam omnibus diebus eius.* 2 Chron. xv. 17.
10 idem. Phil. iii. 15. *quot itaque perfecti sumus, hoc sentiamus.*
Heb. x. 14. *unica enim oblatione consummavit in perpetuum
eos qui sanctificantur.* 1 Ioan. iii. 6. *quisquis in eo manet,
non peccat.* et v. 18. idem. Col. ii. 2. *ut consolationem accipiant eorum corda, instructi in charitate, et in omnes divitias
15 plenitudinis intellectus, in agnitionem mysterii Dei ac patris
et Christi.* Eph. iii. 18, 19. *ut in charitate radicati ac fundati,
valeatis comprehendere cum omnibus sanctis quæ sit illa
latitudo et longitudo et profunditas et sublimitas; et nosse
charitatem illam Christi, omni notitia supereminentiorem; ut
20 impleamini ad omnem usque plenitudinem illam Dei.*

Hence such as are strenuous in this conflict, and earnestly and unceasingly labor to attain perfection in Christ, though they be really imperfect, are yet, by imputation and through the divine mercy, frequently called in Scripture "perfect,"
5 and "blameless," and "without sin"; inasmuch as sin, though still dwelling in them, does not reign over them. Gen. vi. 9. "Noah was a just man and perfect in his generations." xvii. 1. "walk before me, and be thou perfect." 1 Kings xv. 14. "the high places were not removed; nevertheless Asa's heart was
10 perfect with Jehovah all his days." See also 2 Chron. xv. 17. Philipp. iii. 15. "let us therefore as many as be perfect, be thus minded." Heb. x. 14. "by one offering he hath perfected for ever them that are sanctified." 1 John iii. 6. "whosoever abideth in him sinneth not." See also v. 18. Col. ii. 2. "that
15 their hearts might be comforted, being knit together in love, and unto all riches of the full assurance of understanding, to the acknowledgment of the mystery of God and of the Father, and of Christ." Eph. iii. 18, 19, "that ye being rooted and grounded in love, may be able to comprehend with all saints
20 what is the breadth and length and depth and height, and to know the love of Christ, which passeth knowledge, that ye might be filled with all the fulness of God."

CAPUT XXII.

DE IUSTIFICATIONE.

FUIT auctio regenerati hominis absoluta sive interna: sequitur relata sive externa.

Est autem vel ad patrem solum relata vel ad patrem et filium.

5 Relata ad patrem solum est IUSTIFICATIO et ADOPTIO. Rom. viii. 30. *quos prædestinavit, eos etiam vocavit; et quos vocavit, eos etiam iustificavit—.*

IUSTIFICATIO est SENTENTIA DEI GRATUITA QUA REGENERATI, CHRISTOQUE INSITI PROPTER EIUS PLENISSIMAM SATISFACTIONEM
10 PECCATIS ET MORTE ABSOLVUNTUR, ET IUSTI CORAM DEO NON EX OPERIBUS LEGIS SED PER FIDEM REPUTANTUR.

GRATUITA. Rom. iii. 24. *ut qui iustificentur gratis, eius gratia, per redemptionem factam in Christo Iesu.* et v. 16, 17. *neque ut illud quod introiit per unum qui peccavit, ita est*
15 *quod donatur: nam reatus quidem est ex una offensa ad condemnationem; quod autem gratificatur Deus est ex multis offensis ad iustificationem. etenim si per unam offensam, mors regnavit per unum, multo magis ii qui exundantiam illam gratiæ et doni iustitiæ recipiunt, in vita regnabunt per*
20 *unum Iesum Christum.* Tit. iii. 7. *iustificati illius gratia.*

DEI. patris nempe. Rom. iii. 25, 26. *quem proposuit Deus*

CHAPTER XXII.

OF JUSTIFICATION.

HAVING considered the absolute or internal increase of the regenerate, I proceed to speak of that which is relative or external.

This increase has reference either to the Father exclusively,
5 or to the Father and Son conjointly.

That which has reference to the Father exclusively is termed JUSTIFICATION and ADOPTION. Rom. viii. 30. "whom he did predestinate, them he also called, and whom he called, them he also justified—."

10   JUSTIFICATION IS THE GRATUITOUS PURPOSE OF GOD, WHEREBY THOSE WHO ARE REGENERATE AND INGRAFTED IN CHRIST ARE ABSOLVED FROM SIN AND DEATH THROUGH HIS MOST PERFECT SATISFACTION, AND ACCOUNTED JUST IN THE SIGHT OF GOD, NOT BY THE WORKS OF THE LAW, BUT THROUGH FAITH.

15   THE GRATUITOUS PURPOSE. Rom. iii. 24. "being justified freely by his grace, through the redemption that is in Christ Jesus." v. 16, 17. "not as it was by one that sinned, so is the gift: for the judgment was by one to condemnation, but the free gift is of many offences unto justification: for if by one
20 man's offence death reigned by one, much more they which receive abundance of grace and of the gift of righteousness shall reign in life by one, Jesus Christ." Tit. iii. 7. "being justified by his grace."

OF GOD, that is, the Father. Rom. iii. 25, 26. "whom God

placamentum per fidem in sanguine ipsius, ad demonstra-
tionem iustitiæ suæ, prætereundo peccata, quæ antecesserunt,
in illa Dei tolerantia: ad demonstrationem iustitiæ suæ præ-
senti tempore; ut sit ipse iustus, et iustificans eum qui est ex
5 *fide Iesu.* et viii. 33, 34. *Deus is est qui iustificat—.* In filio
per spiritum. 1 Cor. vi. 11. *sed abluti estis, sed sanctificati*
estis, sed iustificati estis in nomine Domini Iesu, et per spiri-
tum Dei nostri.

PROPTER CHRISTI SATISFACTIONEM. Isa. liii. 11. *cognitione sui,*
10 *iustificabit iustus servus meus multos; et iniquitates eorum ipse*
baiulabit. Rom. v. 9. *iustificati igitur nunc eius sanguine,*
servabimur multo magis per eum ab ira illa. et v. 19. *per*
unius obedientiam iusti constituentur multi. et cap. x. 4.
finis legis est Christus ad iustitiam cuivis credenti.

15   Itaque ut peccata nostra imputantur Christo, sic iustitia
sive merita Christi per fidem imputantur nobis. 1 Cor. i. 30.
ex ipso vos estis in Christo Iesu, qui factus est nobis sapientia
a Deo iustitiaque et sanctificatio et redemptio. et 2 Ep. v.
19, 21. *fecit ut qui non noverat peccatum, pro nobis pecca-*
20 *tum esset, ut nos efficeremur iustitia Dei in eo.* Rom. iv. 6.
sicut David declarat beatum eum hominem cui Deus imputat
iustitiam absque operibus. et v. 19. *sicut enim per illam ino-*
bedientiam unius hominis peccatores constituti sunt multi,
ita per unius obedientiam iusti constituentur multi. Iustifica-
25 tio igitur nostra nobis quidem plane gratuita est; Christo non

hath set forth to be a propitiation through faith in his blood, to declare his righteousness for the remission of sins that are passed, through the forbearance of God; to declare, I say, at this time his righteousness, that he might be just, and the

5 justifier of him that believeth in Jesus." viii. 33. "it is God that justifieth." In the Son through the Spirit. 1 Cor. vi. 11. "but ye are washed, but ye are sanctified, but ye are justified in the name of the Lord Jesus, and by the Spirit of our God."

THROUGH THE SATISFACTION OF CHRIST. Isa. liii. 11. "by his

10 knowledge shall my righteous servant justify many; for he shall bear their iniquities." Rom. v. 9. "much more then being now justified by his blood, we shall be saved from wrath through him." v. 19. "by the obedience of one shall many be made righteous." x. 4. "Christ is the end of the law for

15 righteousness to every one that believeth."

As therefore our sins are imputed to Christ, so the merits or righteousness of Christ are imputed to us through faith. 1 Cor. i. 30. "of him are ye in Christ Jesus, who of God is made unto us wisdom, and righteousness, and sanctification,

20 and redemption." 2 Cor. v. 21. "he hath made him to be sin for us who knew no sin, that we might be made the righteousness of God in him." Rom. iv. 6. "even as David also describeth the blessedness of the man unto whom God imputeth righteousness without works." v. 19. "for as by one man's

25 disobedience many were made sinners, so by the obedience of one shall many be made righteous." It is evident therefore that justification, in so far as we are concerned, is gratuitous; in so far as Christ is concerned, not gratuitous; inas-

gratuita: Ille enim peccata nostra persoluto pretio sibi impu-
tator sponte luit et expiavit; nos iustitiam eius nobis imputa-
tam nihil solventes, tantummodo credentes dono accepimus:
hinc Pater placatus omnes credentes Iustos pronuntiat nec
5 ulla ratio satisfactionis clarior aut æquior esse potuit.

Hinc *induti* dicimur. Apoc. xix. 8. *et datum est ei ut ami-*
ciatur byssina veste pura et splendida: byssus enim iustifica-
tiones sunt sanctorum. Et *amici.* Iacob. ii. 23. *credidit Abra-*
ham Deo, et imputatum est ei ad iustitiam, et amicus Dei
10 *vocatus est.*

Peccatis et morte absolvuntur. Act. x. 43. *huic etiam*
omnes prophetæ testimonium dant, remissionem peccatorum
accepturum per nomen eius quemvis qui crediderit in eum.
et xxvi. 18. *ut remissionem peccatorum et sortem inter sanc-*
15 *tificatos accipiant per fidem quæ est in me.* Rom. v. 18. *ita*
per unam iustificationem, beneficium redundavit in omnes
homines ad iustificationem vitæ. et viii. 1. *nulla igitur nunc*
est condemnatio iis qui sunt in Christo Iesu, qui non secun-
dum carnem ambulant, sed secundum spiritum. et v. 34.
20 *quis est qui condemnet? Christus is est qui mortuus est—.*
Col. ii. 14. *ac deleto quod adversum nos erat chirographum*
decretis, quod erat nobis contrarium, ipse vero cruci affixum
sustulit e medio. Peccatis autem vel maximis: 1 Cor. vi. 9,

much as Christ paid the ransom of our sins, which he took upon himself by imputation, and thus of his own accord, and at his own cost, effected their expiation; whereas man, paying nothing on his part, but merely believing, receives as a
5 gift the imputed righteousness of Christ. Finally, the Father, appeased by this propitiation, pronounces the justification of all believers. A simpler mode of satisfaction could not have been devised, nor one more agreeable to equity.

Hence we are said to be "clothed" with the righteousness
10 of Christ. Rev. xix. 8. "to her was granted that she should be arrayed in fine linen, clean and white; for the fine linen is the justification of the saints." For the same reason we are also called the "friends" of God. James ii. 23. "Abraham believed God, and it was imputed unto him for righteousness, and he
15 was called the friend of God."

ARE ABSOLVED FROM SIN AND DEATH. Acts x. 43. "to him give all the prophets witness, that through his name whosoever believeth in him shall receive remission of sins." xxvi. 18. "that they may receive forgiveness of sins and inheritance
20 among them which are sanctified by faith that is in me." Rom. v. 18. "by the righteousness of one the free gift came upon all men unto justification of life." viii. 1. "there is therefore now no condemnation to them which are in Christ Jesus, who walk not after the flesh, but after the Spirit." v. 34.
25 "who is he that condemneth? it is Christ that died—." Col. ii. 14. "blotting out the hand-writing of ordinances that was against us, which was contrary to us, and took it out of the way, nailing it to his cross." Even from the greatest sins.

10, 11. *scortatores, idololatræ—; et hæc eratis quidem, sed abluti estis, sed sanctificati estis, sed iustificati estis—.* Ier. 1. 20. *tempore illo, dictum Iehovæ, si quæratur iniquitas Israelis, nulla extabit; et peccata Iehudæ, nulla invenientur; quia* 5 *condonavero iis quos faciam reliquos.* Isa. i. 18. *si fuerint peccata vestra velut dibapha, tanquam nix exalbescent—.*

ET IUSTI CORAM DEO. Eph. v. 27. *ut sisteret eam sibi gloriosam, ecclesiam non habentem maculam aut rugam, aut quicquam eiusmodi; sed ut sit sancta et inculpata.* Sic illi fideles 10 ante legem et sub lege; *Abel,* Gen. iv. 4; *Enoch,* cap. v. 24; *Noach,* cap. vi. 8. et vii. 1; aliique multi, quorum catalogus Heb. xi. Nec alia ratione dicimur non peccare, nisi quod nobis in Christo peccata non imputantur.

NON EX OPERIBUS LEGIS, SED PER FIDEM. Gen. xv. 6. *tunc* 15 *credidit Abraham Iehovæ, qui imputavit ei illud in iustitiam.* Habac. ii. 4. *iustus ex fide sua vivet.* Ioan. vi. 29. *hoc illud est opus Dei, ut credatis in eum quem ille misit.* Act. xiii. 39. *ab omnibus a quibus non potuistis per legem Mosis iustificari, quemvis credentem per hunc iustificari.* Rom. 20 iii. 20, 21, 22, 23. *propterea ex operibus legis nulla caro iustificabitur in conspectu eius. per legem enim agnitio peccati. nunc vero absque lege iustitia Dei patefacta est, comprobata testimonio legis ac prophetarum. iustitia Dei per*

1 Cor. vi. 9–11. "neither fornicators, nor idolaters" &c. "and such were some of you; but ye are washed, but ye are sanctified, but ye are justified." Jer. l. 20. "in that time, saith Jehovah, the iniquity of Israel shall be sought for, and there
5 shall be none; and the sins of Judah, and they shall not be found; for I will pardon them whom I reserve." Isa. i. 18. "though your sins be as scarlet, they shall be as white as snow."

ACCOUNTED JUST IN THE SIGHT OF GOD. Eph. v. 27. "that he
10 might present it to himself a glorious church, not having spot, or wrinkle, or any such thing; but that it should be holy and without blemish." On the same principle the faithful both before and under the law were accounted just; Abel, Gen. iv. 4. Enoch, v. 24. Noah, vi. 8. and vii. 1. and many others
15 enumerated Heb. xi. Nor is it in any other sense that we are said "not to sin," except as our sins are not imputed unto us through Christ.

NOT BY WORKS OF THE LAW, BUT THROUGH FAITH. Gen. xv. 6. "Abraham believed in Jehovah, and he counted it to him for
20 righteousness." Hab. ii. 4. "the just shall live by his faith." John vi. 29. "this is the work of God, that ye believe on him whom he hath sent." Acts xiii. 39. "by him all that believe are justified from all things from which ye could not be justified by the law of Moses." Rom. iii. 20–23. "therefore by the
25 deeds of the law there shall no flesh be justified in his sight: for by the law is the knowledge of sin; but now the righteousness of God without the law is manifested, being witnessed by the law and the prophets; even the righteousness of God

fidem Iesu Christi in omnes et super omnes qui credunt; non enim est distinctio: omnes enim peccaverunt ac deficiuntur gloria Dei. et v. 27, 28. *ubi igitur est gloriatio? exclusa est. per quam legem? operum? non: sed per legem fidei.* col-
5 *ligimus igitur fide iustificari hominem absque operibus legis.* et 30. *quandoquidem Deus unus est qui iustificabit circumcisionem ex fide et præputium per fidem.* et cap. iv. 2, 3, 4, 5, 6, 7, 8. *nam si Abrahamus ex operibus iustificatus fuit, habet de quo glorietur at non apud Deum. quid enim scrip-*
10 *tura dicit? credidit autem Abrahamus Deo, et imputatum est ei ad iustitiam. atqui ei qui operatur merces non imputatur ei ex gratia, sed ex debito: ei vero qui non operatur, sed credit in eum qui iustificat impium, imputatur fides sua ad iustitiam: sicut etiam David declarat, beatum eum hominem cui Deus*
15 *imputat iustitiam absque operibus, dicens, Beati quibus remissæ sunt legis transgressiones, et quorum tecta sunt peccata: beatus vir cui non imputarit Dominus peccatum.* et ix. 30, 31, 32, 33. *Israelem consectando legem iustitiæ, ad legem iustitiæ non pervenisse. quare? quia non ex fide, sed velut*
20 *ex operibus legis: nempe offenderunt ad lapidem ad quem impingitur.* Gal. ii. 16. *scientes non iustificari hominem ex operibus legis, sed per fidem Iesu Christi: etiam nos in Christum Iesum credidimus, ut iustificaremur ex fide Christi, et non ex operibus legis: propterea quod non iustificabitur ex*
25 *operibus legis ulla caro.* et v. 21. *non irritam facio gratiam Dei.*

which is by faith of Jesus Christ unto all and upon all them
that believe: for there is no difference: for all have sinned,
and come short of the glory of God." v. 27, 28. "where is
boasting then? it is excluded: by what law? of works? nay,
5 but by the law of faith: therefore we conclude that a man is
justified by faith without the deeds of the law." v. 30. "seeing it is one God which shall justify the circumcision by faith,
and uncircumcision through faith." iv. 2–8. "for if Abraham
were justified by works, he hath whereof to glory, but not
10 before God: for what saith the Scripture? Abraham believed
God, and it was counted to him for righteousness: now to
him that worketh, is the reward not reckoned of grace, but
of debt: but to him that worketh not, but believeth on him
that justifieth the ungodly, his faith is counted for righteous-
15 ness: even as David also describeth the blessedness of the man,
unto whom God imputeth righteousness without works, saying, Blessed are they whose iniquities are forgiven, and whose
sins are covered: blessed is the man to whom the Lord will
not impute sin." ix. 30–33. "what shall we say then? that
20 . . . Israel, which followed after the law of righteousness,
hath not attained to the law of righteousness: wherefore?
because they sought it not by faith, but as it were by the works
of the law: for they stumbled at that stumbling-stone." Gal.
ii. 16. "knowing that a man is not justified by the works of
25 the law, but by the faith of Jesus Christ, even we have believed
in Jesus Christ, that we might be justified by the faith of
Christ, and not by the works of the law, for by the works of
the law shall no flesh be justified." v. 21. "I do not frustrate

nam si per legem est iustitia, igitur Christus sine causa mortuus
est. et iii. 8, 9, 10, 11, 12. *quum prævidisset autem scriptura*
Deum ex fide iustificaturum gentes, id ante evangelizavit
Abrahamo, dicens, Benedicentur in te omnes gentes. itaque
5 *qui ex fide sunt, benedicentur cum illo fideli Abrahamo. nam*
quotquot ex operibus legis sunt, sub execratione sunt: scrip-
tum est enim execrabilis est quisquis non manserit in omnibus
quæ scripta sunt in libro legis ut faciat ea. nullum autem per
legem iustificari apud Deum manifestissimum est: quoniam
10 *iustus ex fide vivet. lex autem non est ex fide: sed qui ea*
fecerit, vivet per ea. Phil. iii. 9. *ut comperiar in eo, non*
habens meam iustitiam, quæ est ex lege, sed eam quæ est per
fidem Christi, iustitiam ex Deo per fidem. Heb. xi. 4, &c.
Abel per fidem maioris pretii sacrificium obtulit Deo quam
15 *Cain—.* Eph. ii. 8, 9. *hoc non est ex vobis, sed donum Dei*
est; non ex operibus, ut ne quis glorietur. His tot locis fide et
per fidem et ex fide iustificari nos literæ sacræ docent: an vero
tanquam per instrumentum quoddam, ut vulgo docetur, an
quid aliud scriptura non dicit. Certe si credere est agere,
20 fides actio est, aut habitus non solum infusus verum etiam
crebris actionibus acquisitus; eaque iustificamur, ut toties
supra: actio autem effectum non instrumentum dici solet;
minus principalis fortasse causa melius dicetur. Sin autem

the grace of God; for if righteousness come by the law, then Christ is dead in vain." iii. 8–12. "the Scripture foreseeing that God would justify the heathen through faith, preached before the gospel unto Abraham, saying, In thee shall all
5 nations be blessed: so then they which be of faith, are blessed with faithful Abraham: for as many as are of the works of the law are under the curse; for it is written, Cursed is every one that continueth not in all things which are written in the book of the law to do them: but that no man is justified by the law
10 in the sight of God, it is evident; for, The just shall live by faith: and the law is not of faith, but, The man that doeth them shall live in them." Philipp. iii. 9. "that I may be found in him, not having mine own righteousness, which is of the law, but that which is through the faith of Christ, the right-
15 eousness which is of God by faith." Heb. xi. 4, &c. "by faith Abel offered unto God a more excellent sacrifice than Cain." Eph. ii. 8, 9. "that not of yourselves; it is the gift of God: not of works, lest any man shall boast." In all these numerous passages we are said to be justified by faith, and through faith,
20 and of faith; whether through faith as an instrument, according to the common doctrine, or in any other sense, is not said. Undoubtedly, if to believe be to act, faith is an action, or rather a frame of mind acquired and confirmed by a succession of actions, although in the first instance infused from above;
25 and by this faith we are justified, as declared in the numerous texts above quoted. An action, however, is generally considered in the light of an effect, not of an instrument; or perhaps it may be more properly designated as the less principal

non acquisita sed infusa fides est, eo minus eam verebimur iustificationis causam esse assentiri.

Gravis hic agitatur quæstio acerrimis utrinque adversariis, Solane fides iustificet? Nostri affirmant; et opera quidem effecta esse fidei non causas iustificationis, Rom. iii. 24, 27, 28. Gal. ii. 16. ut supra: alii non sola fide iustificari disputant, freti loco illo Iacobi, cap. ii. 24, nempe, *ex operibus iustificari hominem, et non ex fide tantum.* Quæ duæ sententiæ cum stare simul non posse videantur, respondetur a nostris, Illic loqui Iacobum de iustificatione coram hominibus, non coram Deo. Verum qui a v. 14 ad finem usque capitis attente legerit, de iustificatione coram Deo imprimis illic agi perspiciet: agit nempe de ea fide cuius utilitas quæritur, de ea quæ viva est, quæ servat; non ergo de ea quæ coram hominibus tantummodo iustificat, cum hæc hypocritica esse possit: quæ utilis, quæ vera, quæ viva, quæ salvifica est, ex ea dicit apostolus non sola sed ex operibus etiam nos iustificari. Cum itaque apostoli hoc caput religionis nostræ studiosissime tractent, his autem verbis nusquam concludant, *sola fide hominem iustificari,* sed his fere, *fide iustificari hominem absque*

cause. On the other hand, if faith be not in any degree acquired, but wholly infused from above, there will be the less hesitation in admitting it as the cause of our justification.

An important question here arises, which is discussed with much vehemence by the advocates on both sides; namely, whether faith alone justifies? Our divines answer in the affirmative; adding, that works are the effects of faith, not the cause of justification, Rom. iii. 24, 27, 28. Gal. ii. 16. as above. Others contend that justification is not by faith alone, on the authority of James ii. 24. "by works a man is justified, and not by faith only." As however the two opinions appear at first sight inconsistent with each other, and incapable of being maintained together, the advocates of the former, to obviate the difficulty arising from the passage of St. James, allege that the apostle is speaking of justification in the sight of men, not in the sight of God. But whoever reads attentively from the fourteenth verse to the end of the chapter, will see that the apostle is expressly treating of justification in the sight of God. For the question there at issue relates to the faith which profits, and which is a living and a saving faith; consequently it cannot relate to that which justifies only in the sight of men, inasmuch as this latter may be hypocritical. When therefore the apostle says that we are justified by works, and not by faith only, he is speaking of the faith which profits, and which is a true, living, and saving faith. Considering then that the apostles, who treat this point of our religion with particular attention, nowhere, in summing up their doctrine, use words implying that a man is justified by faith alone, but

operibus legis, Rom. iii. 28. quid venerit in mentem theologis nostris miror ut conclusionis apostolicæ verba coarctarent: quæ si non coarctassent, hæ duæ sententiæ, *fide iustificari hominem absque operibus legis,* et, *ex operibus iustificari*

5 *hominem, non ex fide tantum,* quominus inter se optime conveniant, nihil obstare videretur. Paulus enim non dicit iustificari per fidem simpliciter sine operibus, sed *sine operibus legis;* nec fide sola, sed *fide per charitatem operante* Gal. v. 6. Fides autem sua habet opera, quæ ab operibus legis diversa

10 esse possunt. Fide igitur iustificamur, sed viva, non mortua: ea autem sola fides vivit quæ agit, Iacob. ii. 17, 20, 26. Iustificamur ergo fide absque operibus legis, non absque operibus fidei; eo quod opera a fide viva ac vera abesse non possunt; ab operibus tamen scriptæ legis diversa esse possunt; cuiusmodi

15 fuere illa Abrahami et Raabbæ; cum ille obtulit filium, illa exploratores accepit: quæ duo exempla operum fidei ab Iacobo afferuntur. Duobus his exemplis addo illud Phineæ, cui imputatum est in iustitiam id quod fecerat, Psal. cvi. 31. iisdem verbis quibus imputatum est Abrahamo quod crediderat Gen.

20 xv. 6. Rom. iv. 9. et Phineam quidem iustificatum coram Deo potius quam coram hominibus opusque eius fidei non legis fuisse quod legitur Num. xxv. 11, 12, nemo facile nega-

generally conclude as follows, that "a man is justified by faith without the deeds of the law," Rom. iii. 28. I am at a loss to conjecture why our divines should have narrowed the terms of the apostolical conclusion. Had they not so done, the dec-
5 laration in the one text, that "by faith a man is justified without the deeds of the law," would have appeared perfectly consistent with that in the other, "by works a man is justified, and not by faith only." For St. Paul does not say simply that a man is justified without works, but "without the works of
10 the law"; nor yet by faith alone, but "by faith which worketh by love." Gal. v. 6. Faith has its own works, which may be different from the works of the law. We are justified therefore by faith, but by a living, not a dead faith; and that faith alone which acts is counted living; James ii. 17, 20, 26. Hence
15 we are justified by faith without the works of the law, but not without the works of faith; inasmuch as a living and true faith cannot consist without works, though these latter may differ from the works of the written law. Such were those of Abraham and Rahab, the two examples cited by St. James in illus-
20 tration of the works of faith, when the former was prepared to offer up his son, and the latter sheltered the spies of the Israelites. To these may be added the instance of Phinehas, whose action "was counted unto him for righteousness." Psal. cvi. 31. the very same words being used as in the case of Abraham,
25 whose "faith was reckoned to him for righteousness," Gen. xv. 6. Rom. iv. 9. Nor will it be denied that Phinehas was justified in the sight of God rather than of men, and that his work recorded Num. xxv. 11, 12. was a work of faith, not

verit. Phineas ergo non fide sola, sed operibus quoque est iustificatus fidei. Huius doctrinæ ratio amplius patebit infra, ubi de Evangelio et Libertate Christiana.

Nec tamen merita hoc modo stabiliuntur; quandoquidem
5 et fides ipsa et opera fidei sunt opera spiritus non nostra: Eph. ii. 8, 9, 10. *gratia estis servati per fidem: et hoc non est ex vobis, sed Dei donum est. non ex operibus, ut ne quis glorietur: nam ipsius sumus opus creati in Christo Iesu ad opera bona, quæ præparavit Deus ut in iis ambulemus.* Hic opera de
10 quibus quis glorietur ab operibus distinguuntur quæ gloriationem nullam pariunt, operibus nimirum fidei: sicuti etiam Rom. iii. 27, 28. *ubi igitur est gloriatio? exclusa est. per quam legem? operum? non: sed per legem fidei.* quid autem est lex fidei nisi opera fidei? Quod sicubi post *opera*
15 omittitur vox *legis,* ut Rom. iv. 2. subaudienda tamen est vel *legis* vel *carnis* ex v. 1. non *legis;* cum de Abrahamo sermo sit, qui ante legem vixit: ne contradicat Paulus et sibi ipsi et Iacobo; sibi, si dicat ex operibus quibuscunque habuisse Abrahamum de quibus gloriaretur, cum dixerit superiore capite
20 v. 27, 28. *per legem fidei,* id est, *per opera fidei gloriationem excludi:* Iacobo autem aperte contradicat, affirmanti, ut supra,

of the law. Phinehas therefore was justified not by faith alone, but also by the works of faith. The principle of this doctrine will be developed more fully hereafter, when the subjects of the gospel and of Christian liberty are considered.

5   This interpretation, however, affords no countenance to the doctrine of human merit, inasmuch as both faith itself and its works are the works of the Spirit, not our own. Eph. ii. 8–10. "by grace are ye saved through faith; and that not of yourselves, it is the gift of God; not of works, lest any man 10 should boast: for we are his workmanship, created in Christ Jesus unto good works, which God hath before ordained that we should walk in them." In this passage the works of which a man may boast are distinguished from those which do not admit of boasting, namely, the works of faith. So Rom. iii. 15 27, 28. "where is boasting then? it is excluded: by what law? of works? nay, but by the law of faith." Now what is the law of faith, but the works of faith? Hence, wherever after "works" the words "of the law" are omitted, as in Rom. iv. 2. we must supply either "the works of the law," or, as in the 20 present passage, "of the flesh," with reference to xi. 1. not "of the law," since the apostle is speaking of Abraham, who lived before the law. Otherwise St. Paul would have contradicted himself as well as St. James; he would contradict himself, in saying that Abraham had whereof to glory through 25 any works whatever, whereas he had declared in the preceding chapter, v. 27, 28. that "by the law of faith," that is, "by the works of faith, boasting was excluded"; he would expressly contradict St. James, who affirms, as above, that "by

ex operibus iustificari hominem, et non ex fide tantum. nisi opera fidei intelliguntur, non opera legis. Sic Rom. iv. 13. *non per legem—, sed per iustitiam fidei.* Qualis illa intelligenda est. Matt. v. 20. *nisi abundaverit iustitia vestra plus quam*
5 *scribarum et Pharisæorum, nequaquam—.* ea autem erat secundum legem exactissima. Iacob. i. 25. *quia non fuerit auditor obliviosus, sed effector operis.* Heb. xii. 14. *pacem sectamini cum omnibus et sanctimoniam, sine qua nemo videbit Dominum.* Hinc forte Apoc. ii. 26. *si quis observa-*
10 *verit opera mea.* 1 Ioan. iii. 7. *filioli, nemo vos seducat; qui facit iustitiam, iustus est.*

Nec satisfactioni interim Christi quicquam derogatur, cum et fides nostra imperfecta sit, et proinde opera fidei non alia ratione Deo placere queant, nisi quatenus misericordia Dei
15 iustitiaque Christi nituntur, eaque sola se sustinent. Philipp. iii. 9. *ut comperiar in eo non habens meam iustitiam, quæ est ex lege, sed eam quæ est per fidem Christi, iustitiam ex Deo per fidem.* Tit. iii. 5, 6, 7. *non ex operibus iustis quæ fecerimus nos, sed ex sua misericordia servavit nos per lava-*
20 *crum regenerationis et renovationis spiritus sancti; quem ef-*
fudit super nos copiose per Iesum Christum servatorem no-

works a man is justified, and not by faith only"; unless the expression be understood to mean the works of faith, not the works of the law. Compare Rom. iv. 13. "not through the law, but through the righteousness of faith." In the same
5 sense is to be understood Matt. v. 20. "except your righteousness shall exceed the righteousness of the Scribes and Pharisees, ye shall in no case enter into the kingdom of heaven"; whereas their righteousness was of the exactest kind according to the law. James i. 25. "being not a forgetful hearer, but a
10 doer of the work, this man shall be blessed." Heb. xii. 14. "follow peace with all men, and holiness, without which no man shall see the Lord." Hence perhaps Rev. ii. 26. "he that keepeth my words to the end, to him will I give power—." 1 John iii. 7. "little children, let no man deceive you; he that
15 doeth righteousness, is righteous."

Nor does this doctrine derogate in any degree from Christ's satisfaction; inasmuch as, our faith being imperfect, the works which proceed from it cannot be pleasing to God, except in so far as they rest upon his mercy and the righteousness of
20 Christ, and are sustained by that foundation alone. Philipp. iii. 9. "that I may be found of him, not having mine own righteousness, which is of the law, but that which is through the faith of Christ, the righteousness which is of God by faith." Tit. iii. 5–7. "not by works of righteousness which we have
25 done, but according to his mercy he saved us, by the washing of regeneration and renewing of the Holy Ghost, which he shed on us abundantly through Jesus Christ our Savior; that being justified by his grace, we should be made heirs—."

strum: ut iustificati illius gratia—. 1 Ioan. ii. 29. *nostis, quicunque facit iustitiam, ex ipso natum esse.*

Pontificiis æque absurdum videtur nos aliena iustitia iustos fieri, ac siquis alterius doctrina doctus diceretur: sed dispar est exemplorum ratio, cum homo homini non perinde sit coniunctus, ac fidelis Christo capiti suo. Interim pro absurdo non habent quod est absurdissimum, mortuorum et monachorum iustitiam aliis imputari.

Idem contendunt operibus suis iustificari hominem, ex aliquot scripturæ locis. Psal. xviii. 21, 25. *tribuit mihi Iehova secundum iustitiam meam—*. Rom. ii. 6. *reddet unicuique secundum opera ipsius.* Verum aliud est *secundum* aliud *propter opera* cuique reddere; nec inde sequitur illa opera iustificare vi sua, aut quicquam mereri, cum et siquid recte facimus, et siquid recte factis Deus tribuit, id totum ipsius gratiæ debeatur. Itaque superiore versu eiusdem Psalmi prius dixerat, *liberat me quia delectatur me:* et Psal. lxii. 12. *tuam esse Domine benignitatem, te repensurum cuique secundum opus suum:* deinde, qui tribuit sibi iustitiam, tribuit quoque sibi iniquitatem eodem loco, Psal. xviii. 24. *quum sum integer illi, et caveo ab iniquitate mea.*

1 John ii. 29. "ye know that every one that doeth righteousness is born of him."

The Papists argue, that it is no less absurd to say that a man
is justified by the righteousness of another, than that a man
5 is learned by the learning of another. But there is no analogy
between the two cases, inasmuch as mankind are not one with
each other in the same intimate manner as the believer is one
with Christ his head. In the mean time they do not perceive
the real and extreme absurdity of which they are themselves
10 guilty, in supposing that the righteousness of the dead, or of
monks, can be imputed to others.

They likewise contend, on the authority of a few passages
of Scripture, that man is justified by his own works. Psal.
xviii. 20, 24. "Jehovah rewarded me according to my right-
15 eousness." Rom. ii. 6. "who will render to every man according to his deeds." But to render to every man "according to
his deeds" is one thing, to render to him "on account of his
deeds" is another; nor does it follow from hence that works
have any inherent justifying power, or deserve anything as of
20 their own merit; seeing that, if we do anything right, or if
God assign any recompense to our right actions, it is altogether owing to his grace. Hence the expression in the preceding verse of the same Psalm, "he delivered me, because
he delighted in me"; and Psal. lxii. 12. "unto thee, O Lord,
25 belongeth mercy, for thou renderest to every man according
to his work." Finally, the same Psalmist who attributes to himself righteousness, attributes to himself iniquity in the same
sentence; xviii. 23. "I was also upright before him, and I kept
myself from mine iniquity."

Quod autem dicitur. Matt. xxv. 34, 35. *possidete regnum*—; *esurivi enim et dedistis mihi*—; *respondendum est,* Christum eo die sententiam ferre, non ex interna iustificationis causa, nimirum fide, sed ex effectis fidei et signis, nempe
5 operibus fidei, ut illius sententiæ iustitiam eo manifestius universis hominibus declararet.

Quoties autem quis perfectus aut iustus dicitur coram Deo, ut Luc. i. 6. de Zacharia et uxore eius *erant iusti ambo in conspectu Dei, incedentes in omnibus præceptis et statutis*
10 *Domini inculpate;* id est pro ratione humanæ perfectionis, et si cum aliis quibusvis conferantur, vel animo sincero et integro, non simulato Deut. xviii. 13. *integer esto cum Iehova Deo tuo:* ut vox ista *coram Deo* innuere videtur, Gen. xvii. 1. *indesinenter ambula coram me.* Psal. xix. 13. *atque*
15 *a contumaciis cohibe servum tuum, fac ne dominentur in me,* tunc integer sive *perfectus ero insonsque defectione magna.* Eph. i. 4. *elegit nos ut simus sancti et inculpati in conspectu eius cum charitate.* Vel denique ex gratia et fide iustus a Deo declaratus: sic Noa, Gen. vi. 8. *invenit gratiam in oculis*
20 *Iehovæ;* unde v. 9. *Noa vir iustus, integer erat in ætatibus suis; secundum Deum indesinenter ambulabat,* cum Heb. xi. 7. *eius quæ ex fide est iustitiæ factus est hæres.*

As to the expression in Matt. xxv. 34, 35. "inherit the kingdom . . . for I was an hungred, and ye gave me meat," &c. our answer is, that the sentence which Christ shall pass on that day will not have respect to faith, which is the internal cause of justification, but to the effects and signs of that faith, namely, the works done in faith, that he may thereby make the equity of his judgment manifest to all mankind.

When a man is said to be perfect and just in the sight of God, as Luke i. 6. of Zacharias and his wife, "they were both righteous before God, walking in all the commandments and ordinances of the Lord, blameless," this is to be understood according to the measure of human righteousness, and as compared with the progress of others; or it may mean that they were endued with a sincere and upright heart, without dissimulation, as Deut. xviii. 13. "thou shalt be perfect with Jehovah thy God," which interpretation seems to be favored by the expression "in the sight of God." Gen. xvii. 1. "walk before me, and be thou perfect." Psal. xix. 13. "keep back thy servant also from presumptuous sins, let them not have dominion over me; then shall I be upright, and I shall be innocent from the great transgression." Eph. i. 4. "he hath chosen us . . . that we should be holy and without blame before him in love." Or, lastly, it may mean that they were declared righteous by God through grace and faith. Thus Noah "found grace in the eyes of Jehovah," Gen. vi. 8. compared with v. 9. "Noah was a just man and perfect in his generations, and Noah walked with God," and Heb. xi. 7. "he became heir of the righteousness which is by faith."

Ad illud Luc. vii. 47. *remissa sunt multa illa peccata ipsius, quia dilexit multum,* dicendum est, dilectionem illam non causam, sed indicium vel etiam effectum remissionis fuisse, ut ex ipsa parabola v. 40. perspicuum est: in qua non remis-
5 sum est debitoribus quod multum dilexerint, sed idcirco di-lexerunt, quia multum fuerat remissum; id quod etiam ex verbis sequentibus planum fit; *cui paululum remittitur, pau-lulum diligit:* et planius v. 50. *fides tua te servavit.* sane quæ servavit eadem iustificavit; non dilectio, sed fides; quæ et
10 causa dilectionis illius fuit. Vide etiam infra l. 2. cap. i. in quo de meritis.

Ex iustificationis sensu pax demum oritur, et vera tran-quillitas animi. Rom. v. 1, &c. *iustificati, pacem habemus apud Deum.* 1 Cor. vii. 15. *ad pacem vocavit nos Deus.*
15 Philipp. iv. 7. *pax illa Dei quæ exsuperat omnem intellec-tionem, custodiet corda vestra et cogitationes vestras in Christo Iesu.* Col. iii. 15. *pax Dei omnium arbitra* sive *directrix sit in cordibus vestris, ad quam etiam vocati estis.* Et hæc illa pax est qua apostoli passim ecclesiam salutant.

With regard to Luke vii. 47. "her sins, which are many, are forgiven, for she loved much," it is to be observed that this love was not the cause, but the token or effect of forgiveness, as is evident from the parable itself, v. 40. for the debtors
5 were not forgiven because they had loved much, but they loved much because much had been forgiven. The same appears from what follows; "to whom little is forgiven, the same loveth little"; and still more plainly from v. 50. "thy faith hath saved thee." That which saved, the same also justified;
10 namely, not love, but faith, which was itself the cause of the love in question. Compare Book II. Chap. i. on the subject of merit.

From a consciousness of justification proceed peace and real tranquillity of mind. Rom. v. 1, &c. "being justified by
15 faith, we have peace with God." 1 Cor. vii. 15. "God hath called us to peace." Philipp. iv. 7. "the peace of God, which passeth all understanding, shall keep your hearts and minds through Christ Jesus." Col. iii. 15. "let the peace of God rule in your hearts, to the which also ye are called in one body."
20 This is that peace for which the apostles pray in their salutations addressed to the church.

CAPUT XXIII.

DE ADOPTIONE.

DICTUM est de prima parte auctionis regenerati hominis ad patrem relata. nempe IUSTIFICATIONE: restat altera pars ADOPTIO.

Ea est qua IUSTIFICATOS PER FIDEM DEUS IN FILIOS SIBI
5 ADOPTAT.

Dicimur quidem natura quodammodo filii Dei, utpote ab ipso creati. Luc. iii. 38. *filii Adam, qui fuit Dei.* sicut et angeli. Verum hic de filiis etiam adoptatis; quales illi, ut verisimillimum est, professione saltem, Gen. vi. 2. *videntes*
10 *filii Dei filias hominum.* 1 Chron. xxviii. 6. *elegi ipsum mihi in filium, et ego futurus sum ei in patrem.* Isa. lvi. 5. *nomen melius quam filiorum aut filiarum; nomen perpetuum daturus sum eorum cuique, quod non exscindetur.*

PER FIDEM. Ioan. i. 12. *quotquot eum receperunt, dedit iis*
15 *hoc ius, ut filii Dei sint facti, iis qui credunt in nomen eius.* Gal. iii. 26. *omnes filii Dei estis per fidem in Christo Iesu.* Eph. i. 5. *qui prædestinavit nos quos adoptaret in filios per Iesum Christum in sese, pro benevola voluntate sua.* Heb. ii. 10. *decebat enim ut ipse propter quem sunt hæc omnia,*
20 *et per quem sunt hæc omnia, multos filios in gloriam addu-*

CHAPTER XXIII.

OF ADOPTION.

WE HAVE considered JUSTIFICATION, the first of those particulars connected with the increase of the regenerate which bear reference to the Father; that which remains to be treated of is ADOPTION.

5   ADOPTION is that act whereby GOD ADOPTS AS HIS CHILDREN THOSE WHO ARE JUSTIFIED THROUGH FAITH.

In one sense we are by nature sons of God, as well as the angels, inasmuch as he is the author of our being; Luke iii. 38. "which was the son of Adam, which was the son of God."
10 But the sense here intended is that of adopted children, such as those probably were, though in profession only, who are mentioned Gen. vi. 2. "the sons of God saw the daughters of men that they were fair." 1 Chron. xxviii. 6. "I have chosen him to be my son, and I will be his father." Isa. lvi. 5. "I
15 will give them a name better than of sons and of daughters; I will give them an everlasting name, that shall not be cut off."
THROUGH FAITH. John i. 12. "as many as received him, to them gave he power to become the sons of God, even to them that believe on his name." Gal. iii. 26. "ye are all the chil-
20 dren of God by faith in Christ Jesus." Eph. i. 5. "having pre-destinated us into the adoption of children by Jesus Christ to himself, according to the good pleasure of his will." Heb. ii. 10. "for it became him for whom are all things, and by whom are all things, in bringing many sons unto glory, to make the

cendo, principem salutis ipsorum per perpessiones consum-
maret—. Gal. iv. 4, 5, 6. *emisit Deus filium suum, factum*
ex muliere, factum legi subiectum: ut eos qui legi erant sub-
iecti redimeret, ut adoptionem acciperemus. quoniam autem
5 *estis filii, misit Deus spiritum filii sui in corda vestra claman-*
tem, Abba, pater.

In filios. Rom. viii. 15, 16. *non enim accepistis spiritum*
servitutis rursum ad metum, sed accepistis spiritum adopti-
onis, per quem clamamus, Abba, pater. et ipse spiritus
10 *testatur una cum spiritu nostro, nos esse filios Dei.* et v. 23.
adoptionem expectantes, redemptionem corporis nostri.
Philipp. ii. 15. *filii Dei inculpabiles.* 1 Ioan. iii. 1, 2. *videte*
qualem charitatem dedit nobis pater, ut filii Dei vocemur.
Et quidem *similes Deo,* v. 2. et cap. iv. 17. *per hoc adim-*
15 *pletur charitas nobiscum ut fiduciam habeamus in die iudicii*
quod qualis iste est, tales et nos sumus in hoc mundo.

Ex adoptione oritur primum *libertas,* quæ semper, etiam
sub lege servitutis, Abrahami posteris, utpote filiis Dei nomi-
natis, Deut. xiv. 1. ignota non erat; qua libertate prædti, ne
20 religiosis quidem ritibus plane serviebant quoties charitas
aliud requirebat. Hinc *populum totum qui nati fuerant in*
deserto, in ipso itinere non circumciderant, Ios. v. 4. et Davi-
des fame oppressus, comedebat quod alioqui fas non erat,
1 Sam. xxi. 6. cum Matt. xii. 4. Psal. cxix. 45. *indesinenter*

captain of their salvation perfect through sufferings." Gal. iv.
4–6. "God sent forth his Son, made of a woman, made under
the law, to redeem them that were under the law, that we
might receive the adoption of sons; and because ye are sons,
5   God hath sent forth the Spirit of his Son into your hearts,
crying, Abba, Father."

His CHILDREN. Rom. viii. 15, 16. "ye have not received the
spirit of bondage again to fear, but ye have received the Spirit
of adoption, whereby we cry, Abba, Father: the Spirit itself
10 beareth witness with our spirit, that we are the children of
God." v. 23. "waiting for the adoption, to wit, the redemption of our body." Philipp. ii. 15. "that ye may be blameless
and harmless, the sons of God." 1 John iii. 1, 2. "behold what
manner of love the Father hath bestowed upon us, that we
15 should be called the sons of God." We are also said to be "like
God," v. 2. and chap. iv. 17. "herein is our love made perfect, that we may have boldness in the day of judgment; because as he is, so are we in this world."

From adoption is derived, first, liberty; a privilege which
20 was not unknown to the posterity of Abraham, in virtue of
their title as children of God. Deut. xiv. 1. even under the law
of bondage. In the spirit of this liberty, they did not scruple
even to infringe the ceremonies of religion, when their observance would have been inconsistent with the law of love.
25 Thus they did not circumcise "all the people that were born
in the wilderness by the way," Josh. v. 5. and David "when
he was an hungred, did eat that which was not lawful for him
to eat," Matt. xii. 4. compared with 1 Sam. xxi. 6. Psal. cxix.
45. "I will walk at liberty, for I seek thy precepts." But the

ambulabo in ipsa latitudine, quia mandata tua quæro. Sed quoniam post adventum Christi, sicuti adoptio ita et libertas, unde Christiana dicta est, multo clarius eluxit, de ea tum demum amplius dicetur, cum de evangelio dicendum erit.

5   Ex adoptione *hæredes* etiam in Christo constituimur. Gal. iii. 29. *quod vos estis Christi, nempe Abrahami semen estis, et secundum promissionem hæredes.* et iv. 7. *itaque non amplius es servus, sed filius; quod si filius, etiam hæres Dei per Christum.* Rom. viii. 17. *quod si filii, etiam hæredes;* 10 *hæredes quidem Dei, cohæredes autem Christi.* Tit. iii. 7. *ut iustificati illius gratia hæredes efficeremur, secundum spem vitæ æternæ.* 1 Pet. iii. 9. *ut benedictionem hæreditario iure obtineatis.* Hinc et *primogeniti.* Heb. xii. 22, 23. *accessistis ad ecclesiam primogenitorum.* Et *fratres Christi:* Heb. ii. 15 11, 12. *quam ob causam non erubescit eos vocare fratres; dicens, Annuntiabo nomen tuum fratribus meis.* Et *domestici Dei:* Eph. ii. 19. *non amplius estis peregrini et inquilini, sed concives sanctorum et domestici Dei.* Hinc etiam angeli nobis ministri: Heb. i. 14. *nonne omnes sunt ministerii* 20 *munere fungentes spiritus, qui ministerii causa emittuntur propter hæredes salutis futuros?*

Et tandem nova etiam generatione et quasi natura et gloria filii: Luc. xx. 36. *pares angelis sunt, et filii sunt Dei, quum sint filii resurrectionis.*

clearer and more perfect light in which liberty, like adoption itself, has been unfolded by the gospel, renders it necessary to reserve the fuller exposition of this privilege to that part of our work in which the subject of the Gospel is considered.

5   By adoption we are also made heirs through Christ. Gal. iii. 29. "if ye be Christ's, then are ye Abraham's seed, and heirs according to the promise." iv. 7. "wherefore thou art no more a servant, but a son; and if a son, then an heir of God through Christ." Rom. viii. 17. "if children then heirs; heirs
10 of God, and joint heirs with Christ." Tit iii. 7. "that being justified by his grace, we should be made heirs according to the hope of eternal life." 1 Pet. iii. 9. "knowing that ye are thereunto called, that ye should inherit a blessing." This also confers the title of "first-born." Heb. xii. 22, 23. "ye are
15 come . . . to the general assembly and church of the first-born." And of "brethren of Christ." Heb. ii. 11, 12. "for which cause he is not ashamed to call them brethren, saying, I will declare thy name unto my brethren." Hence we are said to be "of the household of God." Eph. ii. 19. "now there-
20 fore ye are no more strangers and foreigners, but fellow citizens with the saints, and of the household of God." Hence even the angels minister unto us. Heb. i. 14. "are they not all ministering spirits, sent forth to minister for them that shall be heirs of salvation?"

25 Lastly, we become sons of God by a new generation; by the assumption, as it were, of a new nature, and by a conformity to his glory: Luke xx. 36. "they are equal unto the angels, and are the children of God, being the children of the resurrection."

CAPUT XXIV.

DE UNIONE ET COMMUNIONE CUM CHRISTO EIUSQUE MEMBRIS, UBI DE ECCLESIA MYSTICA SIVE INVISIBILI.

HACTENUS regenerati hominis auctio ad patrem solum relata: sequitur relata ad patrem et filium. Relata ad patrem et filium est UNIO et COMMUNIO cum patre in Christo filio, et ad imaginem Christi glorificatio.

5 Unio ista et communio docetur, Ioan. xiv. 20. *in illo die vos cognoscetis me esse in patre meo, et vos in me, et me in vobis.* et v. 23. *si quis diligit me, sermonem meum servabit, et pater meus diliget eum, et ad eum veniemus, et apud eum habitabimus.* et cap. xvii. 21, 22, 23. *ut omnes unum sint,*
10 *sicut tu pater in me, et ego in te; ut et ipsi in nobis unum sint—. et ego gloriam quam dedisti mihi, dedi iis; ut sint unum sicut et nos unum sumus. ego in iis et tu in me, ut sint consummati in unum.* 1 Cor. vi. 17. *qui agglutinatur Domino, unus cum eo spiritus est.* 1 Ioan. ii. 23. *quisquis*
15 *negat filium, nec patrem habet: qui profitetur filium, etiam patrem habet.* et iii. 24. *qui observat eius præcepta, in eo habitat, et ipse in eo: et per hoc novimus eum habitare in*

CHAPTER XXIV.

OF UNION AND FELLOWSHIP WITH CHRIST AND HIS MEMBERS, WHEREIN IS CONSIDERED THE MYSTICAL OR INVISIBLE CHURCH.

HITHERTO the increase of the regenerate has been considered in its relation to the Father alone. We are now to consider that increase which has reference to the Father and Son conjointly.

5   This consists in our UNION and FELLOWSHIP with the Father through Christ the Son, and our glorification after the image of Christ.

Of this union and fellowship mention is made John xiv. 20. "at that day ye shall know that I am in my Father, and ye in 10 me, and I in you." v. 23. "if a man love me, he will keep my words, and my Father will love him, and we will come unto him, and make our abode with him." xvii. 21–23. "that they all may be one, as thou, Father, art in me, and I in thee, that they also may be one in us . . . and the glory which thou 15 gavest me I have given them, that they may be one, even as we are one; I in them, and thou in me, that they may be made perfect in one." 1 Cor. vi. 17. "he that is joined to the Lord, is one spirit." 1 John ii. 23. "whosoever denieth the Son, the same hath not the Father; but he that acknowledgeth the Son, 20 hath the Father also." iii. 24. "he that keepeth his commandments dwelleth in him, and he in him: and hereby we know

nobis, ex spiritu, quem dedit nobis. et cap. i. 3, 6, 7. *et communio nostra sit cum patre et cum filio eius Iesu Christo: si dixerimus nos communionem habere cum eo, et in tenebris ambulamus mentimur, nec sincere agimus. Quod si in luce*
5 *ambulamus, sicut ipse est in luce, communionem habemus cum eo mutuam.* et iv. 13, 15, 16. *per hoc cognoscimus nos in eo habitare et ipsum in nobis, quod de spiritu suo dedit nobis. quisquis professus fuerit Iesum esse filium Dei, Deus in eo habitat, et ipse in Deo. et nos cognovimus et credidimus*
10 *charitatem quam habet Deus erga nos: Deus charitas est; et qui manet in charitate, in Deo manet, et Deus in eo.*

COMMUNIO quæ ex ista unione oritur est omnium donorum ac meritorum Christi participatio per spiritum. Ioan. vi. 56. *qui edit carnem meam et bibit meum sanguinem, in me*
15 *manet et ego in eo.* Rom. viii. 9. *si quis spiritum Christi non habet, is non est eius.* et v. 32. *quomodo non etiam cum eo nobis omnia donabit.* 1 Cor. i. 9. *fidelis est Deus per quem vocati estis in communionem filii ipsius Iesu Christi Domini nostri.* Eph. iii. 17. *inhabitet Christus per fidem in cordibus*
20 *vestris.* Apoc. iii. 20. *si quis audierit vocem meam, et aperuerit ostium, ingrediar ad eum, et cœnabo cum eo, et ipse mecum.* 2 Cor. xiii. 13. *communicatio spiritus.*

Ex hac nostra communione cum Christo oritur mutua membrorum eius communion inter se; quæ SANCTORUM COM-
25 MUNIO in symbolo Apostolico dicitur. Rom. xii. 4, 5. *quem-*

that he abideth in us, by the Spirit which he hath given us."
i. 3, 6, 7. "truly our fellowship is with the Father, and with
his Son Jesus Christ: if we say that we have fellowship with
him, and walk in darkness, we lie, and do not the truth; but
5 if we walk in the light, as he is in the light, we have fellowship one with another." iv. 13, 15, 16. "hereby know we
that we dwell in him, and he in us, because he hath given us
of his Spirit: whosoever shall confess that Jesus is the Son of
God, God dwelleth in him, and he in God: and we have
10 known and believed the love that God hath to us: God is love,
and he that dwelleth in love dwelleth in God, and God in
him."

THE FELLOWSHIP arising from this union consists in a participation, through the Spirit, of the various gifts and merits
15 of Christ. John vi. 56. "he that eateth my flesh, and drinketh
my blood, dwelleth in me, and I in him." Rom. viii. 9. "if
any man have not the Spirit of Christ, he is none of his." v. 32.
"how shall he not with him also freely give us all things?"
1 Cor. i. 9. "God is faithful, by whom ye were called unto the
20 fellowship of his Son Jesus Christ our Lord." Eph. iii. 17.
"that Christ may dwell in your hearts by faith." Rev. iii. 20.
"if any man hear my voice, and open the door, I will come in
to him, and sup with him, and he with me." 2 Cor. xiii. 14.
"the communion of the Holy Ghost."

25 From this our fellowship with Christ arises the mutual
fellowship of the members of Christ's body among themselves,
called in the Apostles' Creed THE COMMUNION OF SAINTS.
Rom. xii. 4, 5. "for as we have many members in one body,

admodum enim in uno corpore membra multa habemus,
membra vero omnia eandem non habent actionem; ita multi
illi unum corpus sumus in Christo, singulatim autem alii
aliorum membra. 1 Cor. xii. 12, 13. *sicut corpus unum est,*
5 *et membra habet multa, omnia vero illa membra corporis*
quod unicum est multa sunt, sed unum est corpus; ita et
Christus. etenim per unum spiritum nos omnes in unum
corpus baptizati sumus, et Iudæi, et Græci, et servi, et liberi:
et omnes poti sumus in unum spiritum. et v. 27. *vos estis*
10 *corpus Christi, et membra particulatim.*

Ex hac unione et communione cum patre et Christo, mem-
brorumque Christi inter se, nascitur illud corpus mysticum
quæ ECCLESIA INVISIBILIS est; cuius caput est Christus. 1 Thess.
i. 1. *ecclesiæ Thessalonicensium, quæ est in Deo patre, et*
15 *Domino Iesu Christo.* et 2 [Thess.] i. 1. idem. Ioan. xi. 52.
nec tantum pro ea gente, sed ut etiam filios Dei dispersos con-
gregaret in unum. 2 Cor. vi. 16. *templum estis Dei.* Gal. iv.
26. *illa vero quæ sursum est Hierusalem, libera est, quæ est*
mater omnium nostrum. Eph. i. 22, 23. *eumque constituit*
20 *caput super omnia ipsi ecclesiæ: quæ est corpus ipsius, et com-*
plementum eius qui omnia implet in omnibus. et iv. 13, 15,
16. *donec deveniamus nos omnes in unitatem fidei et agni-*
tionem filii Dei, in virum adultum, ad mensuram plenæ sta-
turæ Christi—. prorsus adolescamus in eum qui est caput,
25 *Christus. ex quo totum corpus congruenter coagmentatum*
et compactum per omnes suppeditatas commissuras, ex vi
intus agente pro mensura uniuscuiusque membri, incremen-
tum capit corpori conveniens, ad sui ipsius ædificationem

and all members have not the same office; so we, being many, are one body in Christ, and every one members one of another." 1 Cor. xii. 12, 13. "as the body is one, and hath many members, and all the members of that one body, being many,

5 are one body, so also is Christ: for by one Spirit are we all baptized into one body, whether we be Jews or Gentiles, whether we be bond or free; and have been all made to drink into one Spirit." v. 27. "ye are the body of Christ, and members in particular."

10 Lastly, from this union and fellowship of the regenerate with the Father and Christ, and of the members of Christ's body among themselves, results the mystical body called THE INVISIBLE CHURCH, whereof Christ is the head. 1 Thess. i. 1. "unto the church of the Thessalonians which is in God the

15 Father, and in the Lord Jesus Christ." See also 2 Thess. i. 1. John xi. 52. "not for that nation only, but that also he should gather together in one the children of God that were scattered abroad." 2 Cor. vi. 16. "ye are the temple of the living God." Gal. iv. 26. "Jerusalem which is above is free, which is the

20 mother of us all." Eph. i. 22, 23. "he gave him to be the head over all things to the church, which is his body, the fulness of him that filleth all in all." iv. 13, 15, 16. "till we all come in the unity of the faith, and of the knowledge of the Son of God, unto a perfect man, unto the measure of the

25 stature of the fulness of Christ; that we may grow up into him in all things, which is the head, even Christ; from whom the whole body fitly joined together and compacted by that which every joint supplieth, according to the effectual working in

per charitatem. et v. 23. *Christus est caput ecclesiæ, et is est qui salutem dat corpori.* Col. i. 18, 19. *estque caput corporis ecclesiæ.* et ii. 19. *neque retinens caput, ex quo totum corpus per commissuras et connexus suppeditatum et compactum,* 5 *augescit Dei augmento.* et i. 24. *pro corpore ipsius, quod est ecclesia.* Heb. iii. 6. *Christus ut filius domui suæ præest: cuius domus sumus nos—.* et xii. 22, 23. *accessistis ad montem Sion et civitatem Dei vivi, Hierosolymam cœlestem et myriadas angelorum, conventum universalem et concionem* 10 *primogenitorum qui conscripti sunt in cœlis, et iudicem universorum Deum, et spiritus iustorum consummatorum.*

Cum itaque corpus Christi unum mystice sit, communionem quoque membrorum eius necesse est esse mysticam, et non necessario localem, tot nempe gentium longe dissitarum 15 omniumque ab orbe condito ætatum. Rom. ii. 29. *sed qui in occulto est, Iudæus est, et circumcisio cordis, in spiritu, non litera, cuius laus non ex hominibus est, sed ex Deo.* Eph. ii. a v. 19. usque ad finem capitis: *non amplius estis peregrini et inquilini, sed concives sanctorum ac domestici Dei: super-* 20 *structi super fundamentum apostolorum ac prophetarum existente imo angulari eius lapide Iesu Christo. in quo totum ædificium congruenter coagmentatum, crescit ut sit templum sanctum Domino: in quo et vos una ædificamini ut sitis domi-*

the measure of every part, maketh increase of the body unto the edifying of itself in love." v. 23. "Christ is the head of the church, and he is the Savior of the body." Col. i. 18, 19. "he is the head of the body, the church." ii. 19. "not holding
5 the head, from which all the body by joints and bands having nourishment ministered, and knit together, increaseth with the increase of God." i. 24. "for his body's sake, which is the church." Heb. iii. 6. "Christ as a son over his own house, whose house are we." xii. 22, 23. "ye are come unto Mount
10 Sion, and unto the city of the living God, the heavenly Jerusalem, and to an innumerable company of angels, to the general assembly and church of the first-born, which are written in heaven, and to God the Judge of all, and to the spirits of just men made perfect."
15   Seeing then that the body of Christ is mystically one, it follows that the fellowship of his members must also be mystical, and not confined to place or time, inasmuch as it is composed of individuals of widely separated countries, and of all ages from the foundation of the world. Rom. ii. 29. "he is a
20 Jew which is one inwardly, and circumcision is that of the heart, in the spirit, and not in the letter; whose praise is not of men, but of God." Eph. ii. 19–22. "now therefore ye are no more strangers and foreigners, but fellow citizens with the saints, and of the household of God; and are built upon the
25 foundation of the apostles and prophets, Jesus Christ himself being the chief corner-stone; in whom all the building fitly framed together, groweth unto an holy temple in the Lord: in whom ye also are builded together for an habitation of God

cilium Dei per spiritum, Col. ii. 5. *Etsi enim corpore absum, spiritu tamen sum vobiscum, gaudens et cernens vestrum ordinem et soliditatem vestræ in Christum fidei.*

Amor Christi in hanc suam ecclesiam invisibilem et im-
5 maculatam illustratur simili amore coniugali. Apoc. xix. 7. *venerunt nuptiæ agni, et uxor eius paravit se.*

Tuendæ ac docendæ ecclesiæ ratione Christus *pastor* etiam dicitur Ioan. x. 14. *ego sum pastor ille bonus.* et v. 16. *fiet unus grex et unus pastor.* Heb. xiii. 20. *Deus pacis magnum*
10 *illum ovium per sanguinem pacti æterni pastorem, Dominum nostrum Iesum Christum ex mortuis reduxit.* 1 Pet. v. 4. *pastorum princeps.*

CAPUT XXV.

DE GLORIFICATIONE INCHOATA: UBI DE CERTITUDINE SALUTIS, ET PER-SEVERANTIA SANCTORUM.

AUCTIONIS altera pars ad patrem et filium relatæ est GLORIFICATIO.
        Ea est vel INCHOATA vel PERFECTA.

INCHOATA est, qua IUSTIFICATI ADOPTATIQUE A DEO PATRE, CUM PRÆSENTIS GRATIÆ AC DIGNITATIS, TUM FUTURÆ GLORIÆ

through the Spirit." Col. ii. 5. "though I be absent in the flesh, yet am I with you in the spirit, joying and beholding your order, and the steadfastness of your faith in Christ."

The love of Christ towards his invisible and spotless Church is described by the appropriate figure of conjugal love. Rev. xix. 7. "the marriage of the Lamb is come, and his wife hath made herself ready."

Christ is also called "the Shepherd," by reason of his protecting and teaching the church. John x. 14. "I am the good shepherd." v. 16. "there shall be one fold, and one shepherd." Heb. xiii. 20. "now the God of peace, that brought again from the dead our Lord Jesus, that great shepherd of the sheep, through the blood of the everlasting covenant—." 1 Pet. v. 4. "when the chief shepherd shall appear—."

CHAPTER XXV.

OF IMPERFECT GLORIFICATION, WHEREIN ARE CONSIDERED THE DOCTRINES OF ASSURANCE AND FINAL PERSEVERANCE.

OF THAT increase which has reference to the Father and Son conjointly, the remaining part is GLORIFICATION.

Glorification is either IMPERFECT or PERFECT.

IMPERFECT GLORIFICATION is that state wherein, being JUSTIFIED AND ADOPTED BY GOD THE FATHER, WE ARE FILLED WITH A CONSCIOUSNESS OF PRESENT GRACE AND EXCELLENCY, AS WELL AS

SENSU QUODAM IMBUIMUR, ET IAM BEATI ESSE INCIPIMUS. Ioan.
xvii. 22. *Et ego gloriam quam dedisti mihi, dedi iis.*

Ad hanc glorificationem Paulus ab ipsa Dei præscientia
progressione quadam continua nos deducit. Rom. viii. 29, 30.
5 *nam quos prænovit, etiam prædestinavit conformandos ima-*
gini filii sui—: quos vero prædestinavit, eos etiam vocavit;
et quos vocavit, eos etiam iustificavit; quos autem iustificavit,
eos etiam glorificavit. et xv. 7. *assumite alii alios, sicut et*
Christus assumpsit nos in gloriam Dei. Eph. i. 3. *benedictus*
10 *esto Deus et pater Domini nostri Iesu Christi, qui benedixit*
nobis omni benedictione spirituali in cœlis in Christo. et iii.
18, 19. *ut in charitate radicati et fundati, valeatis assequi cum*
omnibus sanctis, quæ sit illa latitudo, et longitudo; et profun-
ditas, et sublimitas: et nosse charitatem illam Christi omni
15 *notitia supereminentiorem; ut impleamini ad omnem usque*
plenitudinem Dei. 1 Thess. ii. 12. *ambulantes sicuti con-*
venit Deo vocanti vos ad suum regnum ac gloriam. et 2 Ep.
ii. 14. *quo vocavit vos per evangelium nostrum ad acquiren-*
dam gloriam Domini nostri Iesu Christi. 1 Pet. v. 10. *qui*
20 *vocavit vos ad gloriam suam in Christo Iesu.* et 2 Ep. i. 3.
qui vocavit nos ad gloriam ac virtutem.

IAM BEATI. Matt. v. 3. &c. *beati pauperes spiritu; quoniam*
ipsorum est regnum cœlorum—.

Regenerationi simul et auctioni accedit confirmatio sive

WITH AN EXPECTATION OF FUTURE GLORY, INSOMUCH THAT OUR BLESSEDNESS IS IN A MANNER ALREADY BEGUN. John xvii. 22. "the glory which thou gavest me, I have given them."

St. Paul traces this glorification by progressive steps, from its original source in the foreknowledge of God himself: Rom. viii. 29, 30. "whom he did foreknow, he also did predestinate to be conformed to the image of his Son . . . moreover, whom he did predestinate, them he also called; and whom he called, them he also justified; and whom he justified, them he also glorified." xv. 7. "receive ye one another, as Christ also received us to the glory of God." Eph. i. 3. "blessed be the God and Father of our Lord Jesus Christ, who hath blessed us with all spiritual blessings in heavenly places in Christ." iii. 17–19. "that ye, being rooted and grounded in love, may be able to comprehend with all saints what is the breadth, and length, and depth, and height, and to know the love of Christ, which passeth knowledge, that ye might be filled with all the fulness of God." 1 Thess. ii. 12. "that ye would walk worthy of God, who hath called you unto his kingdom and glory." 2 Thess. ii. 14. "whereunto he called you by our gospel, to the obtaining of the glory of our Lord Jesus Christ." 1 Pet. v. 10. "who hath called us unto his eternal glory by Christ Jesus." 2 Pet. i. 3. "that hath called us to glory and virtue."

OUR BLESSEDNESS IS IN A MANNER ALREADY BEGUN. Matt. v. 3, &c. "blessed are the poor in spirit, for theirs is the kingdom of heaven."

Both regeneration and increase are accompanied by confirmation, or preservation in the faith, which is also the work

conservatio: opus itidem Dei. 1 Cor. i. 8. *qui confirmabit
vos usque ad finem inculpatos, in diem Domini nostri Iesu
Christi.* et 2 Cor. i. 21, 22. *qui nos confirmat vobiscum in
Christum, Deus est: qui etiam obsignavit nos indiditque ar-*
5 *rhabonem spiritus cordibus nostris.* Eph. iii. 16. *et det vobis
secundum divitias gloriæ suæ, ut fortiter corroboremini per
spiritum suum in interiore homine.* 1 Pet. v. 10. *Deus— qui
vocavit vos—, is inquam compingat vos, stabiliat, roboret,
fundet.* Iudæ 24. *qui potest vos custodire a lapsu immunes,*
10 *et statuere in conspectu gloriæ suæ inculpabiles cum exultatione.*

HÆC TRIA regeneratio, auctio et conservatio, veluti causæ
proximæ a parte Dei, earumque effecta, ut *fides, charitas,* &c.
a parte hominis, sive in homine, CERTITUDINEM SALUTIS et PER-
15 SEVERANTIAM SANCTORUM efficiunt.

A parte Dei causa quidem prima et remotior est eius præ-
destinatio sive electio credentium. Rom. viii. 30. *quos prædestinavit—*, ut supra. et xi. 29. *nam dona illa et illa vocatio
Dei eiusmodi sunt; ut eorum ipsum pœnitere non possit.* Heb.
20 vi. 17, 18. *qua in re Deus volens ex abundanti hæredibus promissionis ostendere immutabilitatem consilii sui, fideiussit
iureiurando: ut per duas res immutabiles in quibus fieri non
potest ut mentitus sit Deus, validam consolationem habeamus
nos* &c. 2 Pet. i. 4. *ex eo quod maxima illa nobis ac pretiosa*
25 *promissa donavit, ut per hæc efficeremini divinæ consortes
naturæ.*

of God. 1 Cor. i. 8. "who shall also confirm you unto the end, that ye may be blameless in the day of our Lord Jesus Christ." 2 Cor. i. 21, 22. "now he which stablisheth us with you in Christ, and hath anointed us, is God; who hath also sealed
5 us, and given us the earnest of the Spirit in our hearts." Eph. iii. 16. "that he would grant you according to the riches of his glory to be strengthened with might by his Spirit in the inner man." 1 Pet. v. 10. "the God of all grace, who hath called us . . . make you perfect, stablish, strengthen, settle you."
10 Jude 24. "unto him that is able to keep you from falling, and to present you faultless before the presence of his glory with exceeding joy."

These three, "regeneration," "increase," and "preservation in the faith," considered as proximate causes on the part of
15 God, and their effects, as "faith," "love," &c. considered as proximate causes on the part of man, or as acting in man, produce ASSURANCE OF SALVATION, and THE FINAL PERSEVERANCE OF THE SAINTS.

On the part of God, however, the primary or more remote
20 cause is his predestination or election of believers. Rom. viii. 30. "whom he did predestinate," &c. as quoted above. xi. 29. "the gifts and calling of God are without repentance." Heb. vi. 17, 18. "wherein God, willing more abundantly to show unto the heirs of promise the immutability of his counsel, con-
25 firmed it by an oath; that by two immutable things, in which it was impossible for God to lie, we might have a strong consolation," &c. 2 Pet. i. 4. "whereby are given unto us exceeding great and precious promises; that by these ye might be partakers of the divine nature."

CERTITUDO itaque SALUTIS est FIDEI QUIDAM GRADUS, QUO QUIS
TESTANTE SPIRITU PERSUASUS EST FIRMITERQUE CREDIT, SE CRE-
DENTEM ATQUE IN FIDE ET CHARITATE PERMANENTEM, IUSTIFI-
CATUM, ADOPTATUM, EX ILLA DENIQUE UNIONE ET COMMUNIONE
5 CUM CHRISTO ET PATRE GLORIFICARI CŒPTUM, SEMPITERNAM
VITAM CONSUMMATAMQUE GLORIAM CERTISSIME ADEPTURUM.

PERSUASUS EST. immo persuasus esse debet. 2 Pet. i. 10.
*potius studete vocationem et electionem vestram salutem
æternam firmam efficere.* id est, vocationis et electionis fruc-
10 tum; vocatio enim ipsa firmior fieri non potest, quippe iam
præterita: sed nihil hoc valet, nisi nos etiam utramque firmam facere studeamus; in nostra igitur potestate quod nostræ
partis est situm esse oportet.

SE CREDENTEM. Ioan. iii. 16. *ut quisquis credit in eum, non
15 pereat, sed habeat vitam æternam:* et vi. 47. idem. Rom.
v. 2. *per quem habemus accessum fide in gratiam istam in
qua stamus, et gloriamur in spe gloriæ Dei.* 2 Cor. xiii. 5. *vos
ipsos tentate, an sitis in fide, vos ipsos explorate: annon ag-
noscitis vosmetipsos, videlicet Iesum Christum in vobis esse?*
20 *nisi reiectandi estis. Inhabitat* autem *Christus in nobis per
fidem,* Eph. iii. 17. fidem ergo, non electionem, quæ sine
fide esse firma non potest, explorare iubemur, ne simus re-
iectanei.

IN FIDE ET CHARITATE PERMANENTEM. Heb. vi. 18, 19, 20, *ut*

Hence ASSURANCE OF SALVATION IS A CERTAIN DEGREE OR GRADATION OF FAITH, WHEREBY A MAN HAS A FIRM PERSUASION AND CONVICTION, FOUNDED ON THE TESTIMONY OF THE SPIRIT, THAT IF HE BELIEVE AND CONTINUE IN FAITH AND LOVE, HAVING

5 BEEN JUSTIFIED AND ADOPTED, AND PARTLY GLORIFIED BY UNION AND FELLOWSHIP WITH CHRIST AND THE FATHER, HE WILL AT LENGTH MOST CERTAINLY ATTAIN TO EVERLASTING LIFE AND THE CONSUMMATION OF GLORY.

HAS A FIRM PERSUASION; or, to speak more properly, ought,

10 and is entitled to have a firm persuasion. 2 Pet. i. 10. "wherefore the rather, brethren, give diligence to make your calling and election sure," that is, the fruit of your calling and election, eternal life; for the calling itself cannot be made more sure, inasmuch as it is already past; but this is of no avail,

15 unless we give diligence to make both sure. It follows, that, as far as this depends upon ourselves, it must be in our own power to make it sure.

IF HE BELIEVE. John iii. 16. "that whosoever believeth in him should not perish, but have everlasting life." See also vi. 47.

20 Rom. v. 2. "by whom also we have access by faith into this grace wherein we stand, and rejoice in hope of the glory of God." 2 Cor. xiii. 5. "examine yourselves whether ye be in the faith; prove your own selves: know ye not your own selves, how that Jesus Christ is in you, except ye be reprobates?" But

25 "Christ dwells in our hearts by faith," Eph. iii. 17. Hence we are enjoined to prove our faith, lest we should be reprobates; not our election, which cannot be sure without faith.

CONTINUE IN FAITH AND LOVE. Heb. vi. 18–20. "that we

validam consolationem habeamus nos, qui confugimus ad
tenendam propositam spem; quam velut animæ anchoram
habemus tutam ac firmam, et ingredientem usque in ea, quæ
sunt intra velum. et x. 22, 23. *accedamus cum vero corde in*
5 *plenitudine fidei, aspersione purgatis cordibus a conscientia*
mala; et abluto corpore aqua pura, retineamus professionem
spei, non vacillantem. 2 Pet. i. 9, 10, 11. *nam cui hæc non*
adsunt, is cæcus est, nihil procul cernens, oblitus sese a vete-
ribus peccatis suis fuisse purificatum: quapropter fratres
10 *potius—: ita enim ample subministrabitur vobis introitus in*
æternum regnum Domini nostri et servatoris Iesu Christi.
1 Ioan. iii. 14. *nos scimus nos translatos esse a morte ad vitam,*
quia diligimus fratres. et iv. 18. *metus non est in charitate,*
sed integra charitas foras eiicit metum. Apoc. ii. 17. *ei qui*
15 *vicerit, tribuam ut edat ex manna illo occulto: et dabo ipsi*
calculum album, et in calculo nomen novum scriptum, quod
nemo novit, nisi qui accepit. datur hic electionis singularis
calculus post victoriam.

IUSTIFICATUM. Rom. v. 9, 10. *iustificati igitur nunc eius san-*
20 *guine, servabimur multo magis per eum ab ira illa: nam si*
cum inimici essemus, reconciliati fuimus Deo per mortem
filii sui, multo magis reconciliati, servabimur per vitam ipsius.
Atqui non iustificamur nisi fide.

ADOPTATUM. Rom. viii. 15, 16. *non accepistis spiritum servi-*

might have a strong consolation who have fled for refuge to lay hold upon the hope set before us; which hope we have as an anchor of the soul both sure and stedfast, and which entereth into that within the veil." x. 22, 23. "let us draw near
5 with a true heart, in full assurance of faith, having our hearts sprinkled from an evil conscience, and our bodies washed with pure water: let us hold fast the profession of our faith without wavering." 2 Pet. i. 9–11. "he that lacketh these things, is blind, and cannot see afar off, and hath forgotten
10 that he was purged from his old sins: wherefore the rather, brethren," &c. "for so an entrance shall be ministered unto you abundantly into the everlasting kingdom of our Lord and Savior Jesus Christ." 1 John iii. 14. "we know that we have passed from death unto life, because we love the brethren."
15 iv. 18. "there is no fear in love, but perfect love casteth out fear." Rev. ii. 17. "to him that overcometh will I give to eat of the hidden manna, and will give him a white stone, and in the stone a new name written, which no man knoweth saving he that receiveth it." Here each is represented as receiving the
20 stone, or pledge of election, after he has individually obtained the victory.

HAVING BEEN JUSTIFIED. Rom. v. 9, 10. "much more then, being now justified by his blood, we shall be saved from wrath through him: for if when we were enemies, we were recon-
25 ciled to God by the death of his Son, much more being reconciled, we shall be saved by his life." We are only justified, however, through faith.

ADOPTED. Rom. viii. 15, 16. "ye have not received the spirit

tutis rursum ad metum, sed accepistis spiritum adoptionis, per quem clamamus, Abba, pater.

Testante spiritu. Rom. viii. 16. *et ipse spiritus testatur una cum spiritu nostro, nos esse filios Dei.* Eph. i. 13, 14. *in quo*
5 *et vos spem posuistis audito illo sermone veritatis illius, felici nuntio salutis vestræ; in quo etiam fide ipsi habita, obsignati estis per spiritum illum promissionis sanctum; qui est arrhabo hæreditatis nostræ, ad obtinendam redemptionem ad laudem gloriæ ipsius.* At cap. iv. 30. *ne tristitia afficite spiritum sanc-*
10 *tum Dei, per quem obsignati estis in diem redemptionis.* I Thess. v. 19. *spiritum ne extinguite.* sane si spiritum tristitia afficimus, si extinguimus per quem obsignati sumus, extingui simul certitudinem salutis necesse est.

Ex hac salutis certitudine, gaudium ineffabile nascitur.
15 Ioan. xv. 10, 11. *manebitis—: hæc locutus sum vobis, ut gaudium illud meum in vobis maneat, et gaudium vestrum compleatur.* Rom. xiv. 17. *non enim est regnum Dei esca et potus, sed iustitia, et pax, et gaudium per spiritum sanctum.* I Pet. i. 8, 9. *in quem, nunc eum non videntes, tamen*
20 *credentes, exultatis gaudio ineffabili et glorioso; reportantes finem fidei vestræ, salutem animarum.*

Perseverantia sanctorum est donum Dei conservantis, quo præcogniti, electi, regeniti et per spiritum sanctum obsignati, in fide et gratia Dei ad finem usque perseverant,

of bondage again to fear, but ye have received the Spirit of adoption, whereby we cry, Abba, Father."

On the testimony of the Spirit. Rom. viii. 16. "the Spirit itself beareth witness with our spirit that we are the children
5 of God." Eph. i. 13, 14. "in whom ye also trusted after that ye heard the word of truth, the gospel of your salvation; in whom also, after that ye believed, ye were sealed with that holy Spirit of promise, which is the earnest of our inheritance until the redemption of the purchased possession, unto the
10 praise of his glory." iv. 30. "grieve not the Holy Spirit of God, whereby ye are sealed unto the day of redemption." 1 Thess. v. 19. "quench not the Spirit." Certainly, if we grieve the Holy Spirit, if we quench that by which we were sealed, we must at the same time quench the assurance of our
15 salvation.

This assurance of salvation produces a joy unspeakable. John xv. 10, 11. "ye shall abide in my love . . . these things have I spoken unto you, that my joy might remain in you, and that your joy might be full." Rom. xiv. 17. "the king-
20 dom of God is not meat and drink, but righteousness and peace and joy in the Holy Ghost." 1 Pet. i. 8, 9. "in whom, though now ye see him not, yet believing, ye rejoice with joy unspeakable and full of glory; receiving the end of your faith, even the salvation of your souls."

25   The final perseverance of the saints is the gift of God's preserving power, whereby they who are foreknown, elect and born again, and sealed by the Holy Spirit, persevere to the end in the faith and grace of God, and never entirely

NEQUE ULLA VI AUT FRAUDE DIABOLI AUT MUNDI PENITUS EXCI-
DUNT, MODO UT IPSI SIBIMET NE DESINT, FIDEMQUE ET CHARI-
TATEM PRO SUA VIRILI PARTE RETINEANT.

DONUM DEI CONSERVANTIS. Psal. xxvi. 1. *Iehovæ confido,*
5 *non vacillaturum.* Luc. xxii. 32. *ego deprecatus sum pro*
te, ne deficiat fides tua. Ioan. vi. 37. *quicquid dat mihi pater,*
ad me veniet; et eum qui venit ad me, nequaquam eicerim
foras. Rom. v. 5. *spes non pudefacit, eo quod charitas Dei*
effusa est in cordibus nostris per spiritum sanctum, qui datus
10 *est nobis.* Iudæ 1. *et Iesu Christo asservatis.*

PRÆCOGNITI. 2 Tim. ii. 19. *solidum fundamentum Dei stat,*
habens sigillum hoc, Novit Dominus eos qui sunt sui; et,
Abscedat ab iniustitia quisquis nominat nomen Christi.

REGENITI. Ioan. viii. 35. *servus non manet in domo perpetuo,*
15 *filius manet perpetuo.*

ULLA VI AUT FRAUDE DIABOLI AUT MUNDI. Matt. xxiv. 24. *ita*
ut seducant (si fieri possit) etiam electos. Ioan. x. 28, 29.
neque rapiet eos quisquam e manu mea: pater meus qui dedit
mihi eas maior omnibus est; nec quisquam potest eas rapere
20 *e manu patris mei.* et xvii. 15. *ut eos a maligno illo conserves.*
Rom. viii. 35, 38, 39. *quis nos separabit a charitate Christi?*
Num afflictio, num angustia, num persecutio, num fames,
num nuditas, num periculum, num gladius? Nam mihi per-
suasum est, neque mortem, neque vitam, neque angelos, neque

FALL AWAY THROUGH ANY POWER OR MALICE OF THE DEVIL OR
THE WORLD, SO LONG AS NOTHING IS WANTING ON THEIR OWN
PARTS, AND THEY CONTINUE TO THE UTMOST IN THE MAINTE-
NANCE OF FAITH AND LOVE.

5 THE GIFT OF GOD'S PRESERVING POWER. Psal. xxvi. 1. "I have
trusted in Jehovah, therefore I shall not slide." Luke xxii. 32.
"I have prayed for thee that thy faith fail not." John vi. 37.
"all that the Father giveth me shall come to me; and him that
cometh to me I will in nowise cast out." Rom. v. 5. "hope
10 maketh not ashamed, because the love of God is shed abroad
in our hearts by the Holy Ghost which is given unto us." Jude
1. "preserved in Jesus Christ."

FOREKNOWN. 2 Tim. ii. 19. "the foundation of God standeth
sure, having this seal, The Lord knoweth them that are his;
15 and, Let every one that nameth the name of Christ depart
from iniquity."

BORN AGAIN. John viii. 35. "the servant abideth not in the
house for ever; but the Son abideth ever."

THROUGH ANY POWER OR MALICE OF THE DEVIL OR THE WORLD.
20 Matt. xxiv. 24. "insomuch that if it were possible, they shall
deceive the very elect." John x. 28, 29. "neither shall any man
pluck them out of my hand: my Father which gave them me
is greater than all, and no man is able to pluck them out of
my Father's hand." xvii. 15. "that thou shouldest keep them
25 from the evil." Rom. viii. 35, 38, 39. "who shall separate us
from the love of Christ? shall tribulation, or distress, or persecution, or famine, or nakedness, or peril, or sword? for I am
persuaded that neither death, nor life, nor angels, nor princi-

principatus, neque potestates, neque præsentia, neque futura,
neque sublimitatem, neque profunditatem, neque ullam rem
aliam creatam posse nos separare a charitate Dei, quæ est in
Christo Iesu Domino nostro.

5   MODO UT IPSI SIBIMET NE DESINT—. hæc ut adiicerem suasit
totus ipse tenor scripturæ. Psal. cxxv. 1, 2. *qui confidunt*
Iehovæ, similes sunt monti Sionis, qui non dimovetur, in sæ-
culum permanet. 2 Chron. xv. 2. *Iehova vobiscum dum vos*
estis cum eo; et si requiretis eum, invenietur a vobis; sin
10 *reliqueritis eum, relinquet vos.* Ier. xxxii. 40. *pangam ipsis*
fœdus perpetuum, fore ut non avertam me a prosequendis
ipsis, beneficiendo ipsis; et reverentiam meam indam animo
ipsorum, ut non recedant a me. promittit quidem hic Deus,
inditurum se reverentiam suam animo ipsorum, ut non rece-
15 dant a se; quod enim suæ sunt partes Deus promittit; suffi-
cientiam nempe gratiæ, ne recedant: attamen fœdus pangit;
in fœdere autem non ab una parte sola, sed utrinque aliquid
præstandum est: deinde, *ut non recedant a me,* id est, a cultu
meo externo, perspicuum est ex toto illo capite a v. 37, et ex
20 sequentis v. 20, 21. *si irritum facere potestis fœdus meum de*
die—, etiam fœdus meum cum Davide servo meo irritum
fiet—, et cum Levitis—. postremo, quibus inditurum se reve-

palities, nor powers, nor things present, nor things to come, nor height, nor depth, nor any other creature, shall be able to separate us from the love of God, which is in Christ Jesus our Lord."

5   So long as nothing is wanting on their own parts. In adding this limitation, I was influenced by what I had observed to be the uniform tenor of Scripture. Psal. cxxv. 1, 2. "they that trust in Jehovah shall be as mount Sion, which cannot be removed, but abideth for ever." 2 Chron. xv. 2.

10 "Jehovah is with you, while ye be with him; and if ye seek him, he will be found of you; but if ye forsake him, he will forsake you." Jer. xxxii. 40. "I will make an everlasting covenant with them, that I will not turn away from them to do them good; but I will put my fear in their hearts, that they

15 shall not depart from me." In promising to "put his fear in their hearts, that they shall not depart from him," God merely engages to perform what is requisite on his part, namely, to bestow such a supply of grace as should be sufficient, if properly employed, to retain them in his way. At the same time

20 he enters into a covenant with them. Now a covenant implies certain conditions to be performed, not by one, but by both the parties. "They shall not depart from me"; that is, from my external worship, as the whole of the context shows, from the thirty-seventh verse to the end of the chapter, compared

25 with the twentieth and twenty-first verses of the following; "if ye can break my covenant of the day . . . then may also my covenant be broken with David my servant . . . and with the Levites." Lastly, it appears that these very persons,

rentiam suam promisit, ut non recederent, illos ipsos recessisse constat: nam et filiis eorum idem promissum est cap. xxxii. 39. unde etiam si Deus reverentiam suam ex fœdere iis indiderit in eum finem ut non recederent, ipsos tamen vitio suo 5 et culpa recessisse eventus docuit: immo omnes Iudæos hic alloquitur et de omnibus; omnes autem non erant electi; non ergo de electis, ut volunt, hic sermo est.

Sic Ezech. xi. 19, 20, 21. *indam ipsis cor unum, et spiritum novum ponam in medio vestri, amovens cor lapideum*—; *ut* 10 *in statutis meis ambulent*—: *at illis quorum animus obibit intima detestabilia*—, *viam suam in capite ipsorum reponam.* Matt. vii. 24, 25. *quisquis audit ex me sermones istos, et eos præstat assimilabo eum viro prudenti, qui ædificavit domum suam super petram.* Ioan. iv. 14. *quisquis biberit ex aqua* 15 *illa*—. et vi. 51. *siquis ederit ex hoc pane, vivet in æternum.* 1 Cor. x. 12. *qui sibi videtur stare, videat ne cadat.* Philipp. ii. 12. *cum timore ac tremore vestram ipsorum salutem conficite.* 1 Ioan. ii. 17. *qui facit voluntatem Dei, manet in æternum.* et v. 28. *manete in eo; ut cum conspicuus factus* 20 *fuerit, habeamus fiduciam, neque pudefiamus coram eo in ipsius adventu.*

Quapropter et hoc adiectum est, FIDEMQUE ET CHARITATEM

in whose hearts he promised to put his fear that they should not depart from him, did actually so depart; for the same promise is made to their children, chap. xxxii. 39. The event therefore proved, that although God had according to com-

5 pact put his fear into their hearts to the very end that they should not depart, they nevertheless departed through their own fault and depravity. Moreover, the words are addressed to, and include, the whole nation; but the whole nation was not elect; it follows therefore that the passage cannot refer to

10 the elect exclusively, as is contended. Ezek. xi. 19–21. "I will give them one heart, and I will put a new spirit within you; and I will take the stony heart out of their flesh . . . that they may walk in my statutes . . . but as for them whose heart walketh after the heart of their detestable things

15 and their abominations, I will recompense their way upon their own heads." Matt. vii. 24, 25. "whosoever heareth these sayings of mine and doeth them, I will liken him unto a wise man that built his house upon the rock." John iv. 14. "whosoever drinketh of the water that I shall give him . . .

20 it shall be in him a well of water springing up into everlasting life." vi. 51. "if any man eat of this bread he shall live for ever." 1 Cor. x. 12. "let him that thinketh he standeth, take heed lest he fall." Philipp. ii. 12. "work out your own salvation with fear and trembling." 1 John ii. 17. "he that doeth

25 the will of God, abideth for ever." v. 28. "abide in him, that when he shall appear, we may have confidence, and not be ashamed before him at his coming."

CONTINUE TO THE UTMOST IN THE MAINTENANCE OF FAITH

PRO SUA VIRILI PARTE RETINEANT. Ioan. xv. 2. *omnem palmitem
in me non ferentem fructum, tollit.* et v. 6. *nisi quis in me
manserit, abiectus extra vineam statim ut palmes, arescet;
deinde congregantur isti palmites, et in ignem abiiciuntur,*
5 *et ardent.* et 10. *si præcepta mea observaveritis, manebitis in
charitate mea; sicut ego patris mei mandata observavi, et
maneo in eius charitate.* Rom. xi. 20. *per incredulitatem
defracti sunt; tu vero per fidem stas.* et v. 22. *vide igitur
benignitatem ac præcisam severitatem Dei; in eos quidem*
10 *qui ceciderunt, præcisam severitatem; in te vero benignitatem,
si permanseris in benignitate; alioquin et tu excideris.* Dona
itaque Dei ἀμεταμέλητα dicuntur, infra v. 29, quia non pœ-
nituit eum promisisse Abrahamo et semini eius; tametsi plurimi defecissent, non quod erga mutantes non mutarit. 2 Cor.
15 i. 24. *fide statis.* Eph. iii. 18. *in charitate radicati ac fundati.*
1 Pet. i. 5. *virtutis Dei præsidio custodimini per fidem.*
2 Ep. i. 5, &c. *et ad hoc ipsum diligentiam omnem adhi-
bentes, adiicite fidei vestræ virtutem*—. *hæc enim si vobis
adsint, et abundent, non segnes vos, vel frustraneos, nec sine*
20 *fructu efficient*—: *hæc enim si feceritis, nunquam impin-
getis*—. Posse autem vel revera fidelem aliquando penitus
deficere, ostendit idem Petrus cap. ii. 18. *inescant per carnis
cupiditates et lascivias alios, qui vere effugerant eos qui in
errore versantur;* si quidem ita legi debet, *vere* vel *re ipsa effu-*
25 *gere,* et non *paulum,* ut alii legunt; deinde, si per *agnitionem*

AND LOVE. This clause is subjoined for the same reason as the preceding. John xv. 2. "every branch in me that beareth not fruit he taketh away." v. 6. "if a man abide not in me, he is cast forth as a branch, and is withered, and men gather them, and cast them into the fire, and they are burned." v. 10. "if ye keep my commandments, ye shall abide in my love, even as I have kept my Father's commandments, and abide in his love." Rom. xi. 20. "because of unbelief they were broken off, and thou standest by faith." v. 22. "behold therefore the goodness and severity of God; on them which fell, severity; but toward thee, goodness, if thou continue in his goodness; otherwise thou also shalt be cut off." Thus the gifts of God are said to be "without repentance," v. 29. inasmuch as he did not repent of his promise to Abraham and his seed, although the greater part of them had revolted; but it does not follow that he did not change his purpose towards those, who had first changed theirs towards him. 2 Cor. i. 24. "by faith ye stand." Eph. iii. 17. "being rooted and grounded in love." 1 Pet. i. 5. "who are kept by the power of God through faith unto salvation." 2 Pet. i. 5–10. "beside this, giving all diligence, add to your faith virtue . . . for if these things be in you, and abound, they make you that ye shall neither be barren nor unfruitful . . . for if ye do these things, ye shall never fall." That a real believer, however, may fall irrecoverably, the same apostle shows, chap. ii. 18. "they allure through the lusts of the flesh, through much wantonness, those that were clean escaped from them who live in error"; if indeed this be the right reading, and not, as others contend, "escaped a little": not to

Domini intelligatur fides salvifica, non historica tantum; postremo, si *pollutiones mundi relictas* interpretemur vitæ puritatem, regeneratam vere et Christianam, non externam puritatem, et philosophicam; sic locus iste ambiguus videtur.
5 Clarior autem est Ezechiel, cap. xviii. 26. *cum avertit se iustus a iustitia sua—, morietur.* hæc vera sit iustitia necesse est, quippe a qua siquis se avertit, morietur. At inquiunt, conditio hæc est, *si averterit se:* nunquam autem se avertet. Respondeo, neque conditionem esse in Hebræo, neque si
10 esset, conditiones impossibiles et absurdas Deo convenire: hic duo tanquam æque verisimilia ponuntur, *si improbus se converterit,* v. 21. *si averterit se iustus,* v. 26. *hæc viarum Domini æquitas est,* v. 25. Eadem repetitur argumentatio cap. xxxiii. 12, 13, &c. Paulus revera fidelis fuit; et tamen, 1 Cor. ix. 27.
15 *contundo corpus meum, et in servitutem redigo; ne quo modo, cum aliis prædicarim, ipse reiectaneus fiam.* Videtur etiam apostolus, Heb. vi. 4, 5, 6. de vero fideli penitus excidente loqui, si extrema illa verba expendantur; *et prolapsos, rursus renovari ad resipiscentiam:* hæc enim effecta regenerationis
20 videntur fuisse. Itaque oravit patrem Christus ne Petri fides

mention, that it appears doubtful whether "the knowledge of the Lord" should be understood here of a saving faith, and not of an historical only; and whether their escape "from the pollutions of the world" implies a truly regenerate and Chris-
5 tian purity of life, and not a mere outward and philosophical morality: so that from this passage nothing certain can be inferred. The text in Ezekiel, xviii. 26. is clearer; "when a righteous man turneth away from his righteousness . . . he shall die." The righteousness here intended must necessarily
10 be true righteousness, being that from which whosoever turns shall die. But, it is replied, the event is conditional, "if he turneth away"; which, on our hypothesis, will never happen. I answer, first, that the Hebrew does not express any condition, and, secondly, that if it were so, an absurd and imprac-
15 ticable condition is inconsistent with the character of God. Two suppositions, both of them equally possible, are here made; v. 21. "if the wicked will turn from all his sins"; v. 26. "when a righteous man turneth away from his righteousness"; hence v. 25. "is not the way of the Lord equal?" The
20 same mode of reasoning occurs again xxxiii. 12, 13, &c. Paul was a true believer, and yet he says, 1 Cor. ix. 27. "I keep under my body and bring it into subjection, lest that by any means when I have preached to others, I myself should be a castaway." The apostle to the Hebrews, vi. 4–6. seems also
25 to speak of the possible final apostasy of the real believer, if the concluding clause of the passage be attentively considered: "if they shall fall away, to renew them again unto repentance"; for the state described in the fourth and fifth verses,

deficiat, Luc. xxii. 32: quippe fides Petri per se potuit deficere, etiamsi gratia Dei ordinaria Petrum non deficeret: oravit igitur Christus non, ut ne gratia Dei, sed ut ne fides Petri deficeret; quod eo tempore verendum erat, nisi gratia Dei extraordinaria rogatu Christi succurreret. 1 Tim. i. 19. *retinens fidem et bonam conscientiam; qua expulsa, nonnulli naufragium fidei fecerunt.* certe vel illam fidem et bonam conscientiam quam nonnulli expulerunt, vel illam fidem cuius naufragium fecerunt fuisse veram, negari non potest.

Non igitur electi, sed perseverantes salutem adipisci dicuntur. Matt. xxiv. 12, 13. *refrigescet charitas multorum: sed qui permanserit ad finem usque, is servabitur.* et x. 22. idem. Heb. iii. 6. *cuius domus sumus nos, si modo fiduciam et spem illam de qua gloriamur, ad finem usque firmam retinuerimus.* et v. 14. *Christi consortes facti sumus, si modo principium illud quo sustentamur, firmum retinuerimus ad finem usque.* 1 Ioan. ii. 24. *si in vobis manserit quod audivistis a principio, vos quoque in filio et patre manebitis.* Apoc. ii. 10. *esto fidelis usque ad mortem, et dabo tibi coronam vitæ.* et iii. 11. *retine quod habes, ut nemo accipiat coronam tuam.* Ioan. viii. 31. *si vos manseritis in sermone meo, vere discipuli mei eritis.*

and from which they are represented as having fallen, can
scarcely have been other than a regenerate state. Christ therefore prayed to the Father that the faith of Peter might not
fail, Luke xxii. 32. For it was possible for his faith to fail
through his own fault, without any failure in the ordinary
gifts of God's grace; wherefore Christ prayed, not that the
grace of God, but that the faith of Peter, might not fail; which
was to be dreaded at that time, unless he were strengthened
by an extraordinary effusion of the grace of God at the request
of Christ, 1 Tim. i. 19. "holding faith and a good conscience,
which some having put away concerning faith have made
shipwreck." It cannot be doubted that the faith and good
conscience which some had put away, as well as the faith concerning which some had made shipwreck, was genuine.

Accordingly, not the elect, but those who continue to the
end, are said to obtain salvation. Matt. xxiv. 12, 13. "the love
of many shall wax cold; but he that shall endure unto the end,
the same shall be saved." See also x. 22. Heb. iii. 6. "whose
house are we, if we hold fast the confidence and the rejoicing
of the hope even to the end." v. 14. "we are made partakers
of Christ, if we hold the beginning of our confidence stead-
fast unto the end." 1 John ii. 24. "if that which ye have heard
from the beginning shall remain in you, ye also shall continue
in the Son." Rev. ii. 10. "be thou faithful unto death, and I
will give thee a crown of life." iii. 11. "hold that fast which
thou hast, that no man take thy crown." John viii. 31. "if ye
continue in my word, then are ye my disciples indeed." From
this last passage, however, our opponents draw the inverse

At vice versa, si estis vere mei discipuli, manebitis. Sic enim disserunt ex 1 Ioan. ii. 19. *si fuissent ex nobis, mansissent utique nobiscum: sed egressi sunt ex nobis, ut manifestum fieret, non omnes esse ex nobis.* Respondeo, hæc inter se non
5 repugnare; neque enim esse hanc regulam de universis fidelibus, neque ex causis necessario deductam; sed iudicium apostoli de quibusdam Antichristis ab eventu factum, ut plerumque solet evenire. Itaque non dicit, *si fuissent ex nobis, non potuissent non nobiscum mansisse,* neque causas dicit cur non
10 potuissent; hoc solum dicit, *mansissent utique:* ac si sic disseruisset; quandoquidem raro admodum fit ut verus discipulus non maneat in fide, mansissent utique illi si veri fuissent: sed *egressi sunt.* quare? non ut ostenderent veros fideles nunquam potuisse egredi, sed ut ostenderent ex eo quod veri
15 rarissime faciunt, non omnes fuisse veros qui cum apostolis versabantur: ut si quis diceret, si verus amicus fuisset, nunquam deseruisset; propterea quod amicus verus rarissime id facit; non quo nequeat ullo tempore hoc facere. Hanc autem non esse regulam de omni semper et reciproce veram, perspi-
20 cuum est si hoc modo invertas; si mansissent, ex nobis utique fuissent; multi nempe hypocritæ ad obitum usque in ecclesia

inference, "if ye be my disciples indeed, ye will continue";
in other words, your continuance will be a proof of your being
really my disciples; in support of which they quote 1 John
ii. 19. "if they had been of us, they would no doubt have con-
5 tinued with us; but they went out, that it might be made
manifest that they were not all of us." I reply, that these texts
do not contradict each other, inasmuch as the apostle is not
here laying down a rule applicable to believers in general,
formally deduced from necessary causes; but merely giving
10 his judgment concerning certain antichrists, which judgment,
according to a common practice, he had formed from the
event. He does not say, therefore, "if they had been of us, it
was impossible but that they should have continued with us,"
nor does he mention the causes of this impossibility; but he
15 merely says, "they would have continued." His argument
is as follows; since it is very rare that a true disciple does not
continue in the faith, it is natural to suppose that they would
have continued in it, if they had been true disciples. But "they
went out from us." Why? Not to show that true believers
20 could never depart from the faith, but that all who walked
with the apostles were not true believers, inasmuch as true
believers very rarely acted as they had done. In the same way
it might be said of an individual, "if he had been a real friend,
he would never have been unfaithful"; not because it is im-
25 possible that a real friend should ever be unfaithful, but because the case very seldom happens. That the apostle could
not have intended to lay down a rule of universal application,
will be shown by inverting the hypothesis; "if they had con-

manent, nunquam egrediuntur. Ut igitur qui manent, non ex eo cognoscuntur esse vere fideles, quia manent, ita qui non manent, non omnes hinc demonstrantur nunquam fuisse vere fideles quia non manent, sed hoc duntaxat; tum quidem
5 non fuisse veros cum egrederentur: neque vero Christus, cui certe Ioannes non contradicit, hoc modo argumentatur; *estis vere discipuli si manseritis* sed, *si manseritis (vere* scilicet, id enim utrinque intelligendum est), *vere discipuli mei eritis:* ergo *si non manseritis, non eritis.*

10 At in eadem epistola cap. iii. 9. *omnis qui natus est ex Deo, non facit peccatum, quoniam semen eius manet in ipso: neque potest peccare, quia ex Deo natus est.* Unde sic disputatur; si non potest peccare, multo minus potest a fide deficere. At vero non est singularis aliquis versus ita praecise a caeteris quasi
15 intercipiendus, ut non sit cum aliis versibus eiusdem et capitis et epistolae, immo cum aliis etiam scripturae totius locis diligenter conferendus, ne Ioannes vel secum vel cum aliis divinis auctoribus confligere videatur. Docet hoc versu 9. quam firmum praesidium contra peccatum a Deo sit in nobis collocatum:
20 docuerat supra v. 3. quid etiam a nobis requiratur; *quisquis*

tinued, they would no doubt have been of us;" whereas many
hypocrites continue in outward communion with the church
even till their death, and never go out from it. As therefore
those who continue are not known to be real believers simply
5 from their continuing, so neither are those who do not continue proved thereby never to have been real believers; this
only is certain, that they were not real believers when they
went out from the church. For neither does Christ, with
whom John undoubtedly agreed, argue thus, "ye are my
10 disciples indeed, if ye continue in my word," but thus; "if ye
continue indeed (for this latter word must be taken with both
members of the sentence) then will ye be indeed my disciples"; therefore, "if ye do not continue, ye will not be my
disciples."
15 It is said, however, in the same epistle, chap. iii. 9. "whosoever is born of God doth not commit sin; for his seed remaineth in him, and he cannot sin, because he is born of
God"; from which they argue as follows: if he cannot sin,
much less can he depart from the faith. We are not at liberty,
20 however, thus to separate a particular verse from its context,
without carefully comparing its meaning with other verses
of the same chapter and epistle, as well as with texts bearing
on the same subject in other parts of Scripture; lest the apostle
should be made to contradict either himself, or the other
25 sacred writers. He is declaring, in the verse above quoted, the
strength of that internal aid with which God has provided us
against sin; having previously explained what is required on
our own part, v. 3. "every man that hath this hope in him,

habet hanc spem in eo sitam, purificat se sicut et ille purus est.
et infra versu sequenti 10. *in hoc manifesti sunt filii Dei et*
filii diaboli: omnis qui non facit iustitiam, non est ex Deo;
et qui non diligit fratrem suum. Et cap. iv. 16. *Deus charitas*
5 *est; et qui manet in charitate, in Deo manet et Deus in eo.*
et v. 18. *quisquis natus est ex Deo, non peccat; sed qui genitus*
est ex Deo, conservat seipsum. Quisquis igitur natus est ex
Deo, non potest peccare, adeoque nec deficere; sed hoc simul
intellecto, ut pro virili sua parte se quoque purificet, ut faciat
10 iustitiam, ut diligat fratrem suum, ut ipse maneat in charitate,
quo Deus Deique semen in ipso quoque maneat; ut seipsum
denique conservet. Deinde quid hoc est, *non potest peccare;*
cum dictum iam sit cap. i. 8. *si dixerimus nos peccatum non*
habere, nosmetipsos fallimus? Proculdubio igitur, *non potest*
15 *peccare* intelligendum hic est, non facile peccat, non sua voluntate ac consilio, non dedita opera, non de industria; sed, invitus
ac dolens; nec in peccandi consuetudine persistit; unde et peccatum ei, maximeque propter Christum, non imputatur.
Quod si in hac voce *peccare* tanta est interpretandi cautione
20 utendum, debemus etiam cæteras huius versiculi voces non
minus caute interpretari, nec ea styli simplicitate, qua perpetua
usus est hic apostolus, ad doctrinam alioqui absurdam indu-
cendam abuti. *Non posse* enim, ut recte monuerunt Theologi
Remonstrantes, non semper, neque in communi usu loquendi,
25 neque in aliis scripturæ locis Impossibilitatem significat. Sic

purifieth himself, even as he is pure." He recurs again to the
same point v. 10. "in this the children of God are manifest,
and the children of the devil: whosoever doeth not righteousness is not of God, neither he that loveth not his brother." iv.
5 16. "God is love, and he that dwelleth in love, dwelleth in
God, and God in him." v. 18. "whosoever is born of God,
sinneth not, but he that is begotten of God keepeth himself—." Whosoever, therefore, is born of God, cannot sin,
and therefore cannot depart from the faith, provided that he
10 at the same time purify himself to the utmost of his power,
that he do righteousness, that he love his brother, that he
remain himself in love, in order that God and his seed may
also remain in him; that finally he keep himself. Further, in
what sense is it said, "he cannot sin," when the apostle has
15 already declared chap. i. 8. "if we say that we have no sin,
we deceive ourselves, and the truth is not in us?" Doubtless
we ought to understand by this phrase that he does not easily
fall into sin, not voluntarily and intentionally, not wilfully
and presumptuously, but with reluctance and remorse; and
20 that he does not persist in the habit of sinning; for which
reasons, and above all for Christ's sake, sin is not imputed to
him. If then so much caution be necessary in explaining the
word "sin," we ought to proceed with no less care in the
interpretation of the remaining part of the verse; and not to
25 take advantage of the simplicity of style peculiar to this
apostle, for the purpose of establishing a doctrine in itself
absurd. For "not to be able," as the Remonstrant divines have
rightly observed, does not always signify absolute impossi-

frequenter dicimus, Non possum hoc facere, id [est], non possum commode, honeste, facile, salva conscientia, verecundia, honore, dignitate, iureiurando: sic dicitur Luc. xi. 7. *non possum surgere et dare tibi* &c. et tamen statim surrexit

5 et Act. iv. 20. *non possumus quæ vidimus et audivimus, non loqui.* Matt. xii. 34. *quomodo potestis bona loqui, cum sitis improbi?* Certe bona loqui in promptu est vel hypocritis: ita hic, *Non potest peccare,* id [est], non potest facile peccare, adeoque nec facile deficere. Eadem perspicacia ac diligentia

10 explicatur a Theologis illis ratio illa quæ redditur, *quia semen Dei manet in ipso:* ita ut *manet* idem sit quod *est in ipso.* Sic. Ioan. xiv. 17. *apud vos manet, et in vobis erit.* Et v. 14. huius ipsius capitis de quo nunc agitur; *qui non diligit fratrem, manet in morte:* quamdiu nempe non diligit fratrem;

15 alioqui impossibile esset qui unquam fratrem non dilexisset, mortem effugere. *Omnis* igitur *qui natus est ex Deo non potest peccare, quia semen eius manet* vel *est in ipso;* est autem in ipso quamdiu ab ipso non extinguitur; potest nempe et spiritus extingui: manet etiam in ipso quamdiu is manet

20 in charitate.

Veruntamen cum *Deus fidelis sit qui nos conservat,* totque

bility, either in common language or in Scripture. Thus we often say that a particular thing cannot be done, meaning that it cannot be done with convenience, honor, or facility, or with a safe conscience, or consistently with modesty, or credit, or

5 dignity, or good faith. In this sense it is said, Luke xi. 7. "I cannot rise and give thee," although the speaker shortly afterwards rises. So also Acts iv. 20. "we cannot but speak the things which we have seen and heard." Matt. xii. 34. "how can ye, being evil, speak good things?" whereas it is easy even

10 for hypocrites to "speak good things." In like manner, when it is said in the present passage "he cannot sin," the meaning is, that he cannot easily fall into sin, and therefore cannot easily depart from the faith. The same divines have displayed equal sagacity and research in their explanation of the reason

15 assigned by the apostle, "for his seed remaineth in him"; where they show that "to remain in him" means the same as "to be in him." So John xiv. 7. "he dwelleth with you, and shall be in you." Thus also in the fourteenth verse of the very chapter under consideration; "he that loveth not his brother

20 abideth in death"; that is, so long as he does not love his brother; for in any other sense it would be impossible for a man to escape death who had ever been guilty of not loving his brother. "Whosoever" therefore "is born of God cannot sin, because his seed remaineth" or "is in him"; it is in him

25 as long as he does not himself quench it, for even the Spirit can be quenched; it remains in him moreover, as long as he himself remains in love.

Those, however, who do not persevere in the faith, are in

nobis pignora salutis, electionem nempe credentium, regenerationem, iustificationem, adoptionem, unionem et communionem secum et cum Christo una cum spiritu arrhabone
et obsignatore dederit, glorificationem etiam nostram inchoa-
5 verit, hinc qui non perseverant, pro non regenitis et non vere
fidelibus plerumque habendi sunt. Prov. xxiv. 16. *nam ut
septies cadat iustus, exsurgit tamen; improbi vero corruunt
malo.* Matt. xxv. 3. *quæ fatuæ erant, sumptis lampadibus
suis, non ceperunt oleum secum.* Luc. viii. 13. *radicem non
10 habent.* 2 Pet. ii. 22. *canis et sus lota.* 1 Ioan. ii. 19. *e nobis
egressi sunt.*

Aut defecisse a fide quæ creditur, non qua creditur cen-
sendi. 1 Tim. iv. 1. *spiritus diserte dicit, fore ut posterioribus
præstitutis temporibus desciscant quidam a fide, attenti spiri-
15 tibus deceptoribus ac doctrinis dæmoniorum.* Gal. v. 4. *evanuistis separati a Christo, quicunque per legem justificamini, et
a gratia excidistis.* Utcunque hæc se habent, Deus assiduis
precibus nobis est orandus cum apostolo, 2 Thess. i. 11. *ut
nos dignetur ista vocatione, et compleat totum suæ bonitatis
20 beneplacitum et opus fidei potenter.*

Et de inchoata quidem glorificatione hactenus: perfectam
quoniam in hac vita non assequimur, de ea in ultimo huius
libri capite dicemus.

ordinary cases to be accounted unregenerate and devoid of genuine belief; seeing that God who "keeps us" is faithful, and that he has given believers so many pledges of salvation, namely, election, regeneration, justification, adoption, union
5 and fellowship with him conjointly with Christ and the Spirit, who is the earnest and seal of the covenant; seeing also that the work of glorification is in them already begun. Prov. xxiv. 16. "a just man falleth seven times, and riseth up again, but the wicked shall fall into mischief." Matt. xxv. 3. "they
10 that were foolish took their lamps, and took no oil with them." Luke viii. 13. "these have no root." 2 Pet. ii. 22. "the dog is turned to his own vomit again, and the sow that was washed to her wallowing in the mire." 1 John ii. 19. "they went out from us."

15 Or perhaps they are to be considered as apostates from the faith, in that sense of faith in which it is the object, not the cause of belief. 1 Tim. iv. 1. "the Spirit speaketh expressly, that in the latter times some shall depart from the faith, giving heed to seducing spirits, and doctrines of devils." Gal. v. 4.
20 "Christ is become of no effect unto you, whosoever of you are justified by the law; ye are fallen from grace." However this may be, it is our duty to entreat God with constant prayer, in the words of the apostle, 2 Thess. i. 11. "that our God would count us worthy of this calling, and fulfil all the good pleas-
25 ure of his goodness, and the work of faith with power."

Thus far of the beginnings of glorification. As its perfection is not attainable in the present life, this part of the subject will be reserved for the concluding chapter of the present book.

CAPUT XXVI.

DE MANIFESTATIONE FŒDERIS GRATIÆ: UBI ET DE LEGE DEI.

FUIT renovationis ratio quoad in hac vita progreditur. Reliqua est eius in fœdere gratiæ MANIFESTATIO sive EXHIBITIO.

FŒDUS ipsum GRATIÆ ex parte Dei promulgatur primum,
5 Gen. iii. 15. *præterea inimicitiam pono inter te et mulierem hanc; similiterque inter semen tuum et semen eius: hoc conteret tibi caput, tu autem conteres huic calcaneum* cum Rom. xvi. 20. *Deus pacis conteret Satanam sub pedes vestros cito.* et 1 Ioan. iii. 8. *ad hoc manifestus factus est filius Dei, ut*
10 *dissolvat opera diaboli.* Ex parte hominum significatur, ex quo homines Deum coluisse narrantur.

MANIFESTATIO FŒDERIS GRATIÆ est eius exhibitio et obsigna-tio: utraque et sub lege fuit, et est sub evangelio.

Sub lege quidem, obscurius licet, et redemptor et redemp-
15 tionis necessitas percipitur. Heb. ix. 8, &c. *nondum factam fuisse manifestam ad sacrarium viam, priore tabernaculo adhuc consistente: quod erat exemplar pro tempore illo tunc*

CHAPTER XXVI.

OF THE MANIFESTATION OF THE COVE-
NANT OF GRACE; INCLUDING
THE LAW OF GOD.

THE nature and process of renovation, so far as it is developed in this life, have been considered. We are now to trace its manifestation and exhibition in the covenant of grace.

5   THE COVENANT OF GRACE itself, on the part of God, is first declared Gen. iii. 15. "I will put enmity between thee and the woman, and between thy seed and her seed; it shall bruise thy head, and thou shalt bruise his heel"; compared with Rom. xvi. 20. "the God of peace shall bruise Satan under your feet
10   shortly." 1 John iii. 8. "for this purpose the Son of God was manifested, that he might destroy the works of the devil." On the part of man its existence may be considered as implied from the earliest period at which it is recorded that mankind worshipped God.

15   THE MANIFESTATION OF THE COVENANT OF GRACE consists in its exhibition and its ratification. Both existed under the law, and both continue under the gospel.

Even under the law the existence of a Redeemer and the necessity of redemption are perceptible, though obscurely
20   and indistinctly. Heb. ix. 8, &c. "the way into the holiest of all was not yet made manifest, while as the first tabernacle was yet standing; which was a figure for the time then pres-

præsente, quo dona sacrificiaque offeruntur, quæ non pos-
sunt in conscientia consummare cultorem. In cibis duntaxat
et potionibus et diversis ablutionibus ac iustificationibus sive
iudiciis carnis usque ad præstitutum tempus directionis im-
5 *posita.* Sub evangelio, apertius, et redemptor et redemptionis
veritas cognoscitur. Ioan. i. 17. *lex per Mosen data est; gratia*
et veritas per Iesum Christum præstita est.

Lᴇx Dᴇɪ est non scripta vel scripta.

Non scripta est naturalis illa primo homini data, cuius
10 reliquiæ et quoddam lumen omnium mortalium cordibus
permansit; in regeneratis vero spiritus sancti opera indies
ad perfectionem primævam renovatur. Rom. i. 19. *ostendit*
enim illis. 32. *qui Dei iure agnito (nempe eos qui talia faciunt*
dignos esse morte) tamen non solum ea faciunt, sed etiam
15 *facientibus consentiunt ultro.* Et ii. 14, 15. *gentes quæ legem*
non habent, natura quæ legis sunt faciunt: isti enim sibi ipsis
sunt lex; ut qui ostendant opus legis scriptum in cordibus suis.

Unde lex pro Doctrina sacra seu voluntate Dei sive sub lege
sive sub evangelio sæpe accipitur. Ier xxxi. 33. *indam legem*
20 *meam menti eorum.* Ioan. x. 34. *nonne scriptum est in lege*
vestra, Ego dixi dii estis? quod scriptum in psalmis, non in
lege, reperitur.

ent, in which were offered both gifts and sacrifices, that could not make him that did the service perfect, as pertaining to the conscience; which stood only in meats and drinks, and divers washings, and carnal ordinances, or "righteousness of the
5 flesh," imposed on them until the time of reformation. Under the gospel both the Redeemer and the truth of his redemption are more explicitly understood. John i. 17. "the law was given by Moses, but grace and truth came by Jesus Christ."

10 THE LAW OF GOD is either written or unwritten.

The unwritten law is no other than that law of nature given originally to Adam, and of which a certain remnant, or imperfect illumination, still dwells in the hearts of all mankind; which, in the regenerate, under the influence of the Holy
15 Spirit, is daily tending towards a renewal of its primitive brightness. Rom. i. 19. "God hath showed it unto them." v. 32. "who knowing the judgment of God, that they which commit such things are worthy of death, not only do the same, but have pleasure in them that do them." ii. 14, 15.
20 "the Gentiles, which have not the law, do by nature the things contained in the law, these having not the law, are a law unto themselves; which show the work of the law written in their hearts."

Hence "the law" is often used for heavenly doctrine in the
25 abstract, or the will of God, as declared under both covenants. Jer. xxxi. 33. "I will put my law in their inward parts." John x. 34. "is it not written in your law, I said, Ye are gods?" though the passage alluded to is found in the Psalms, not in the law properly so called.

Fœderis gratuiti manifestatio sub lege, vel ante Mosen fuit vel sub Mose.

Ante Mosen aliqua ex parte tradita iam lex erat, etsi non scripta. Gen. iv. 3, 4. *obtulit Cain de fructu terræ munus*
5 *Iehovæ.* et v. 26. *tunc cœptum est invocari nomen Iehovæ.* et cap. vii. 1, 2. *te perspexi iustum coram me. Ex omnibus pecudibus mundis—.* Et viii. 20, 21, &c. *extruxit Noa altare Iehovæ—.* 2 Pet. ii. 5. *Noe iustitiæ præconem.* Eadem de cæteris patriarchis ante Mosen leguntur, Gen. xii. 4, 5. *et*
10 xiii. 18. et xxv. 22. et xxviii. 18. Et purificatio, cap. xxxv. 2. *mundate vos ac mutate vestimenta vestra.* Et v. 14. Sic Exod. xvii. 5.

Fœderis manifestatio quædam et veluti umbra sub Mose fuit primum redemptio, per liberationem ex Ægypto, ductu
15 Mosis: deinde, serpens æneus, Ioan. iii. 14, 15, 16.

Expiationis et redemptionis symbola et ante Mosen et sub Mose erant sacrificia et sacerdotes, Melchesedecus et Aharon cum posteris suis. Heb. viii. 5. *ut qui exemplari et umbræ cultum præstent rerum cœlestium—.*

20 LEX MOSAICA ERAT MULTORUM PRÆCEPTORUM, ISRAELITIS DUN-
TAXAT, SCRIPTA INSTITUTIO, CUM PROMISSIONE VITÆ IIS QUI EA
PRÆSTITISSENT, MALEDICTIONE AUTEM QUI NON PRÆSTITISSENT,
UT HUMANI GENERIS PRAVITATEM, ADEOQUE SUAM, INDE AGNO-
SCENTES, AD IUSTITIAM PROMISSI CHRISTI CONFUGERENT, UTQUE

The manifestation of this gratuitous covenant under the law was partly anterior to, and partly coincident with Moses.

Even before Moses the law was already in part delivered, although not in a written form. Gen. iv. 3, 4. "Cain brought
5 of the fruit of the ground an offering unto Jehovah." v. 26. "then began men to call upon the name of Jehovah." vii. 1, 2. "thee have I seen righteous before me in this generation: of every clean beast," &c. viii. 20, 21, &c. "Noah builded an altar unto Jehovah." 2 Pet. ii. 5. "Noah, a preacher of right-
10 eousness." The same is said of the other patriarchs before Moses. Gen. xii. 4, 5. xiii. 18. xxv. 22. xxviii. 18. Cere-monial purification is likewise mentioned, xxxv. 2. "be clean and change your garments." Compare v. 14. Exod. xvii. 5.

A certain manifestation or shadowing forth of the cove-
15 nant was exhibited under Moses, first, in the redemption from bondage by the liberation from Egypt under the guidance of Moses; secondly, in the brazen serpent, John iii. 14–16.

The symbols of expiation and redemption, both before and under Moses, were the sacrifices and the priests, Melchizedec
20 and Aaron with his posterity. Heb. viii. 5. "who serve unto the example and shadow of heavenly things."

THE MOSAIC LAW WAS A WRITTEN CODE CONSISTING OF MANY PRECEPTS, INTENDED FOR THE ISRAELITES ALONE, WITH A PROMISE OF LIFE TO SUCH AS SHOULD KEEP THEM, AND A CURSE ON SUCH AS
25 SHOULD BE DISOBEDIENT; TO THE END THAT THEY, BEING LED THEREBY TO AN ACKNOWLEDGMENT OF THE DEPRAVITY OF MAN-KIND, AND CONSEQUENTLY OF THEIR OWN, MIGHT HAVE RECOURSE TO THE RIGHTEOUSNESS OF THE PROMISED SAVIOR; AND THAT

AB ILLA QUASI PUERILI ATQUE SERVILI RUDIMENTORUM DISCIPLINA
AD ÆTATEM ADULTAM NOVÆ CREATURÆ ET LIBERTATEM SUB EVAN-
GELIO VIRILEM FILIISQUE DIGNAM, OMNES POSTEA GENTES ERUDI-
REMUR. Heb. ix. 8, &c. ut supra.

5   ISRAELITIS DUNTAXAT. Exod. xix. 5, 6. *si sedulo attendetis voci*
meæ, et observabitis fœdus meum, utique eritis mihi pecu-
lium præ omnibus aliis populis: nam mea est tota terra.
Vosque eritis mihi regnum sacerdotale et gens sancta. Deut.
v. 2. *hæ testificationes illæ, statutaque et iudicia quæ locutus*
10 *est Moses apud filios Israelis, quum exivissent ex Ægypto.*
1 Reg. viii. 21. *disposui locum pro arca; in qua est fœdus*
Iehovæ, quod pepigit cum patribus nostris, quum educeret
eos e terra Ægypti. Psal. cxlvii. 19, 20. *verba sua Iacobo* &c.
statuta et iudicia sua Israeli. non sic ulli genti &c. Rom. ii. 4.
15 Hic paries intergerinus ille inter Gentes nempe et Israelitas
morte Christi tandem dirutus et solutus. Eph. ii. 14. ante
hunc solutum Gentes alienatæ ab omni fœdere fuere v. 12.
alienatæ a republica Israelis. Act. xiv. 16, 17. *Qui præteritis*
sæculis sivit omnes gentes incedere viis ipsarum Nec tamen
20 *se sine testimonio* &c. Et xvii. 27, 28, 30. *Ut quærerent Do-*
minum si forte palparent invenirentque; quamquam non
procul &c. *tempora igitur ignorantiæ præteriens Deus,* &c.

THEY, AND IN PROCESS OF TIME ALL OTHER NATIONS, MIGHT BE
LED UNDER THE GOSPEL FROM THE WEAK AND SERVILE RUDIMENTS
OF THIS ELEMENTARY INSTITUTION TO THE FULL STRENGTH OF
THE NEW CREATURE, AND A MANLY LIBERTY WORTHY THE SONS
5 OF GOD. Heb. ix. 8, &c. as above.

INTENDED FOR THE ISRAELITES ALONE. Exod. xix. 5, 6. "if ye
will obey my voice indeed, and keep my covenant, then ye
shall be a peculiar treasure unto me above all people; for
all the earth is mine: and ye shall be unto me a kingdom of
10 priests, and a holy nation." Deut. iv. 45. "these are the testimonies, and the statutes, and the judgments, which Moses
spake unto the children of Israel, after they came forth out of
Egypt." 1 Kings viii. 21. "I have set there a place for the ark,
wherein is the covenant of Jehovah, which he made with our
15 fathers when he brought them out of the land of Egypt."
Psal. cxlvii. 19, 20. "he showeth his word unto Jacob, his
statutes and his judgments unto Israel: he hath not dealt so
with any nation, and as for his judgments, they have not
known them." This wall of partition between the Gentiles
20 and Israelites was at length broken down by the death of
Christ, Eph. ii. 14. until which time the Gentiles were aliens
from the whole of the covenant, v. 12. "being aliens from
the commonwealth of Israel." Acts xiv. 16, 17. "who in times
past suffered all nations to walk in their own ways: neverthe-
25 less he left not himself without witness," &c. xvii. 27, 28, 30.
"that they should seek the Lord, if haply they might feel after
him, and find him, though he be not far from every one of
us . . . the times of this ignorance God winked at."

CUM PROMISSIONE VITÆ. Huius nimirum non æternæ ut
Lev. xxvi. *toto capite apparet.* Lev. xviii. 5. *homo qui fecerit
ea, vivet in iis.* Deut. vi. 24, 25. *et iustitia erit nobis si observantes fecerimus totam præceptionem hanc coram Deo nostro*
5 *quemadmodum præcepit nobis.* Gal. iii. 12. *lex non est ex
fide; sed, Qui fecerit ea, vivet per eam.* Vitam autem æternam
etsi lex non promittit, prophetæ tamen sic innuere videntur.
Zech. iii. 7. *disponam tibi qui ambulent inter adstantes istos.*
Luc. x. 25, 28. Ioan. v. 39. et infra de resurrectione.

10 ET MALEDICTIONE IIS &c. Deut. xxvii. 26. *maledictus qui non
præstiterit verba legis huius, faciendo ea.* Gal. iii. 10. *quotquot ex operibus legis sunt, sub execratione sunt: scriptum est
enim; Execrabilis est quisquis—.*

UT PRAVITATEM—. Rom. iii. 20. *per legem agnitio peccati* et
15 iv. 15. *lex operatur iram.* et v. 20. *lex præterea introiit, ut
redundaret delictum; sed ubi redundavit delictum, ibi super-
abundavit gratia illa.* et vii. 5. *cum essemus in carne, affectus
peccatorum per legem existentes, agebant in membris nostris
ad fructum ferendum morti.* et v. 7, 8, 9. *peccatum non*
20 *cognovi, nisi per legem—: sed peccatum, occasione per illud
præceptum sumpta, effecit in me—.* et 12, 13. *lex ipsa quidem sancta, et præceptum illud sanctum ac iustum et bonum*

WITH A PROMISE OF LIFE; namely, temporal life, as is obvious from the whole of the twenty-sixth chapter of Leviticus. Lev. xviii. 5. "ye shall keep my statutes, which if a man do, he shall live in them." Deut. vi. 25. "it shall be our righteousness, if we observe to do all these commandments before Jehovah our God, as he hath commanded us." Gal. iii. 12. "the law is not of faith; but the man that doeth them shall live in them." Though the law, however, does not promise eternal life, this latter seems to be implied in the language of the prophets. Zech. iii. 7. "I will give thee places to walk among these that stand by." Luke x. 25–28. John v. 39. See also below, on the resurrection.

A CURSE ON SUCH AS SHOULD BE DISOBEDIENT. Deut. xxvii. 26. "cursed be he that confirmeth not all the words of this law to do them." Gal. iii. 10. "as many as are of the works of the law are under the curse; for it is written, Cursed is every one that continueth not in all things which are written in the law to do them."

ACKNOWLEDGING THE DEPRAVITY. Rom. iii. 20. "by the law is the knowledge of sin." iv. 15. "the law worketh wrath." v. 20. "moreover the law entered, that the offence might abound; but where sin abounded, grace did much more abound." vii. 5. "when we were in the flesh, the motions of sin which were by the law did work in our members to bring forth fruit unto death." v. 7–9. "I had not known sin, but by the law—: but sin taking occasion by the commandment, wrought in me all manner of concupiscence." v. 12, 13. "wherefore the law is holy, and the commandment holy, and

est. ergo quod bonum, mihi factum est mors? absit. sed pec-
catum; ut appareret esse peccatum mihi per id quod bonum
est efficiens mortem; ut peccatum fieret admodum peccans
per illud praeceptum. Gal. iii. 19. *quid igitur lex? transgres-*
5 *sionum gratia adiecta est, usque quo venisset semen illud cui*
facta est promissio. Hinc omnibus nondum regenitis lex
naturæ; data est in eundem finem atque data est Israelitis lex
Mosaica. Rom. iii. 19. *scimus autem quæcunque lex dicit,*
iis qui in lege sunt dicere; ut omne os obstruatur, et obnoxius
10 *fiat totus mundus condemnationi Dei.* cum i. 19. *ostendit*
enim eis Deus.

AD IUSTITIAM CHRISTI. Hinc illa Christi invitatio, Matt. xi.
28. *venite ad me omnes qui fatigati estis et onerati, et ego*
faciam ut requiescatis; a maledictione scilicet legis. Hinc illa
15 Pauli sub legis maledictione æstuatio, gratiæque Deo actæ
propter Christum, Rom. vii. 24, 25. *ærumnosus ego homo,*
quis me eripiet—? x. 4. *finis legis est Christus ad iustitiam*
cuivis credenti. Gal. iii. 11. *nullum per legem iustificari apud*
Deum, manifestum est, quoniam iustus ex fide vivet. et v. 13.
20 *Christus nos redemit ab execratione legis—.* et 21. *si data*
fuisset lex quæ posset vivificare, vere ex lege esset iustitia. et
22. *sed conclusit illa scriptura sub peccatum omnia, ut pro-*

just, and good: was then that which is good made death unto me? God forbid: but sin, that it might appear sin, working death in me by that which is good; that sin by the commandment might become exceeding sinful." Gal. iii. 19. "where-

5 fore then serveth the law? it was added because of transgressions, till the seed should come to whom the promise was made." Hence to those who are not yet regenerate, the law of nature has the same obligatory force, and is intended to serve the same purposes, as the law of Moses to the Israelites.

10 Rom. iii. 19. "we know that whatsoever things the law saith, it saith to them that were under the law, that every mouth may be stopped, and all the world may become guilty before God," compared with i. 19. "that which may be known of God is manifest in them, for God hath showed it unto them."

15 THE RIGHTEOUSNESS OF THE PROMISED SAVIOR. Hence Christ's invitation, Matt. xi. 28. "come unto me, all ye that labor, and are heavy laden, and I will give you rest"; that is, from the curse of the law. Hence also the conflict in the mind of Paul while under the curse of the law, and the thanks which he

20 renders to God for the atonement of Christ; Rom. vii. 24, 25. "O wretched man that I am, who shall deliver me from the body of this death?" x. 4. "Christ is the end of the law for righteousness to every one that believeth." Gal. iii. 11. "that no man is justified by the law in the sight of God, it is evident,

25 for the just shall live by faith." v. 13. "Christ hath redeemed us from the curse of the law." v. 21. "if there had been a law given which could have given life, verily righteousness should have been by the law." v. 22. "but the Scripture hath con-

missio ex fide Iesu Christi daretur credentibus. conclusit id
est *reos peccati omnes declaravit.* et 24. *itaque lex pædagogus
noster fuit in Christum respiciens, ut ex fide iustificaremur.*
2 Cor. iii. 6. *Littera occidit,* id est, Littera Legis sive *Elemen-*
5 *tum,* ut alias dicitur; *occidit,* id est, vitam æternam non promisit. Col. ii. 14. *ac deleto quod adversum nos erat chirographo decretis; quod erat nobis contrarium.* Itaque in ipsa
Mosis persona imperfectio legis manifesta fuit: Moses enim
qui legis typus erat, non potuit in terram Canaan, id est, in
10 æternam requiem, perducere Israelis filios; sed ductu Iosuæ,
id est, Iesu, ingressus iis est datus. Unde et salutem æternam
per solum Christum, licet nondum revelatum, sub lege quoque unam et eandem fuisse testatur Petrus: Act. xv. 10, 11.
quid tentatis Deum ad imponendum iugum cervici discipulo-
15 *rum, quod neque patres nostri neque nos portare valuimus?
immo per gratiam Domini Iesu Christi credimus nos servatum
iri, quemadmodum et illos.* Heb. xiii. 8. *Iesus Christus heri
et hodie idem est, et in sæcula.* Iustificabantur quidem sub
Lege quotquot mandata eius omnia observare poterant, sed
20 ad hanc solum vitam beate agendam Deut. vi. 24, 25. *præcepit nobis Iehova exercere omnia statuta ista* &c. *ut bene sit
nobis omnibus diebus* &c. *et iustitia erit nobis, si observantes*
&c. Fides autem in Deum per Christum assecuta est et quod
Lex ipsa et quod Legis observatores præstare nequiverunt,
25 idque ad vitam sempiternam.

cluded all under sin, that the promise by faith of Jesus Christ
might be given to them that believe"; "concluded," that is, declared all guilty of sin. v. 24. "wherefore the law was our
schoolmaster to bring us unto Christ, that we might be justi-
5 fied by faith." 2 Cor. iii. 6. "the letter killeth," that is, the
letter of the law (elsewhere called "the elements") "killeth,"
in other words, does not promise eternal life. Col. ii. 14.
"blotting out the handwriting of ordinances that was against
us, which was contrary to us." Thus the imperfection of the
10 law was manifested in the person of Moses himself; for Moses,
who was a type of the law, could not bring the children of
Israel into the land of Canaan, that is, into eternal rest; but
an entrance was given to them under Joshua, or Jesus. Hence
Peter testifies that eternal salvation was through Christ alone
15 under the law, equally as under the gospel, although he was
not then revealed: Acts xv. 10, 11. "why tempt ye God, to
put a yoke upon the neck of the disciples, which neither our
fathers nor we were able to bear? but we believe that through
the grace of the Lord Jesus Christ we shall be saved, even as
20 they." Heb. xiii. 8. "Jesus Christ the same yesterday, and
to-day, and for ever." For although, under the law, as many
as were able to keep all the commandments were justified, the
promise extended only to happiness in this life: Deut. vi. 24,
25. "Jehovah commanded us to do all these statutes, to fear
25 Jehovah our God, for our good always, that he might preserve
us alive," &c. "and it shall be our righteousness if we observe
to do all these commandments." But what neither the law
itself nor the observers of the law could attain, faith in God
through Christ has attained, and that even to eternal life.

CAPUT XXVII.

DE EVANGELIO, ET LIBERTATE CHRISTIANA.

EVANGELIUM est NOVA DISPENSATIO FŒDERIS GRATIÆ, EXCELLENTIOR MULTO LEGE ET PERFECTIOR, PRIMUM A MOSE ET PROPHETIS, OBSCURIUS, DEINDE AB IPSO CHRISTO EIUSQUE APOSTOLIS ET EVANGELISTIS PLENA LUCE ANNUNIATA,
5 INDE FIDELIUM CORDIBUS PER SANCTUM SPIRITUM INSCRIPTA, ET AD FINEM MUNDI PERMANSURA, SUB PROMISSIONE VITÆ ÆTERNÆ OMNIBUS PER OMNES GENTES CREDENTIBUS IN CHRISTUM EXHIBITUM, ET COMMINATIONE MORTIS ÆTERNÆ NON CREDENTIBUS DENUNTIATA.

10   NOVA. Ier. xxxi. 31, 32, 33. cum Heb. viii. 8, 9. *peragam cum domo Israelis et cum domo Iudæ pactum novum: non secundum pactum quod feci cum patribus ipsorum—*. Et *novum testamentum* dicitur, Matt. xxvi. 28. Marc. xiv. 24. Luc. xxii. 20. I Cor. xi. 25. et 2 Ep. iii, 6. Sed vox διαθήκη,
15 Hebraice בְּרִיה, pro συνθήκη sive *pacto* apud scriptores biblicos fere usurpatur, et Latine vertitur: 2 Cor. iii. 14. *veteris pacti.* Gal. iv. 24. *duo pacta;* et alibi. *Testamentum* autem proprie semel tantum dicitur, addita peculiari ratione Heb. ix. 15, 16, &c. *ob id novi testamenti mediator est, ut morte ad re-*
20 *demptionem earum transgressionum intercedente, quæ fue-rant sub priore pacto, qui vocati erant, promissam æternam*

CHAPTER XXVII.

OF THE GOSPEL AND CHRISTIAN LIBERTY.

THE GOSPEL IS THE NEW DISPENSATION OF THE COVENANT OF GRACE, FAR MORE EXCELLENT AND PERFECT THAN THE LAW, ANNOUNCED FIRST OBSCURELY BY MOSES AND THE PROPHETS, AFTERWARDS IN THE CLEAREST TERMS BY CHRIST 5 HIMSELF, AND HIS APOSTLES AND EVANGELISTS, WRITTEN SINCE BY THE HOLY SPIRIT IN THE HEARTS OF BELIEVERS, AND ORDAINED TO CONTINUE EVEN TO THE END OF THE WORLD, CONTAINING A PROMISE OF ETERNAL LIFE TO ALL IN EVERY NATION WHO SHALL BELIEVE IN CHRIST WHEN REVEALED TO THEM, AND A THREAT OF 10 ETERNAL DEATH TO SUCH AS SHALL NOT BELIEVE.

THE NEW DISPENSATION. Jer. xxxi. 31–33, compared with Heb. viii. 8, 9. "I will make a new covenant with the house of Israel, and with the house of Judah, not according to the covenant that I made with their fathers." It is called "the new 15 testament," Matt. xxvi. 28. Mark xiv. 24. Luke xxii. 20. 1 Cor. xi. 25. 2 Cor. iii. 6. But the word $\delta\iota\alpha\theta\eta\varkappa\eta$, in the Hebrew בְּרִית, is generally used by the inspired writers for $\sigma\upsilon\nu\theta\eta\varkappa\eta$, "covenant," and is rendered in Latin by the word *pactum*, 2 Cor. iii. 14. Gal. iv. 24. *veteris pacti.* The Gospel is only once 20 called "testament" in a proper sense, and then for a particular reason which is subjoined. Heb. ix. 15, 16, &c. "for this cause he is the mediator of the new testament, that by means of death for the redemption of the transgressions that were under the first testament, they which are called might receive the prom-

hæreditatem acciperent: nam ubi testamentum est, mors intercedat necesse est testatoris.

EXCELLENTIOR—. Matt. xiii. 17. *multi prophetæ et iusti desiderarunt conspicere quæ conspicitis, et non conspexerunt;*
5 *et audire quæ auditis, et non audierunt.* 2 Cor. iii. 11, &c. *si quod evanidum erat, fuit gloriosum; multo magis est gloriosum id quod manet. Itaque cum huiusmodi spem habeamus, multa in loquendo evidentia utimur; nec simus sicut Moses*—. Heb. vii. 18, 19, 20, 22. *nihil enim consummavit*
10 *lex; sed superintroducta spes potior, per quam appropinquamus Deo. Etiam quatenus non absque iureiurando: nam illi quidem absque iureiurando sacerdotes facti sunt, hic vero cum iureiurando*—: *tanto melioris pacti sponsor factus est Iesus.* Et viii. 6, &c. *quanto præstantioris pacti est mediator,*
15 *quod præstantioribus promissis sancitum est,* &c. *Indam leges meas menti eorum*—. Iacob. i. 25. *at is qui introspexerit in perfectam illam legem libertatis, et permanserit in ea, quia non fuerit auditor obliviosus, sed effector operis, is beatior erit in opere suo.* 1 Pet. i. 10, &c. *de qua salute exquisierunt,*
20 *et quam scrutati sunt prophetæ, qui de ventura in vos gratia prophetarunt*—: *per emissum e cœlo spiritum sanctum; in quæ cupiunt angeli introspicere.* Vocatur itaque *ministerium* et *sermo reconciliationis,* 2 Cor. v. 18, 19. *cum lex iram efficiat,* Rom. iv. 15.
25 A MOSE ET PROPHETIS. Ioan. v. 39. *illæ testantur de me.* et

ise of eternal inheritance; for where a testament is, there must also of necessity be the death of the testator."

MORE EXCELLENT AND PERFECT THAN THE LAW. Matt. xiii. 17. "many prophets and righteous men have desired to see those
5 things which ye see, and have not seen them, and to hear those things which ye hear, and have not heard them." 2 Cor. iii. 11, &c. "if that which was done away was glorious, much more that which remaineth is glorious. Seeing then that we have such hope, we use great plainness of speech; and not as
10 Moses—." Heb. vii. 18–20, 22. "the law made nothing perfect, but the bringing in of a better hope did, by the which we draw nigh unto God: and inasmuch as not without an oath he was made priest; for those priests were made without an oath, but this with an oath . . . by so much was Jesus made
15 a surety of a better covenant." viii. 6, &c. "by how much more also he is the mediator of a better covenant, which was established upon better promises," &c. "I will put my laws into their mind." James i. 25. "whoso looketh into the perfect law of liberty, and continueth therein, he being not a forget-
20 ful hearer, but a doer of the work, this man shall be blessed in his deed." 1 Pet. i. 10, &c. "of which salvation the prophets have inquired and searched diligently, who prophesied of the grace that should come unto you . . . with the Holy Ghost sent down from heaven; which things the angels desire to look
25 into." The Gospel is also called "the ministry" and "word of reconciliation," 2 Cor. v. 18, 19. whereas on the contrary "the law worketh wrath," Rom. iv. 15.

BY MOSES AND THE PROPHETS. John v. 39. "they are they

46. *si crederetis Mosi, crederetis mihi; nam ille de me scripsit;* nempe Gen. iii. 15. et xxii. 18. et xlix. 10. Deut. xviii. 15. Luc. xxiv. 27. *exorsus a Mose——.* et v. 44. *oportere impleri omnia, quæ scripta sunt in lege Mosis et prophetis et psalmis*
5 *de me.* Act. xvii. 11. *examinantes scripturas, an——.* et xxvi. 22, 23. *nihil extra dicens quam ea quæ prophetæ ac Moses——.* Rom. iii. 21. *comprobata testimonio legis ac prophetarum.* 1 Pet. i. 10, &c. *qui de ventura in vos gratia prophetarunt.*

CORDIBUS INSCRIPTA. Isa. lix. 21. *de me autem, hoc erit fœdus*
10 *meum cum istis, ait Iehova, spiritus meus qui est in te et verba mea quæ posui in ore tuo, non recedent ex ore tuo, aut ex ore seminis tui, aut ex ore seminis seminis tui, ait Iehova, ex hoc tempore usque in sæculum.* Ier. xxxi. 31, 32, 33. *ecce dies venturi sunt——: nam hoc est illud fœdus quod pangam cum*
15 *domo Israelis post dies hos, dictum Iehovæ* (attende hoc ipsum quid sit in quo excellentiam novi fœderis præ vetere ponit) *indam legem meam menti eorum, et cordi eorum inscribam eam——,* cum Heb. viii. 10, &c. *hoc est pactum——. indam leges meas menti eorum——; et ero ipsis Deus, et ipsi*
20 *erunt mihi populus——.* Ioel. ii. 28. *erit postea, ut effundam spiritum meum super omnem carnem——; quinetiam super servos et super ancillas diebus illis effundens spiritum meum.*

which testify of me." v. 46. "had ye believed Moses, ye would have believed me, for he wrote of me"; namely Gen. iii. 15. xxii. 18. xlix. 10. Deut. xviii. 15. Luke xxiv. 27. "beginning at Moses and all the prophets, he expounded unto them in all
5 the scriptures the things concerning himself." Acts xvii. 11. "searching the scriptures daily, whether those things were so." xxvi. 22, 23. "saying none other things than those which the prophets and Moses did say should come." Rom. iii. 21. "being witnessed by the law and the prophets." 1 Pet. i. 10.
10 "who prophesied of the grace which should come unto you."

WRITTEN IN THE HEARTS OF BELIEVERS. Isa. lix. 21. "as for me, this is my covenant with them, saith Jehovah; My Spirit which is upon thee, and my words which I have put in thy mouth, shall not depart out of thy mouth, nor out of the
15 mouth of thy seed, nor out of the mouth of thy seed's seed, saith Jehovah, from henceforth and for ever." Jer. xxxi. 31–33. "behold the days come . . . but this shall be the covenant that I will make with the house of Israel; After those days, saith Jehovah," a declaration particularly worthy of at-
20 tention, as it specifies in what respect the new covenant is more excellent than the old, "I will put my law in their inward parts, and write in their hearts," compared with Heb. viii. 10, &c. "this is the covenant . . . I will put my laws into their mind . . . and I will be to them a God, and they shall be to
25 me a people." Joel ii. 28. "it shall come to pass afterward, that I will pour out my Spirit upon all flesh . . . and also upon the servants and upon the handmaids in those days will I pour out my Spirit." To these may be added, from the chap-

Adde ex loco illo Ieremiæ v. 34. *quotquot erunt, cognoscent me a minimo eorum usque ad maximum eorum.* et Ioelis v. 28. *prophetabunt filii vestri et filiæ vestræ; seniores vestri somnia somniabunt, iuvenes vestri visiones videbunt,* cum
5 Act. ii. 16, 17, 18. Etenim vere fideles aut prophetant, aut prophetiæ et somniorum et visionum instar in se habent spiritum sanctum. 2 Cor. iii. 3. *vos esse epistolam Christi subministratam a nobis, inscriptam non atramento, sed spiritu Dei vivi; non in tabulis lapideis, sed in carneis tabulis cordis.*
10 et v. 6. *ministri novi pacti; non litteræ, sed spiritus: nam littera occidit, spiritus autem vivificat.* Iacob. i. 21. *cum lenitate excipite insititium illum sermonem, qui potest servare animas vestras.*

PER SPIRITUM SANCTUM. nempe donum Dei, evangelio pecu-
15 liare. Ioan. vii. 39. *Nondum enim erat spiritus Sanctus, quia* &c. et xiv. 26. *advocatus ille, id est, Spiritus Sanctus quem mittit pater in nomine meo ille vos docebit omnia* &c. Luc. xii. 12. idem. Act. i. 8. *Recipietis virtutem Spiritus sancti.* et ii. 1, &c. v. 38. *Resipiscite* &c. *et accipietis donum*
20 *Spiritus Sancti.* Rom. v. 5. *Per Spiritum Sanctum qui datus est nobis.* 1 Cor. ii. 13. *sermonibus quos docet Spiritus Sanctus.* 2 Cor. xiii. 13. *communicatio Spiritus Sancti.* 1 Thess. iv. 8. *Spiritum Sanctum qui dedit nobis.* Rom. viii. 9. 1 Cor. xii. 3. 1 Pet. i. 12. 1 Ioan. iv. 13.
25 PERMANSURA. 2 Cor. iii. 11. *multo magis est gloriosum id*

ter of Jeremiah quoted above, v. 34. "they shall all know me, from the least of them unto the greatest of them." Joel ii. 28. "your sons and your daughters shall prophesy, your old men shall dream dreams, your young men shall see visions." Com-
5 pare Acts ii. 16–18. For although all real believers have not the gift of prophecy, the Holy Spirit is to them an equivalent and substitute for prophecy, dreams, and visions. 2 Cor. iii. 3. "ye are manifestly declared to be the epistle of Christ minis-tered by us, written not with ink, but with the Spirit of the
10 living God, not in tables of stone, but in fleshy tables of the heart." v. 6. "ministers of the new testament, not of the letter, but of the spirit; for the letter killeth, but the spirit giveth life." James i. 21. "receive with meekness the engrafted word, which is able to save your souls."

15   By the Holy Spirit, the gift of God, and peculiar to the gospel. John vii. 39. "the Holy Ghost was not yet given, be-cause that Jesus was not yet glorified." xiv. 26. "the Com-forter, which is the Holy Ghost, whom the Father will send in my name, he shall teach you all things." See also Luke xii. 12.
20 Acts i. 8. "ye shall receive power after that the Holy Ghost is come upon you." See also ii. 1, &c. v. 38. "repent," &c. "and ye shall receive the gift of the Holy Ghost." Rom. v. 5. "by the Holy Ghost which is given unto us." 1 Cor. ii. 13. "in words which the Holy Ghost teacheth." 2 Cor. xiii. 14. "the
25 communion of the Holy Ghost." 1 Thess. iv. 8. "who hath also given unto us his Holy Spirit." See also Rom. viii. 9. 1 Cor. xii. 3. 1 Pet. i. 12. 1 John iv. 13.

    Ordained to continue even to the end of the world.

quod manet. Eph. iv. 13. *donec perveniamus nos omnes in virum adultum, ad mensuram plenæ staturæ Christi.*

SUB PROMISSIONE VITÆ ÆTERNÆ—. Marc. xvi. 15. *profecti prædicate evangelium—: qui crediderit et baptizatus fuerit,* 5 *servabitur.* Rom. i. 16, 17. *potentia siquidem Dei est ad salutem.*

CREDENTIBUS. Ioan. iii. 15, 16. *quisquis credit in eum.* Rom. i. 16, 17. *cuivis credenti.* 1 Ioan. ii. 25. *Hæc est promissio quam ipse pollicitus est nobis, nempe vita æterna.* Cætera 10 loca vide supra de fide et obiecto fidei. Credentium nomine pœnitentes etiam comprehendimus: pœnitentiam enim et fidem coniunctim annuntiatio prima evangelii proponit: Matt. iii. 1, &c. et iv. 17. Marc. i. 15. Luc. xxiv. 47. Act. ii. 39, 40, 41. et x. 34. *quemvis qui eum timeat, et operam det* 15 *iustitiæ.* et xix. 3, 4, et xx. 21, et alibi.

ET COMMINATIONE MORTIS &c. Matt. x. 14, 15. *quicunque non audierit sermones vestros, exeuntes—. amen dico vobis, tolerabilior erit conditio Sodomorum—.* et xxi. 37, &c. *misit ad eos filium suum— Agricolæ vero—: Dicunt ei, malos* 20 *ipsos male perdet—.* Marc. xvi. 16. *qui vero non crediderit, condemnabitur.* Ioan. iii. 19. *hæc est autem condemnatio;*

2 Cor. iii. 11. "much more that which remaineth is glorious."
Eph. iv. 13. "till we all come . . . unto a perfect man, unto
the measure of the stature of the fulness of Christ."

A PROMISE OF ETERNAL LIFE. Mark xvi. 15, 16. "go ye into
5 all the world, and preach the gospel . . . he that believeth
and is baptized shall be saved." Rom. i. 16. "the power of God
unto salvation."

To ALL WHO SHALL BELIEVE. John iii. 15, 16. "whosoever
believeth in him," &c. Rom. i. 16, 17. "to every one that be-
10 lieveth." 1 John ii. 25. "this is the promise that he hath promised us, even eternal life." See other passages to the same effect
above, in the chapter on faith and its objects. Under the name
of believers the penitent are comprehended, inasmuch as in
the original annunciation of the gospel repentance and faith
15 are jointly proposed as conditions of salvation. Matt. iii. 1, &c.
iv. 17. Mark i. 15. Luke xxiv. 47. Acts ii. 39–41. x. 35. "he
that feareth him and worketh righteousness, is accepted of
him." xix. 3, 4. xx. 21. and elsewhere.

A THREAT OF ETERNAL DEATH TO SUCH AS SHALL NOT BELIEVE.
20 Matt. x. 14, 15. "whosoever shall not receive you nor hear
your words, when ye depart out of that city, shake off the dust
of your feet: verily I say unto you, It shall be more tolerable
for the land of Sodom—." xxi. 37, &c. "he sent unto them his
son . . . but when the husbandmen saw the son, they said
25 . . . let us kill him . . . they say unto him, He will miser-
ably destroy those wicked men." Mark xvi. 16. "he that believeth not shall be damned." John iii. 19. "this is the condemnation, that light is come into the world, and men loved

quod lux venit in mundum, sed—. Act. iii. 23. *omnis anima qua non audierit prophetam illum, disperdatur e populo.* 2 Thess. i. 8, 9. *infligens ultionem iis qui Deum nesciunt, neque auscultant evangelio*—. Heb. x. 26, &c. *nam si ultro* 5 *peccaverimus post acceptam cognitionem veritatis, non adhuc pro peccatis reliqua est hostia; sed horrenda quædam expectatio iudicii.*

NON CREDENTIBUS autem IN CHRISTUM de iis est intelligendum cui Christus annuntiatur. *quomodo enim credent ei, de* 10 *quo non audierint,* Rom. x. 14?

PER OMNES GENTES. Matt. xxiv. 14. *prædicabitur istud evangelium regni in toto terrarum orbe; ut sit testimonio omnibus gentibus; et tunc veniet finis.* Marc. xvi. 15. *omni creaturæ.* Ioan. x. 16. *alias etiam oves habeo, quæ non sunt ex hac caula.* 15 Act. x. 34, 35. *vere deprehendo, Deum non respicere ad personam; sed in quavis gente acceptum esse ei quemvis.* Rom. x. 18. *in omnem terram exivit sonus eorum; et ad ultima orbis terrarum verba eorum.* Quod prædictum est: Isa. ii. 2, &c. *erit ultimis temporibus*—. Mic. iv. 1, &c. idem. Isa. xix. 20 18, &c. *tempore illo erunt quinque civitates*—. et xxv. 6, &c. *omnibus populis*—. et xlii. 4, &c. *in doctrina eius regiones expectationem habebunt.* et xlv. 22, 23. *respicite ad me, et servemini omnes fines terræ*— et lv. 4, 5. *testem nationum*—. et lvi. 3, &c. *ne loquatur alienigena*—. et lxvi. 21. *atque* 25 *etiam ex istis assumam in sacerdotes et Levitas, ait Iehova.*

darkness rather than light." Acts iii. 23. "every soul which
will not hear that prophet, shall be destroyed from among the
people." 2 Thess. i. 8, 9. "taking vengeance on them that
know not God, and that obey not the gospel." Heb. x. 26, &c.
5 "if we sin wilfully after that we have received the knowledge
of the truth, there remaineth no more sacrifice for sins, but a
certain fearful looking for of judgment." By unbelievers,
however, those only can be meant to whom Christ has been
announced in the gospel; for "how shall they believe in him of
10 whom they have not heard?" Rom. x. 14.

   IN EVERY NATION. Matt. xxiv. 14. "this gospel of the kingdom shall be preached in all the world, for a witness unto all
nations, and then shall the end come." Mark xvi. 15. "to
every creature." John x. 16. "other sheep I have, which are
15 not of this fold." Acts x. 34, 35. "of a truth I perceive that
God is no respecter of persons; but in every nation he that
feareth him, and worketh righteousness, is accepted of him."
Rom. x. 18. "their sound went into all the earth, and their
words unto the ends of the world." This was predicted, Isa.
20 ii. 2, &c. "it shall come to pass in the last days," &c. See also
Mic. iv. 1. Isa. xix. 18, &c. "in that day shall five cities in the
land of Egypt speak the language of Canaan," &c. xxv. 6, &c.
"unto all people." xlii. 4, &c. "the isles shall wait for his
law." xlv. 22, 23. "look unto me, and be ye saved, all the ends
25 of the earth." lv. 4, 5. "a witness to the people," &c. lvi. 3,
&c. "neither let the son of the stranger . . . speak, saying,
Jehovah hath utterly separated me from his people." lxvi. 21.
"I will also take of them for priests and Levites, saith Jeho-

Ier. iii. 12. *recta confluent eo omnes gentes.* et xxv. 8, &c. *eo quod non auscultastis verbis meis; ecce ego missurus sum, ut assumam omnes nationes—.* Hag. ii. 7. *ut veniant desiderati omnium gentium,—* Zech. viii. 20, &c. *venient populi—.*

5 Introducto evangelio per fidem in Christum fœdere novo, vetus omne, id est, tota lex Mosaica aboletur. Ier. xxxi. 31, 32, 33. ut supra. Luc. xvi. 16. *lex et prophetæ usque ad Ioannem.* Act. xv. 10. *nunc ergo, quid tentatis Deum ad imponendum iugum cervici discipulorum, quod neque patres nostri neque* 10 *nos portare valuimus.* Rom. iii. 21, 22. *nunc vero absque lege iustitia Dei patefacta est.* et vi. 14. *non estis sub lege, sed sub gratia.* et vii. 4. *mortificati estis legi in corpore Iesu Christi; ut essetis alterius, eius qui ex mortuis est suscitatus, ut fructum feratis Deo.* et v. 6. *nunc autem liberati sumus* 15 *a lege, mortuo eo in quo detinebamur, ut serviamus in novitate spiritus, et non in vetustate litteræ.* Neque secus liberari nos a lege ostendit Paulus initio illius capitis, atque uxor liberatur mortuo viro. et v. 7. *peccatum non cognovi, nisi per legem:* totam scilicet; *nam concupiscentiam quoque non nossem, nisi* 20 *lex dixisset, non concupisces:* decalogus nimirum; decalogo igitur ipso quoque liberamur. et cap. viii. 15. *non accepistis*

vah." Jer. iii. 17. "all the nations shall be gathered unto it."
xxv. 8, &c. "because ye have not heard my words, behold, I
will send and take all the families of the north——." Hag. ii.
7. "the desire of all nations shall come." Zech. viii. 20. "there
5 shall come people, and the inhabitants of many cities."

On the introduction of the gospel, or new covenant through
faith in Christ, the whole of the preceding covenant, in other
words the entire Mosaic law, was abolished. Jer. xxxi. 31–33.
as above. Luke xvi. 16. "the law and the prophets were until
10 John." Acts xv. 10. "now therefore why tempt ye God, to put
a yoke upon the neck of the disciples, which neither our fathers nor we were able to bear?" Rom. iii. 21. "now the righteousness of God without the law is manifested." vi. 14. "ye
are not under the law, but under grace." vii. 4. "ye also are
15 become dead to the law by the body of Christ, that ye should
be married to another, even to him that is raised from the
dead, that we should bring forth fruit unto God." v. 6. "now
we are delivered from the law, that being dead wherein we
were held, that we should serve in newness of spirit, and not
20 in the oldness of the letter." In the beginning of the same
chapter the apostle illustrates our emancipation from the law
by the instance of a wife who is loosed from her husband who
is dead. v. 7. "I had not known sin but by the law," that is, the
whole law, for the expression is unlimited, "for I had not
25 known lust, except the law had said, Thou shalt not covet."
It is in the decalogue that the injunction here specified is contained; we are therefore absolved from subjection to the decalogue as fully as to the rest of the law. viii. 15. "ye have not

spiritum servitutis rursum ad metum. et xiv. 20. *omnia quidem munda*—: cum Tit. i. 15. *omnia munda mundis: pollutis autem et incredulis nihil est mundum; sed polluta est eorum et mens et conscientia.* 1 Cor. vi. 12. *omnia mihi*
5 *licent, at non omnia conducunt; omnia mihi licent, at nequaquam ego redigar sub ullius rei potestatem.* et x. 23. *omnia mihi licent, at non omnia conferunt; omnia mihi licent, sed non omnia ædificant.* 2 Ep. iii. 3. *non in tabulis lapideis, sed in corneis tabulis cordis.* et v. 6, 7, 8. *ministri novi pacti;*
10 *non litteræ, sed spiritus: nam littera occidit, spiritus autem vivificat. quod si mortis ministerium in litteris positum et informatum in lapidibus, fuit gloriosum;—qui non potius ministerium spiritus erit gloriosum.* et 11. *si quod evanidum erat, fuit gloriosum; multo magis est gloriosum id quod*
15 *manet.* et 13. *ne defigerent oculos filii Israelis, ad finem eius quod evanidum erat.* et cap. v. 17. *siquis est in Christo, nova est creatio; vetera præterierunt, ecce nova facta sunt omnia.* Gal. iii. 19. *quid igitur lex? transgressionum gratia adiecta est, usque quo venisset semen illud, cui facta est promissio.*
20 et v. 25. *at postquam venit fides, non amplius sub pædagogo sumus.* et iv. 1, &c. *quamdiu hæres infans est, nihil differt a servo*—, *usque ad tempus quod pater præstituerit; ita et nos, cum essemus*—, *eramus in servitutem redacti; at postquam*

received the spirit of bondage again to fear." xiv. 20. "all things indeed are pure," compared with Tit. i. 15. "unto the pure all things are pure; but unto them that are defiled and unbelieving is nothing pure, but even their mind and con-
5 science is defiled." 1 Cor. vi. 12. "all things are lawful to me, but all things are not expedient; all things are lawful for me, but I will not be brought under the power of any." x. 23. "all things are lawful for me, but all things are not expedient; all things are lawful for me, but all things edify not." 2 Cor.
10 iii. 3. "not in tables of stone, but in fleshy tables of the heart." v. 6–8. "ministers of the new testament, not of the letter, but of the spirit; for the letter killeth, but the spirit giveth life: but if the ministration of death, written and engraven in stones, was glorious . . . how shall not the ministration of
15 the spirit be rather glorious?" v. 11. "if that which was done away was glorious, much more that which remaineth is glorious." v. 15. "the children of Israel could not stedfastly look to the end of that which is abolished." v. 17. "if any man be in Christ, he is a new creature; old things are passed away;
20 behold, all things are become new." Gal. iii. 19. "wherefore then serveth the law? it was added because of transgressions, till the seed should come, to whom the promise was made." v. 25. "after that faith is come, we are no longer under a schoolmaster." iv. 1, &c. "the heir, as long as he is a child,
25 differeth nothing from a servant . . . until the time appointed of the father: even so we, when we were children, were in bondage under the elements of the world; but when the fulness of the time was come, God sent forth his Son,

venit plenum illud tempus, emisit Deus filium suum, factum
ex muliere, factum legi subiectum; ut eos qui legi erant sub-
iecti, redimeret; ut adoptionem acciperemus. et v. 21. ad eos
qui sub lege volebant esse; v. 24. de Agare et Sara; *hæ sunt*
5 *duæ illæ pactiones; Agar generans prolem ad servitutem:*
altera, v. 26. libera est: inde v. 30. *eiice ancillam et filium*
eius; nequaquam enim hæres erit filius ancillæ cum filio
liberæ. et cap. v. 18. *quod si Spiritu ducimini, non estis sub*
lege. Eph. ii. 14, 15. *intergerini parietis septum,* id est, *inim-*
10 *icitias, dissolvit carne sua; lege illa præceptorum, quæ in*
decretis posita est, irrita facta. lex autem non cæremonialis
modo, sed tota Mosaica positiva, præceptorum erat, et in decretis posita, nec cæremoniali tantum, ut hic vult Zanchius,
sed tota lege Mosaica dissidebant Iudæi a Gentibus; *abalienatis*
15 *nempe a civili statu Israelis, et extraneis quod ad pactorum*
promissionem, v. 12. promissio autem facta est totius legis
operibus, non cæremoniis tantum; nec illæ solum causæ erant
inimicitiæ inter nos et Deum, v. 16. Sic Col. ii. 14, 15, 16, 17.
ac deleto quod adversum nos erat chirographo decretis, quod
20 *erat nobis contrarium—, sustulit e medio.* Heb. vii. 12, &c.
mutato enim hoc sacerdotio, necessario quoque legis mutatio
fit. Exoritur sacerdos alius, qui non ex lege cuius præceptum

made of a woman, made under the law, to redeem them that were under the law, that we might receive the adoption of sons." Compare also v. 21, addressed to those who desired to be under the law; and v. 24, of Hagar and Sarah, "these

5 are the two covenants; the one from the mount Sinai, which gendereth to bondage, which is Agar . . . but Jerusalem which is above," v. 26. "is free": hence v. 30. "cast out the bondwoman and her son; for the son of the bondwoman shall not be heir with the son of the freewoman." v. 18. "if

10 ye be led of the Spirit, ye are not under the law." Eph. ii. 14, 15. "who hath broken down the middle wall of partition between us, having abolished in his flesh the enmity, even the law of commandments contained in ordinances." Now not only the ceremonial code, but the whole positive law of Moses,

15 was a law of commandments, and contained in ordinances; nor was it the ceremonial law which formed the sole ground of distinction between the Jews and Gentiles, as Zanchius on this passage contends, but the whole law; seeing that the Gentiles, v. 12. "were aliens from the commonwealth of

20 Israel, and strangers from the covenant of promise," which promise was made to the works of the whole law, not to those of the ceremonial alone; nor was it to these latter only that the enmity between God and us was owing, v. 16. So Col. ii. 14–17. "blotting out the hand-writing of ordinances that was

25 against us . . . he took it out of the way," &c. Heb. vii. 12, 15, 16. "the priesthood being changed, there is made of necessity a change also in the law . . . there ariseth another priest, who is made not after the law of a carnal commandment."

sit carnale—. et v. 18. fit enim irritum præcedens præceptum,
propter ipsius infirmitatem et inutilitatem; operum scilicet.
et cap. viii. 13. *dum novum dicit, antiquavit prius; porro*
quod antiquatur ac senescit, prope est ut evanescat. et xii. 18,
5 &c. *non accessistis ad contrectabilem montem, et ardentem*
ignem, ac turbinem, et caliginem; et procellam; tubæque
sonitum, et vocem verborum, quam qui audierant, cum ex-
cusatione petierunt, ne amplius sibi fieret sermo—: sed
accessistis ad montem Sion—, et ad novi pacti mediatorem
10 *Iesum.*

Vulgo occurritur, de lege duntaxat cæremoniali abolita,
intelligi hæc loca omnia debere. Verum hoc ex ipsa primum
legis definitione, quæ causas ferendæ legis omnes continet, ut
superiore capite videre est, facile refutatur: causis enim totius
15 legis omnibus obsoletis et abrogatis, abrogari totam legem
ipsam necesse est. Quæ causæ totius legis ferendæ afferuntur
præcipuæ, ad pravitatem videlicet nostram irritandam, ad iram
inde operandam, ad metum servilem incutiendum, quia inimicitiæ, quia chirographum contra nos accusatorium erat, atque
20 ut esset pædagogus ad iustitiam Christi, et similia, eas omnes
causas et abrogari superius citata loca confirmant, et ad cære-
monias quam minime pertinere.

v. 18. "there is verily a disannulling of the commandment going before," that is, of the commandment of works, "for the weakness and unprofitableness thereof." viii. 13. "in that he saith, a new covenant, he hath made the first old; now that which decayeth and waxeth old, is ready to vanish away." xii. 18, &c. "ye are not come unto the mount that might be touched, and that burned with fire, nor unto blackness, and darkness, and tempest, and the sound of a trumpet, and the voice of words; which voice they that heard entreated that the word should not be spoken to them any more . . . but ye are come unto mount Sion . . . and to Jesus the mediator of the new covenant."

It is generally replied, that all these passages are to be understood only of the abolition of the ceremonial law. This is refuted, first, by the definition of the law itself, as given in the preceding chapter, in which are specified all the various reasons for its enactment: if therefore, of the causes which led to the enactment of the law considered as a whole, every one is revoked or obsolete, it follows that the whole law itself must be annulled also. The principal reasons then which are given for the enactment of the law are as follows: that it might call forth and develop our natural depravity; that by this means it might work wrath; that it might impress us with a slavish fear through consciousness of divine enmity, and of the handwriting of accusation that was against us; that it might be a schoolmaster to bring us to the righteousness of Christ; and others of a similar description. Now the texts quoted above prove clearly, both that all these causes are now abrogated,

Primum idcirco lex maxime aboletur, quia est lex operum,
ut locum det gratiæ. Rom. iii. 27. *per quam legem? operum?*
non: sed per legem fidei. et xi. 6. *si per gratiam, iam non ex*
operibus: alioqui gratia iam non est gratia. Atqui lex ope-
5 rum non erat cæremonialis tantum, sed tota lex.

2. *lex iram efficit: ubi enim non est lex, ibi nec transgres-*
sio, cap. iv. 15. At non pars utique solum, sed tota lex iram
efficit; totius enim, non partis tantum, est transgressio. Et
lex quidem iram efficit, evangelium autem gratiam: ut igitur
10 ira et gratia stare simul non possunt, ita neque lex et evangelium.

3. quæ lex vitam atque salutem pollicebatur iis qui facerent quæcunque erant scripta ut fierent, Lev. xviii. 5. Gal.
iii. 12. non facientibus autem, execrationem, Deut. xxvii. 26.
15 Gal. iii. 10. ea erat tota lex; Christusque nos ab illius legis
execratione redemit, v. 13; quam videlicet implere non potui-
mus: cæremonialem autem implere haud difficili negotio
potuissemus; tota ergo ea est lex Mosaica a qua Christus nos
redemit. Cum autem execratio sit totam non implentibus
20 legem, ab eius nos execratione certe non redemit, nisi totam
nobis legem abrogavit: si totam abrogavit, nulla certe illius
parte obligamur.

and that they have not the least connection with the ceremonial law.

First then, the law is abolished principally on the ground of its being a law of works; that it might give place to the law
5 of grace. Rom. iii. 27. "by what law? of works? nay, but by the law of faith." xi. 6. "if by grace, then is it no more of works; otherwise grace is no more grace." Now the law of works was not solely the ceremonial law, but the whole law.

Secondly, iv. 15. "the law worketh wrath; for where no
10 law is, there is no transgression." It is not however a part, but the whole of the law that worketh wrath; inasmuch as the transgression is of the whole, and not of a part only. Seeing then that the law worketh wrath, but the gospel grace, and that wrath is incompatible with grace, it is obvious that the
15 law cannot co-exist with the gospel.

Thirdly, the law of which it was written, "the man that doeth them shall live in them," Gal. iii. 12. Lev. xviii. 5. and, "cursed is every one that continueth not in all things which are written in the book of the law to do them," Deut. xxvii.
20 26. Gal. iii. 10. was the whole law. From "the curse of" this "law Christ hath redeemed us," v. 13. inasmuch as we were unable to fulfil it ourselves. Now to fulfil the ceremonial law could not have been a matter of difficulty; it must therefore have been the entire Mosaic law from which Christ delivered
25 us. Again, as it was against those who did not fulfil the whole law that the curse was denounced, it follows that Christ could not have redeemed us from that curse, unless he had abrogated the whole law; if therefore he abrogated the whole, no part of it can be now binding upon us.

4. docemur, eam legem esse *mortis ministerium* adeoque *evanidam, quæ tabulis lapideis scripta erat,* 2 Cor. iii. erat autem ea ipse decalogus.

5. quæ lex igitur peccati est et mortis: peccati, quia peccatum irritat; mortis, quia mortem parit, et legi spiritus vitæ opponitur; ea procul dubio cæremonialis duntaxat non est, sed tota lex: ea autem aboletur: Rom. viii. 2. *lex spiritus vitæ, qui est in Christo Iesu, liberavit me a lege peccati et mortis.*

6. per quam legem affectus peccatorum vigebant in membris nostris ad fructum ferendum morti, Rom. vii. 5. ea certe non est duntaxat cæremonialis: ab ea autem lege, cum et nos ei mortificati simus, v. 4. et illa nobis sit mortua, v. 6. sic liberamur, ut a mortuo viro uxor, v. 3. liberamur ergo non a lege cæremoniali duntaxat, sed a lege Mosaica tota, v. 7. ut supra.

7. omnes credentes cum a Deo per fidem iustificati sint, iusti procul dubio sunt habendi: iustis autem nullam esse legem, diserte asserit Paulus Gal. v. 22, 23. 1 Tim. i. 9. Quod si lex ulla posita esset iustis, ea sola esset, quæ iustificet: lex autem non cæremonialis tantum, sed ne tota quidem Mosaica

Fourthly, we are taught, 2 Cor. iii. 7. that the law "written and engraven in stones" was "the ministration of death," and therefore "was done away." Now the law engraven in stones was not the ceremonial law, but the decalogue.

5 Fifthly, that which was, as just stated, a law of sin and death—of sin, because it is a provocative to sin; of death, because it produces death, and is in opposition to the law of the spirit of life—is certainly not the ceremonial law alone, but the whole law. But the law to which the above descrip-
10 tion applies, is abolished; Rom. viii. 2. "the law of the spirit of life in Christ Jesus hath made me free from the law of sin and death."

Sixthly, it was undoubtedly not by the ceremonial law alone that "the motions of sin which were by the law, wrought in
15 our members to bring forth fruit unto death," Rom. vii. 5. But of the law which thus operated it is said that we "are become dead thereto," v. 4. and "that being dead wherein we were held," v. 6. "we are delivered from it," as a wife is free "from the law of her husband who is dead," v. 3. We are
20 therefore "delivered," v. 6. not from the ceremonial law alone, but from the whole law of Moses.

Seventhly, all believers, inasmuch as they are justified by God through faith, are undoubtedly to be accounted righteous; but Paul expressly asserts that "the law is not made for
25 a righteous man," 1 Tim. i. 9. Gal. v. 22, 23. If however any law were to be made for the righteous, it must needs be a law which should justify. Now the ceremonial law alone was so far from justifying, that even the entire Mosaic law had

iustificat, ut ex iustificationis doctrina iam constat; Gal. iii.
11. et passim: ergo tota lex, non cæremonialis tantum, quia
non iustificat, est abrogata.

His adde, quæ lex non solum iustificare non potest, verum
5 etiam fideles turbat et labefactat, quæ etiam Deum tentat, si
nos eam præstare tentamus, quæ nullam promissionem habet,
immo quæ promissiones omnes, hæreditatem, adoptionem,
ipsam gratiam, ipsum denique spiritum tollit atque frustratur, immo quæ maledictos nos reddit; ea certe aboletur: ea
10 autem non cæremonialis tantum, sed tota lex erat, lex videlicet
operum; tota igitur lex aboletur.   Hæc singulatim ordine ex
clarissimis locis demonstrabuntur: Act. xv. 24. *quosdam e*
nobis egressos audivimus vos turbasse verbis, labefactantes
animas vestras; dicentes, oportere vos circumcidi, et servare
15 *legem*—. et v. 10. *quid tentatis Deum ad imponendum*
iugum—? Pharisæi qui crediderant, totam legem imponi
credentibus volebant, v. 5. totam ergo legem amovendam a
cervicibus discipulorum disserebat Petrus. Quæ autem lex
promissionem non habet, eam esse non cæremonialem dun-
20 taxat legem, sed totam, ex eo evincitur, quod pars eius aliqua

not power to effect this, as has been already shown in treating
of justification: Gal. iii. 11, &c. therefore it must be the
whole law, and not the ceremonial part alone, which is abrogated by reason of its inability in this respect.

5   To these considerations we may add, that that law which
not only cannot justify, but is the source of trouble and sub-
version to believers; which even tempts God if we endeavor
to perform its requisitions; which has no promise attached to
it, or, to speak more properly, which takes away and frustrates
10 all promises, whether of inheritance, or adoption, or grace,
or of the Spirit itself; nay, which even subjects us to a curse;
must necessarily have been abolished. If then it can be shown
that the above effects result, not from the ceremonial law
alone, but from the whole law, that is to say, the law of works
15 in a comprehensive sense, it will follow that the whole law is
abolished; and that they do so result, I shall proceed to show
from the clearest passages of Scripture. With regard to the
first point, Acts xv. 24. "we have heard that certain which
went out from us have troubled you with words, subverting
20 your souls, saying, Ye must be circumcised, and keep the law."
v. 10. "why tempt ye God, to put a yoke upon the neck of the
disciples?" Certain of the Pharisees which believed, said that
"it was needful for them to keep the whole law," v. 5. when
therefore Peter in opposition to this doctrine contends, that
25 the yoke of the law ought to be removed from the necks of
the disciples, it is clear that he must mean the whole law.
Secondly, that the law which had not the promise was not the
ceremonial law only, but the whole law, is clear from the

si promissionem haberet, satis profecto hoc esset: at ea lex de qua Paulus toties loquitur, nulla ex parte promissionem habet. Rom. iv. 13, 16. *non per legem promissio cessit Abrahamo, aut semini eius, ut hæres esset mundi; sed per iustitiam fidei.* Gal. iii. 18. *si ex lege est hæreditas, non iam ex promissione. Atqui Abrahamo per promissionem largitus est Deus hæreditatem.* non ergo per legem, aut ullam eius partem: eam itaque totam aboleri, aut aboleri ipsam promissionem demonstrat ipse Paulus, Rom. iv. 14. *etenim si ii qui ex lege sunt, hæredes sunt, inanis facta est fides, et cassa reddita est promissio.* et Gal. iii. 18. ut supra. Promissione abolita, aboletur hæreditas, aboletur adoptio, reducitur metus et servitus, quæ cum adoptione stare non possunt, Rom. viii. 15. Gal. iv. 1, &c. et v. 21, 24, 26, 30, ut supra; dissolvitur unio et communio cum Christo, Gal. v. 4. *evanuistis, separati a Christo quicunque per legem iustificamini:* unde amittitur et glorificatio; aboletur et ipsa gratia, nisi lex tota aboleatur, Gal. v. 4. *quicunque per legem iustificamini, a gratia excidistis.* de tota lege hoc dici et versus superior testatur, in quo totius legis servandæ fit mentio, et alioqui perspicuum est. Pellitur denique ipse spiritus, Gal. v. 18. *quod si spiritu ducimini, non estis sub lege;* ergo, vice versa, si estis sub lege, spiritu non

consideration, that it would be sufficient if one part had the promise, although the other were without it; whereas the law which is so often the subject of discussion with St. Paul has no promise attached to either of its branches. Rom. iv. 13, 16. "the promise that he should be the heir of the world, was not to Abraham, or to his seed through the law, but through the righteousness of faith." Gal. iii. 18. "if the inheritance be of the law, it is no more of promise; but God gave it to Abraham by promise"; and therefore not by the law, or any part of it; whence St. Paul shows that either the whole law, or the promise itself, must of necessity be abolished, Rom. iv. 14. "if they which are of the law be heirs, faith is made void, and the promise is made of none effect." Compare also Gal. iii. 18. as above. By the abolition of the promise, the inheritance and adoption are abolished; fear and bondage, which are incompatible with adoption, are brought back, Rom. viii. 15. Gal. iv. 1, &c. v. 21, 24, 26, 30. as above; union and fellowship with Christ are dissolved, Gal. v. 4. "Christ is become of no effect unto you, whosoever of you are justified by the law," whence follows the loss of glorification; nay, grace itself is abolished, unless the abolition of the law be an entire abolition: Gal. v. 4. "whosoever of you are justified by the law, ye are fallen from grace," where by the word "law" is intended the entire code, as appears not only from the preceding verse, "he is a debtor to do the whole law," but from other considerations; finally, the Spirit itself is excluded; Gal. v. 18. "if ye be led of the Spirit, ye are not under the law"; therefore, vice versa, if ye be under the law, ye are not led of the Spirit.

ducimini: relinquitur execratio, Gal. iii. 10. *quotquot ex operibus legis sunt, sub execratione sunt; scriptum est enim, execrabilis est quisquis non manserit in omnibus quæ scripta sunt in libro legis, ut faciat ea:* ergo omnia quæ scripta sunt

5 in lege, non cæremoniæ tantum, maledictioni obnoxios nos reddunt: Christus itaque cum ab execratione nos redemerit, v. 13. redemit etiam ab execrationis causis, nempe legis operibus, vel, quod idem est, tota lege operum; ea autem cæremonialis sola non est, ut supra ostendimus. Et sane quamvis

10 hoc non sequeretur, tamen legem observare quæ promissionem non habeat, non est operæ pretium; observare quam nisi totam impleas nihil agas, totam autem implere nullo modo possis, est operæ ludibrium; succedente præsertim in eius locum præstantiore lege fidei, ad quam implendam Deus

15 et voluntatem nobis et vires in Christo suppeditat.

Ex his omnibus cum auctoritatibus tum argumentis evincitur, totam legem Mosaicam per Evangelium aboleri. Et hac tamen legis abolitione, re quidem vera non abrogatur lex, id est, summa legis, sed finem suum assequitur in dilectione illa

20 Dei et proximi, quæ ex fide per spiritum nascitur. Hinc vere Christus legem asseruit, Matt. v. 17, &c. *ne existimate me venisse, ut dissolvam legem aut prophetas: non veni, ut dis-*

We are consequently left under the curse: Gal. iii. 10. "as many as are of the works of the law, are under the curse; for it is written, Cursed is every one that continueth not in all things which are written in the book of the law, to do them";

5 therefore "all things which are written in the law," and not the things of the ceremonial law alone, render us obnoxious to the curse. Christ therefore, when he "redeemed us from the curse," v. 13. redeemed us also from the causes of the curse, namely, the works of the law, or, which is the same,

10 from the whole law of works; which, as has been shown above, is not the ceremonial part alone. Even supposing, however, that no such consequences followed, there could be but little inducement to observe the conditions of a law which has not the promise; it would be even ridiculous to attempt to

15 observe that which is of no avail unless it be fulfilled in every part, and which nevertheless it is impossible for man so to fulfil; especially as it has been superseded by the more excellent law of faith, which God in Christ has given us both will and power to fulfil.

20 It appears therefore as well from the evidence of Scripture, as from the arguments above adduced, that the whole of the Mosaic law is abolished by the gospel. It is to be observed, however, that the sum and essence of the law is not hereby abrogated; its purpose being attained in that love of God and

25 our neighbor, which is born of the Spirit through faith. It was with justice therefore that Christ asserted the permanence of the law, Matt. v. 17. "think not that I am come to destroy the law, or the prophets; I am not come to destroy, but to

solvam; sed ut impleam, &c. Rom. iii. 31. *legem igitur cassam reddimus per fidem? absit: immo legem stabilimus.* et viii. 4. *ut ius illud legis compleatur in nobis qui non secundum carnem ambulamus, sed secundum spiritum.*

5   Vulgari obiectioni occurrit ipse Paulus, et peccatum hac legis abrogatione tolli aut certe frangi potius, quam roborari perspicue docet: Rom. vi. 14, 15. *peccatum vobis non dominabitur; non enim estis sub lege, sed sub gratia. Quid igitur? peccabimus, quod non simus sub lege, sed sub gratia? absit—.*
10 Summa igitur legis, ut ante diximus, dilectio nimirum Dei et proximi, nequaquam existimanda est aboleri; sed veluti mutato solum codice in cordibus fidelium, scriptore spiritu, exarari: ita tamen, ut in præceptis particularibus aliud atque littera velle spiritus nonnunquam videatur, si litteram non
15 retinendo rectius dilectioni Dei et proximi consulemus. Sic Christus a legis littera discessit, Marc. ii. 27, cum *sabbathum propter hominem factum esse, non hominem propter sabbathum* dixit, si quartum præceptum conferas. sic Paulus de coniugio cum infideli non dissolvendo, quod contra sub lege
20 severissime iniungitur. 1 Cor. vii. 12. *ego, non Dominus:* in utrisque enim illis et de sabbatho et coniugio mandatis interpretandis, ratio habita charitatis, omni scriptæ legi præponitur; quemadmodum et in reliquis omnibus præponi debet.

fulfil." Rom. iii. 31. "do we then make void the law through faith? God forbid: yea, we establish the law." viii. 4. "that the righteousness of the law might be fulfilled in us, who walk not after the flesh, but after the Spirit."

5   The common objection to this doctrine is anticipated by St. Paul himself, who expressly teaches that by this abrogation of the law, sin, if not taken away, is at least weakened rather than increased in power: Rom. vi. 14, 15. "sin shall not have dominion over you; for ye are not under the law, but
10 under grace: what then? shall we sin, because we are not under the law, but under grace? God forbid." Therefore, as was said above, the end for which the law was instituted, namely, the love of God and our neighbor, is by no means to be considered as abolished; it is the tablet of the law, so to
15 speak, that is alone changed, its injunctions being now written by the Spirit in the hearts of believers with this difference, that in certain precepts the Spirit appears to be at variance with the letter, namely, wherever by departing from the letter we can more effectually consult the love of God and our
20 neighbor. Thus Christ departed from the letter of the law, Mark ii. 27. "the sabbath was made for man, and not man for the sabbath," if we compare his words with the fourth commandment. St. Paul did the same in declaring that a marriage with an unbeliever was not to be dissolved, contrary to
25 the express injunction of the law; 1 Cor. vii. 12. "to the rest speak I, not the Lord." In the interpretation of these two commandments, of the sabbath and marriage, a regard to the law of love is declared to be better than a compliance with the

Matt. xxii. 37, 39, 40. *ab istis duobus præceptis* (dilectione videlicet Dei et proximi) *tota lex et prophetæ pendent.* neutrum tamen horum decalogi disertum præceptum est; sed illud Deut. vi. 5. hoc Lev. xix. 18. primum occurrit nec 5 decalogum solum sed plus decalogo totam nempe legem et prophetas per eminentiam, quod aiunt, complectitur: et Matt. vii. 12. *quæcunque volueritis ut faciant vobis homines, ita et vos facite iis: ista enim est lex et prophetæ.* Rom. xiii. 8, 10. *qui diligit alterum, legem implevit: charitas est completio* 10 *legis.* Gal. v. 14. *tota lex uno dicto impletur; isto, diliges proximum tuum ut teipsum.* 1 Tim. i. 5. *finis mandati est charitas ex puro corde, et conscientia bona, et fide minime simulata:* mandati nempe Mosaici, multo magis evangelici. Iacob. ii. 8. *si legem regiam præstatis secundum scripturam,* 15 *diliges proximum tuum ut teipsum.* Itaque præcepta illa Christi in monte sani omnes ex charitatis sensu, non ex littera interpretantur: et illud Pauli 1 Cor. xi. 4. *omnis vir orans aut prophetans operto capite*—: de quo vide infra, l. 2. cap. 4. ubi de habitu orantium. Hinc Rom. iv. 15. *ubi non est lex,*

whole written law; a rule which applies equally to every other
instance. Matt. xxii. 37–40. "on these two commandments,"
namely, the love of God and our neighbor, "hang all the law
and the prophets." Now neither of these is propounded in
5 express terms among the ten commandments, the former oc-
curring for the first time Deut. vi. 5. the latter, Lev. xix. 18.
and yet these two precepts are represented as comprehending
emphatically, not only the ten commandments, but the whole
law and the prophets. Matt. vii. 12. "all things whatsoever ye
10 would that men should do unto you, do ye even so to them;
for this is the law and the prophets." Rom. xiii. 8, 10. "he
that loveth another hath fulfilled the law; love is the fulfilling
of the law." Gal. v. 14. "all the law is fulfilled in one word,
even in this, Thou shalt love thy neighbor as thyself." 1 Tim.
15 i. 5. "the end of the commandment is charity out of a pure
heart, and of a good conscience, and of faith unfeigned." If
this is the end of the Mosaic commandment, much more is it
the end of the evangelic. James ii. 8. "if ye fulfil the royal law
according to the scripture, Thou shalt love thy neighbor as
20 thyself, thou shalt do well." Hence all rational interpreters
have explained the precepts of Christ, in his sermon on the
mount, not according to the letter, but in the spirit of the law
of love. So also that of St. Paul, 1 Cor. xi. 4. "every man pray-
ing or prophesying, having his head covered, dishonoreth his
25 head"; a text which will come under consideration in Book
II. chap. iv. on the outward deportment befitting prayer.
Hence it is said, Rom. iv. 15. "where no law is, there is no
transgression"; that is, no transgression in disregarding the

ibi nec transgressio; litteræ videlicet, si summa servetur in dilectione Dei et proximi, duce spiritu.

Hanc ego veritatem cum tot locorum luce collata contra omnium fere, quos legeram, Theologorum sententiam, qui
5 totam Mosaicam legem abrogatam negant, asseruisse mihi videbar, Zanchium forte in epistolam ad Ephes. cap. ii. fuse scribentem in eadem mecum sententia reperi: qui addit, et recte quidem, *in huius quæstionis explicatione, non minimam partem Theologiæ consistere: nec probe intelligi posse ne*
10 *scripturas quidem, præsertim doctrinam de iustificatione et bonis operibus,* totum evangelium ego quidem dixerim, *nisi articulus iste de legis abrogatione intelligatur;* remque satis accurate probat; sed probatis non strenue utitur; multis postea exceptionibus involutus ac fluctuans, quæ lectorem paulo mi-
15 nus attentum, incertiorem dimittunt. Cameronis etiam eandem esse alicubi de abolenda lege tota sententiam animadverti.

Cæteri fere igitur, qui dogma illud Pharisæorum creden-tium adhuc retinent, legem sub evangelio etiam observari oportere (quod dogma initiis ecclesiæ haud parum olim
20 molestiæ attulit) multos esse aiunt usus legis etiam nobis

letter of the law, provided that under the direction of the
Spirit the end of the institution be attained in the love of God
and our neighbor.

On the united authority of so many passages of Scripture,
5 I conceived that I had satisfactorily established the truth in
question against the whole body of theologians, who, so far
as my knowledge then extended, concurred in denying the
abrogation of the entire Mosaic law. I have since however
discovered, that Zanchius, in his commentary on the second
10 chapter of Ephesians, declares himself of the same opinion,
remarking, very justly, that "no inconsiderable part of divin-
ity depends on the right explanation of this question; and that
it is impossible to comprehend the Scriptures properly, especially those parts which relate to justification and good
15 works,"—he might have added, the whole of the New Testament—"unless the subject of the abrogation of the law be
thoroughly understood." He proves his point with sufficient
accuracy, but neglects to follow up his conclusions; losing
himself in a multitude of minute exceptions, and apparently
20 fluctuating between the two opinions, so as to leave the
reader, if not extremely attentive, in a state of uncertainty. I
have also observed that Cameron somewhere expresses the
same opinion respecting the abolition of the whole law.

It is asserted, however, by divines in general, who still main-
25 tain the tenet of the converted Pharisees, that it is needful for
those who are under the gospel to observe the law (a doctrine
which in the infancy of the church was productive of much
mischief) that the law may be highly useful, in various ways,

Christianis; nempe, ut eo magis impellamur ad peccatum
agnoscendum, gratiamque amplectendam, Deique voluntatem intelligendam. Respondeo, primum sententia nostra non
ponit eos quibus impulsione ad Christum opus est, sed iam
5 credentes, id est, Christo iam arctissime coniunctos: deinde,
voluntas Dei ex ipsa doctrina evangelii et promisso spiritu
veritatis duce, Dei lege denique cordibus fidelium inscripta
rectissime cognoscitur: peccatum autem agnoscimus, et ad
gratiam Christi impellimur, legem duntaxat cognoscendo,
10 non præstando; siquidem operibus legis non propius ad
Christum accedimus, sed longius a Christo aberramus; ut
scriptura toties monet.

　　Secundo, distinguunt, et nominatim Polanus, *non esse sub*
lege, non est, Non teneri obedientia legis; sed, Liberum esse a
15 *maledictione et coactione legis, et peccati irritatione.* Verum
si hoc ita est, quid assequuntur fideles per evangelium; quandoquidem fideles etiam sub lege liberati maledictione et
peccati irritatione iam tum erant: coactione autem legis
liberum esse, quid aliud est obsecro, quam plane id quod
20 defendimus; omnino sub lege non esse? Lex enim quamdiu
est, cogit, quia servitutis lex est: coactio autem et servitus a

even to us who are Christians; inasmuch as we are thereby led
to a truer conviction of sin, and consequently to a more thank-
ful acceptance of grace; as well as to a more perfect knowledge
of the will of God. With regard to the first point, I reply, that
I am not speaking of sinners, who stand in need of a prelimin-
ary impulse to come to Christ, but of such as are already
believers, and consequently in the most intimate union with
Christ; as to the second, the will of God is best learnt from the
gospel itself under the promised guidance of the Spirit of
truth, and from the divine law written in the hearts of believers. Besides, if the law be the means of leading us to a
conviction of sin and an acceptance of the grace of Christ, this
is effected by a knowledge of the law itself, not by the performance of its works; inasmuch as through the works of the
law, instead of drawing nearer to Christ, we depart farther
from him; as Scripture is perpetually inculcating.

In the next place, a distinction is made; and Polanus in particular observes, that "when it is said that we are not under
the law, it is not meant that we are not under an obligation to
obey it, but that we are exempt from the curse and restraint of
the law, as well as from the provocation to sin which results
from it." If this be the case, what advantage do believers reap
from the gospel? since even under the law they at least were
exempted from the curse and provocation to sin; and since to
be free from the restraint of the law can mean nothing but that
for which I contend, an entire exemption from the obligation
of the law. For as long as the law exists, it constrains, because
it is a law of bondage; constraint and bondage being as in-

lege separari non potest, uti nec libertas ab evangelio, quod statim liquebit.

Instat Polanus, ad illud Gal. iv. 4, 5. *ut eos qui legi erant subiecti, redimeret; Christianos esse redemptos a subiectione* legis *et non esse sub lege, non simpliciter, quasi nullam amplius obedientiam legi deberent; sed, secundum quid; nempe quatenus non amplius tenentur perfectissime in hac vita implere legem Dei, quam Christus pro ipsis implevit.* Quod quis non videt longe aliter se habere? a Christianis enim non minus perfecta vita requiritur, immo perfectior potius quam ab iis, qui sub lege erant; id quod omnia præcepta Christi sonant. Hoc tantum interest, quod Moses litteram sive externam legem imponebat vel invitis; Christus internam Dei legem per spiritum suum fidelium cordibus inscribit, volentesque ducit: sub lege, etiam per fidem iustificabantur homines Deo fidentes, sed non sine operibus legis; Rom. iv. 12. *Pater circumcisionis* &c. evangelium iustificat per fidem sine operibus legis. Unde nos ab operibus legis liberati, non litteram sequimur, sed spiritum; non legis opera, sed fidei. Nobis itaque non dicitur, *quicquid ex lege non est, peccatum est;* sed, *quicquid ex fide non est.* nostra igitur norma non

separable from the dispensation of the law, as liberty from the dispensation of the gospel; of which shortly.

Polanus contends, on Gal. iv. 4, 5. "to redeem them that were under the law," that "when Christians are said to be redeemed from subjection to the law, and to be no longer under the law, this is not to be taken in an absolute sense, as if they owed no more obedience to it. What then do the words imply? They signify, that Christians are no longer under the necessity of perfectly fulfilling the law of God in this life, inasmuch as Christ has fulfilled it for them." That this is contrary to the truth, is too obvious not to be acknowledged. So far from a less degree of perfection being exacted from Christians, it is expected of them that they should be more perfect than those who were under the law; as the whole tenor of Christ's precepts evinces. The only difference is, that Moses imposed the letter, or external law, even on those who were not willing to receive it; whereas Christ writes the inward law of God by his Spirit on the hearts of believers, and leads them as willing followers. Under the law, those who trusted in God were justified by faith indeed, but not without the works of the law; Rom. iv. 12. "the father of circumcision to them who are not of the circumcision only, but who also walk in the steps of that faith of our father Abraham, which he had being yet uncircumcised." The gospel, on the contrary, justifies by faith without the works of the law. Wherefore, we being freed from the works of the law, no longer follow the letter, but the spirit; doing the works of faith, not of the law. Neither is it said to us, "whatever is not of the law is sin," but, "whatever

est lex, sed fides. Ex quo sequitur, cum fides cogi non possit, neque opera fidei cogi posse. Plura vide supra cap. xv. de regio Christi munere, et interna lege spiritus, qua is ecclesiam gubernat; et infra l. 2. c. i. ubi de forma bonorum operum.

5 Abrogata per evangelium lege servitutis, sequitur Libertas Christiana: quamquam est quidem libertas primario adoptionis fructus, et proinde legis temporibus, ut supra diximus cap. xxiii. non ignota: sed quoniam ante adventum Christi liberatoris libertas nostra perfecta aut manifesta esse non 10 potuit, idcirco libertas ad evangelium maxime pertinet, eiusque est comes: primum, quia sub evangelio maxime est veritas; Ioan. i. 17. *gratia et veritas per Iesum Christum præstita est:* Veritas autem in libertatem vindicat; cap. viii. 31, 32. *si vos manseritis in sermone meo, vere discipuli mei* 15 *critis: et cognoscetis veritatem, et veritas vos in libertatem vindicabit.* et v. 36. *itaque si vos filius in libertatem vindicarit, vere liberi estis.* Secundo, quia evangelii præcipue donum est spiritus: *ubi autem spiritus domini, illic libertas,* 2 Cor. iii. 17.

20 Libertas Christiana est qua liberatore Christo, a servitute peccati, adeoque legis hominumque præscripto velut

is not of faith is sin"; faith consequently, and not the law, is our rule. It follows, therefore, that as faith cannot be made matter of compulsion, so neither can the works of faith. See more on this subject in the fifteenth chapter, on Christ's
5 kingly office, and on the inward spiritual law by which he governs the church. Compare also Book II. chap. i. where the form of good works is considered.

From the abrogation, through the gospel, of the law of servitude, results Christian liberty; though liberty, strictly
10 speaking, is the peculiar fruit of adoption, and consequently was not unknown during the time of the law, as observed in the twenty-third chapter. Inasmuch, however, as it was not possible for our liberty either to be perfected or made fully manifest till the coming of Christ our deliverer, liberty must
15 be considered as belonging in an especial manner to the gospel, and as consorting therewith: first, because truth is principally known by the gospel, John i. 17. "grace and truth came by Jesus Christ," and truth has an essential connection with liberty; viii. 31, 32. "if ye continue in my word, then are
20 ye my disciples indeed; and ye shall know the truth, and the truth shall make you free." v. 36. "if the Son therefore shall make you free, ye shall be free indeed." Secondly, because the peculiar gift of the gospel is the Spirit; but "where the Spirit of the Lord is, there is liberty," 2 Cor. iii. 17.
25   CHRISTIAN LIBERTY is that whereby WE ARE LOOSED AS IT WERE BY ENFRANCHISEMENT, THROUGH CHRIST OUR DELIVERER, FROM THE BONDAGE OF SIN, AND CONSEQUENTLY FROM THE RULE OF THE LAW AND OF MAN; TO THE INTENT THAT BEING MADE SONS

MANUMISSI LIBERAMUR, UT FILII EX SERVIS FACTI, EX PUERIS
ADULTI, DEO PER SPIRITUM VERITATIS DUCEM IN CHARITATE SER-
VIAMUS. Gal. v. 1. *in libertate igitur qua Christus nos liberavit,
perstate; et ne rursus iugo servitutis implicamini.* Rom. viii. 2.
5 *lex spiritus vitæ qui est in Christo Iesu, liberavit me a lege
peccati et mortis.* et v. 15. *non enim accepistis spiritum servitutis rursum ad metum; sed spiritum adoptionis, per quem
clamamus Abba, id est, pater.* Gal. iv. 7. *non amplius es
servus, sed filius.* Heb. ii. 15. *ut liberos redderet quotquot
10 metu mortis per omnem vitam damnates erant servitutis.*
1 Cor. vii. 23. *pretio empti estis, ne fiatis servi hominum.*
Iacob. i. 25. *qui inspicit in legem perfectam illam libertatis*
et ii. 12. *Ita loquimini atque ita facite ut qui ex lege libertatis
iudicandi sitis.*

15   UT DEO SERVIAMUS. Matt. xi. 29, 30. *attollite iugum meum
in vos—: nam iugum meum bonum* sive *facile est, et onus
meum leve est,* cum 1 Ioan. v. 3, 4, 5. *hæc est enim charitas
Dei, ut præcepta eius observemus; et præcepta eius gravia non
sunt—.* Rom. vi. 18. *liberati a peccato, servi facti estis ius-
20 titiæ.* et v. 22. *nunc liberati a peccato, servi autem facti Deo,
habetis fructum vestrum in sanctimoniam—.* et vii. 6. *nunc
autem liberati sumus a lege, mortuo eo in quo detinebamur,
ut serviamus in novitate spiritus, ac non in vetustate litteræ.*
Rom. xii. 1, 2. *rationalem cultum.* et ne conformemini
25 *huic sæculo, sed transformemini renovatione mentis vestræ*

INSTEAD OF SERVANTS, AND PERFECT MEN INSTEAD OF CHILDREN, WE MAY SERVE GOD IN LOVE THROUGH THE GUIDANCE OF THE SPIRIT OF TRUTH. Gal. v. 1. "stand fast therefore in the liberty wherewith Christ hath made us free; and be not entangled
5 again with the yoke of bondage." Rom. viii. 2. "the law of the Spirit of life in Christ Jesus hath made me free from the law of sin and death." v. 15. "ye have not received the spirit of bondage again to fear; but ye have received the Spirit of adoption, whereby we cry, Abba, Father." Gal. iv. 7. "wherefore
10 thou art no more a servant, but a son." Heb. ii. 15. "that he might deliver them who through fear of death were all their lifetime subject to bondage." 1 Cor. vii. 23. "ye are bought with a price; be not ye the servants of men." James i. 25. "whoso looketh into the perfect law of liberty, and continueth
15 therein." ii. 12. "so speak ye, and so do, as they that shall be judged by the law of liberty."

THAT WE MAY SERVE GOD. Matt. xi. 29, 30. "take my yoke upon you . . . for my yoke is easy, and my burden is light," compared with 1 John v. 3–5. "this is the love of God, that we
20 keep his commandments, and his commandments are not grievous." Rom. vi. 18. "being then made free from sin, ye became the servants of righteousness." v. 22. "now being made free from sin, and become servants to God, ye have your fruit unto holiness." vii. 6. "now we are delivered from the
25 law, that being dead wherein we were held, that we should serve in newness of spirit, and not in the oldness of the letter." xii. 1, 2. "present your bodies . . . a reasonable service; and be not conformed to this world; but be ye transformed by the

ad explorandum quænam sit voluntas Dei illa bona et accepta et perfecta. Iacob. i. 25. *at is qui introspexerit in perfectam illam legem libertatis, et permanserit in ea, quia non fuerit auditor obliviosus, sed effector operis, is beatior erit in opere*
5 *suo.* 1 Pet. ii. 16. *ut liberi, ac non veluti malitiæ velamen habentes libertatem; sed ut servi Dei.* Hinc iudiciis hominum multo magis coactione et tribunalibus in religione liberamur: Rom. xiv. 4. *tu quis es qui condemnas alienum famulum? proprio Domino perstat aut cadit.* et v. 8. *sive vivimus sive*
10 *morimur, Domini sumus.* Matt. vii. 1. *ne iudicate, ut ne iudicemini.* Rom. xiv. 10. *tu vero cur condemnas fratrem tuum, aut etiam tu cur pro nihilo habes fratrem tuum? omnes enim sistemur apud tribunal Christi.* Certe si in sermone communi iudicare aut condemnare fratres de rebus quæ ad religionem
15 et conscientiam spectant, prohibemur, quanto magis in foro civili, id est, plane alieno; cum Paulus ista omnia ad Christi, non ad hominum tribunal referat? Iacob. ii. 12. *ita loquimini et ita facite, ut per legem libertatis iudicandi:* a Deo nempe, non ab hominibus in rebus religiosis; in quibus si
20 Deus nos iudicaturus est per legem libertatis, cur homo nos præiudicat per legem servitutis?

PER SPIRITUM VERITATIS DUCEM IN CHARITATE. Rom. xiv. toto capite; et parte capitis xv. usque ad v. 15. Duo autem imprimis in his capitibus cavenda esse admonet Paulus: primum

renewing of your mind, that ye may prove what is that good
and acceptable and perfect will of God." James i. 25. "whoso
looketh into the perfect law of liberty, and continueth therein,
he being not a forgetful hearer, but a doer of the work, this
5 man shall be blessed in his deed." 1 Pet. ii. 16. "as free, and
not using your liberty for a cloak of maliciousness, but as the
servants of God." Hence we are freed from the yoke of
human judgments, much more of civil decrees and penalties
in religious matters. Rom. xiv. 4. "who art thou that judgest
10 another man's servant? to his own master he standeth or
falleth." v. 8. "whether we live or die, we are the Lord's."
Matt. vii. 1. "judge not, that ye be not judged." Rom. xiv. 10.
"why dost thou judge thy brother? or why dost thou set at
nought thy brother? for we shall all stand before the judg-
15 ment-seat of Christ." If we are forbidden to judge or condemn our brethren respecting matters of religion or conscience
in common discourse, how much more in a court of law,
which has confessedly no jurisdiction here; since St. Paul
refers all such matters to the judgment-seat of Christ, not of
20 man? James ii. 12. "so speak ye, and so do, as they that shall
be judged by the law of liberty"; namely, by God, not by
fallible men in things appertaining to religion; wherein if he
will judge us according to the law of liberty, why should man
prejudge us according to the law of bondage?
25   BY THE GUIDANCE OF THE SPIRIT OF TRUTH IN LOVE. Rom.
xiv. throughout the whole of the chapter; and chap. xv. 1–15.
In these chapters Paul lays down two especial cautions to be
observed; first, that whatever we do in pursuance of this our

ut quicquid agamus in hac nostra libertate utenda, id certa fide agamus, persuasi nobis licitum id esse: v. 5. *unusquisque in animo suo plene certus esto.* et 23. *quicquid ex fide non est, peccatum est:* deinde, ne infirmo fratri iustam offensam

5 offeramus, v. 20, 21. *ne cibi causa destrue opus Dei: omnia quidem munda; sed malum est homini qui edens offendit—.* 1 Cor. viii. 13. *si esca offendiculo est fratri meo, non edam carnes in æternum, ne sim offendiculo fratri meo:* qui tamen Pauli insignis potius erga fratres amor fuit, quam officii onus

10 cuique impositum, ut quis in perpetuum carne abstineret, si infirmus frater vesci solis oleribus licere crederet. Et cap. ix. 19, 20, 21, 22. *nam quamvis liber sim ab omnibus, omnibus meipsum servum feci, ut plures lucrifacerem: Iudæis ut Iudæus—; iis qui sub lege sunt, ut si essem sub lege—; exle-*

15 *gibus ut exlex, non exlex Deo, sed sublex Christo—: infirmis ut infirmus—; omnibus omnia—.* et x. 23. *omnia mihi licent, at non omnia conferunt—,* ut supra. Gal. v. 13. *vos ad libertatem vocati estis fratres; tantum ne libertatem vertite in datam carni occasionem; sed ex charitate servite alii aliis.*

20 2 Pet. ii. 19. *libertatem iis pollicendo, cum ipsi servi sint cor-ruptelæ.* 1 Cor. viii. 9. *videte ne quo modo istud quod vobis licitum est, impingendi causa fiat infirmis.*

Ob hanc solam rationem videtur præceptum esse ecclesiis,

liberty, we should do it in full assurance of faith, nothing doubting that it is permitted us. v. 5. "let every man be fully persuaded in his own mind." v. 23. "whatever is not of faith, is sin." Secondly, that we should give no just cause of offence to a weak brother, v. 20, 21. "for meat destroy not the work of God: all things indeed are pure, but it is evil for that man who eateth with offence." 1 Cor. viii. 13. "if meat make my brother to offend, I will eat no flesh while the world standeth, lest I make my brother to offend"; which resolution, however, must be considered as an effect of the extraordinary love which the apostle bore his brethren, rather than a religious obligation binding on every believer to abstain from flesh for ever, in case a weak brother should think vegetable food alone lawful. ix. 19–22. "though I be free from all men, yet have I made myself servant unto all, that I might gain the more; unto the Jews I became as a Jew . . . to them that are under the law, as under the law . . . to them that are without law, as without law; being not without law to God, but under the law to Christ . . . to the weak became I as weak . . . I am made all things to all men." x. 23. "all things are lawful for me, but all things are not expedient." Gal. v. 13. "for, brethren, ye have been called unto liberty; only use not liberty for an occasion to the flesh; but by love serve one another." 2 Pet. ii. 19. "while they promise themselves liberty, they themselves are the servants of corruption." 1 Cor. viii. 9. "take heed lest by any means this liberty of yours become a stumbling-block to them that are weak."

This appears to have been the sole motive for the command

Act. xv. 28, 29. *ut sanguine et suffocato abstinerent;* ne scilicet Iudæis nondum satis confirmatis, offensioni essent. Sanguinis enim prohibitio cæremonialis fuisse liquet, Lev. xvii. 11. ex ratione allata; *nam anima cuiusque carnis in san-* 5 *guine est; ego vero*—. Sic etiam, in lege, adipis esus prohibetur, cap. vii. 23, &c. nemo tamen idcirco defensum sibi esse adipis esum existimat, cum illa prohibitio tantummodo sacrificiorum sæcula spectaret, Act. x. 13, &c.

Malitiosorum autem aut pertinacium ducenda ratio nulla 10 est: Gal. ii. 4, 5. *sed propter irreptitios falsos fratres, qui fuerant clam ingressi ad explorandum libertatem nostram quam habemus in Christo Iesu, ut nos in servitutem redige- rent: quibus ne ad momentum quidem nos subiiciendo cessi- mus; ut veritas evangelii permaneret apud vos.* 1 Cor. xiv. 38. 15 *qui vero ignarus est, ignarus esto.* Scandalum Pharisæis esse datum Christus non laboravit, sed discipulos tum qui manus ante cibum non lavabant Matt. xv. 2, 3. tum qui spicas velle- bant defendit; quod tunc temporis illicitum die sabbathi ha- bebatur, Luc. vi. 1, &c. Christus pedes suos a fœmina tam 20 sumptuose perungi, mollique divitis puellæ capillitio abstergi non fuisset passurus, immo factum non defendisset atque laudasset, Ioan. xii. 3, &c. nec prosequentium se quacunque iret mulierum officiis ac liberalitate fuisset usurus, Luc. viii. 2, 3. si malitiosis et invidis esset perpetuo satisfaciendum.

given to the churches, Acts xv. 28, 29. "to abstain from blood, and from things strangled"; namely, lest the Jews who were not yet sufficiently established in the faith should take offence. For that the abstinence from blood was purely ceremonial, is evident from the reason assigned Lev. xvii. 11. "the life of the flesh is in the blood, and I have given it to you upon the altar to make an atonement for your souls." Thus the eating of fat was forbidden by the law, vii. 23, &c. yet no one infers from hence that the use of fat is unlawful, this prohibition applying only to the sacrificial times: Acts x. 13, &c.

No regard, however, is to be paid to the scruples of the malicious or obstinate. Gal. ii. 4, 5. "and that because of false brethren unawares brought in, who came in privily to spy out our liberty which we have in Christ Jesus, that they might bring us into bondage; to whom we gave place by subjection, no, not for an hour; that the truth of the gospel might continue with you." 1 Cor. xiv. 38. "if any man be ignorant, let him be ignorant." Christ was not deterred by the fear of giving offence to the Pharisees, from defending the practice of his disciples in eating bread with unwashen hands, Matt. xv. 2, 3. and plucking the ears of corn, which it was considered unlawful to do on the sabbath-day, Luke vi. 1, &c. Nor would he have suffered a woman of condition to anoint his feet with precious ointment, and to wipe them with her hair, still less would he have vindicated and praised the action, John xii. 3, &c. neither would he have availed himself of the good offices and kindness of the women who ministered unto him whithersoever he went, if it were necessary on all occasions to satisfy

Ne fratrum quidem, si minus sincere agant. Gal. ii. 11, &c. *quum autem venisset Petrus Antiochiam, in os ei obstiti, eo quod condemnandus esset—*.

Debebunt etiam infirmi firmiorum libertatem non temere
5 iudicare, sed erudiendos potius se praebere. Rom. xiv. 13. *ne amplius igitur alii alios iudicemus.*

Non igitur hæc ratio, ne præfatio hæc quidem consulendi scilicet infirmis idonea satis est ad conficienda magistratuum edicta quibus congantur fideles, aut libertatis ulla parte spo-
10 lientur. Sic enim disserit Paulus, 1 Cor. ix. 19. *quamvis liber sim ab omnibus, omnibus meipsum servum feci. meipsum feci,* non factus sum ab alio: *ab omnibus liber;* certe ergo a magistratu his quidem in rebus. Quam libertatem si magistratus tollit, tollit ipsum Evangelium: tollit saltem bonos
15 iuxta et malos; contra illud præceptum notissimum, Matt. xiii. 29, 30. *ne colligendo zizania eradicetis simul cum eis triticum, sinite utraque crescere usque ad messem.*

the unreasonable scruples of malicious or envious persons. Nay, we must withstand the opinions of the brethren themselves, if they are influenced by motives unworthy of the gospel. Gal. ii. 11, &c. "when Peter was come to Antioch, I
5 withstood him to the face, because he was to be blamed." Nor ought the weak believer to judge rashly of the liberty of a Christian brother whose faith is stronger than his own, but rather to give himself up to be instructed with the more willingness. Rom. xiv. 13. "let us not therefore judge one another
10 any more."

Neither this reason, therefore, nor a pretended consideration for the weaker brethren, afford a sufficient warrant for those edicts of the magistrate which constrain believers, or deprive them in any respect of their religious liberty. For so
15 the apostle argues 1 Cor. ix. 19. "though I be free from all men, yet have I made myself servant unto all"; I was not made so by others, but became so of my own accord; "free from all men," and consequently from the magistrate, in these matters at least. When the magistrate takes away this liberty,
20 he takes away the gospel itself; he deprives the good and the bad indiscriminately of their privilege of free judgment, contrary to the spirit of the well known precept, Matt. xiii. 29, 30. "lest while ye gather up the tares ye root up also the wheat with them: let both grow together until the harvest."

CAPUT XXVIII.

DE OBSIGNATIONE FŒDERIS GRATIÆ EXTERNA.

FUIT EXHIBITIO FŒDERIS GRATIÆ sub lege et evangelio: sequitur eius OBSIGNATIO, vel potius per externa quædam signa repræsentatio;

Ea etiam est et sub lege et sub evangelio.

5   Sub lege CIRCUMCISIO fuit et PASCHA: sub evangelio BAPTIS-MUS et CŒNA DOMINICA.

Hæc præsertim Duo posteriora recepto in ecclesia vocabulo SACRAMENTA præcipue nominantur.

Sacramentum est quo gratiam salvificam sive Christi satis-
10 factionem per signum visibile divinitus institutum nobis cre-dentibus Deus obsignat, nos Deo fidem et obedientiam no-stram sincero animo proposito, et grata recordatione testamur.

DE CIRCUMCISIONE Gen. xvii. 10, &c. *hoc est fœdus meum inter me et vos, et semen tuum post te, quod servabitis, ut*
15 *circumcidatur vobis omnis mas. circumcidetis carnem præ-putii vestri, ut sit signum fœderis inter me et vos——.* Rom. iv. *11, 12. et signum accepit circumcisionis: quod esset sigillum*

CHAPTER XXVIII.

OF THE EXTERNAL SEALING OF THE COVENANT OF GRACE.

THE MANIFESTATION OF THE COVENANT OF GRACE, under the law and the gospel respectively, has been considered; we are now to speak of the SEALING OF THAT COVENANT, or rather of its representation under certain out-
5 ward signs.

This representation, like the covenant itself and its manifestation, is common both to the law and the gospel: under the former it consisted in CIRCUMCISION and the PASSOVER; under the latter it consists in BAPTISM and the SUPPER OF THE LORD.
10 These ceremonies, particularly the two latter, are generally known by the name of SACRAMENTS.

Sacrament is a visible sign ordained by God, whereby he sets his seal on believers in token of his saving grace, or of the satisfaction of Christ; and whereby we on our part testify our
15 faith and obedience to God with a sincere heart and a grateful remembrance.

Respecting CIRCUMCISION, compare Gen. xvii. 10, &c. "this is my covenant which ye shall keep between me and you, and thy seed after thee; every man child among you shall be cir-
20 cumcised; and ye shall circumcise the flesh of your foreskin; and it shall be a token of the covenant between me and you." Rom. iv. 11, 12. "he received the sign of circumcision, a seal of the righteousness of faith which he had yet being uncircum-

iustitiæ fidei receptæ in præputio; ut esset pater omnium cre-
dentium in præputio, imputata etiam ipsis iustitia: et pater cir-
cumcisionis, iis qui non solum sunt ex circumcisione, sed qui
etiam incedunt vestigiis fidei patris nostri Abrahami, quæ fuit
5 *in præputio.* Deut. x. 16. *circumcidetis præputium cordis*
vestri, et cervicem vestram ne obduretis amplius. et xxx. 6.
circumcidet Iehova Deus tuus animum tuum et animum
seminis tui ad diligendum Iehovam—. Ier. iv. 4. *circum-*
cidite vos Iehovæ, et amovete præputia animi vestri. Non-
10 nunquam itaque sanctificationem etiam sub evangelio significat. Col. ii. 11. *in quo etiam circumcisi estis circumcisione*
quæ fit sine manibus, exuendo corpus peccatorum carnis, per
circumcisionem Christi.

Post legem tamen datam circumcisio signum fœderis ope-
15 rum fuisse videtur. Rom. iv. 12. *et Pater circumcisionis iis qui*
non solum sunt ex circumcisione. cap. ii. 25. *nam circum-*
cisio quidem prodest si legem observes; quod si transgressor
legis fueris, circumcisio tua facta est præputium. Gal. v. 3.
testor omni homini qui circumciditur, eum esse debitorem
20 *totius legis servandæ.* Hinc a Mose dicitur data Ioan. vii.
22, 23.

DE PASCHATE Exod. xii. 3, &c. *in ipso decimo die huius men-*
sis; ut accipiant sibi quisque parvam pecudem pro familia
paterna &c. v. 13. *erit autem sanguis ille pro vobis in signum*

cised; that he might be the father of all them that believe, though they be not circumcised, that righteousness might be imputed unto them also; and the father of circumcision to them who are not of the circumcision only, but who also walk
5 in the steps of that faith of our father Abraham, which he had being yet uncircumcised." Deut. x. 16. "circumcise the foreskin of your heart, and be no more stiff-necked." xxx. 6. "Jehovah thy God will circumcise thine heart, and the heart of thy seed, to love Jehovah thy God—." Jer. iv. 4. "circum-
10 cise yourselves to Jehovah, and take away the foreskins of your heart." Sometimes, by a similar figure, it signifies sanctification even under the gospel. Col. ii. 11. "in whom also ye are circumcised with the circumcision made without hands, in putting off the body of the sins of the flesh by the
15 circumcision of Christ."

Subsequently, however, to the giving of the law circumcision seems to have typified the covenant of works. Rom. iv. 12. "the father of circumcision to them who are not of the circumcision only." ii. 25. "for circumcision verily profiteth,
20 if thou keep the law; but if thou be a breaker of the law, thy circumcision is made uncircumcision." Gal. v. 3. "I testify again to every man that is circumcised, that he is a debtor to do the whole law." Hence it is said to have been given by Moses, John vii. 22, 23.

25 Respecting the PASSOVER, compare Exod. xii. 3, &c. "in the tenth day of this month they shall take to them every man a lamb, according to the house of their fathers, a lamb for an house," &c. v. 13. "the blood shall be to you for a token upon

super illas domos ubi eritis; ut videns sanguinem illum tran-
seam præter vos; sic non erit in vobis plaga exitialis quum
cædam primogenitos in terra Ægypti. et 15. *septem dies*
panes azymos comedite; ipso die primo amovebitis vetus
5 *fermentum e domibus vestris—.*

Paschatis autem significatio erat Christus mactatus eiusque
sanguinis aspersi efficacia ad salutem eis qui festum illud
puro corde celebrarent; Ioan. i. 29. *vidit Ioannes Iesum veni-*
entem ad se, et ait, ecce agnus ille Dei qui tollit peccata mundi.
10 et xix. 36. *facta sunt hæc ut scriptura impleretur, dicens, non*
conteretur ullum os ipsius. et 1 Cor. v. 7. *expurgate vetus*
fermentum, ut sitis nova massa, sicut estis fermenti expertes.
etenim pascha nostrum pro nobis sacrificatum est, nempe
Christus.

15 BAPTISMUS est primum sub evangelio sacramentum vulgo
dictum quo CREDENTIUM ET PURITATEM VITÆ SPONDENTIUM COR-
PORA IN PROFLUENTEM AQUAM IMMERGUNTUR AD SIGNIFICANDAM
NOSTRAM PER SPIRITUM SANCTUM REGENERATIONEM, NOSTRAM
ETIAM CUM CHRISTO COALITIONEM PER MORTEM, SEPULTURAM
20 ET RESURRECTIONEM EIUS.

CREDENTIUM. Matt. xxviii. 19. *docete omnes gentes, bap-*
tizantes eas—. Marc. xvi. 15, 16. *prædicate evangelium—.*
qui crediderit et baptizatus fuerit, servabitur. Act. viii. 36, 37.
quid prohibet me baptizari? si credis ex toto corde licet.
25 Eph. v. 26. *purificans lavacro aquæ per verbum.* 1 Pet. iii.
21. *cui rei nunc respondens exemplar baptismi nos quoque*

the houses where ye are, and when I see the blood I will pass
over you, and the plague shall not be upon you to destroy you,
when I smite the land of Egypt." v. 15. "seven days shall ye
eat unleavened bread; even the first day ye shall put away
5 leaven out of your houses."

The passover typified the sacrifice of Christ, and the
efficacy of the sprinkling of his blood for the salvation of such
as celebrated the feast with purity of heart. John i. 29. "John
seeth Jesus coming unto him, and saith, Behold the Lamb of
10 God, which taketh away the sin of the world." xix. 36. "these
things were done that the scripture should be fulfilled, A bone
of him shall not be broken." 1 Cor. v. 7. "purge out therefore the old leaven, that ye may be a new lump, as ye are
unleavened: for even Christ our passover is sacrificed for us."
15 Under the gospel, the first of the sacraments commonly so
called is BAPTISM, wherein THE BODIES OF BELIEVERS WHO EN-
GAGE THEMSELVES TO PURENESS OF LIFE ARE IMMERSED IN
RUNNING WATER, TO SIGNIFY THEIR REGENERATION BY THE HOLY
SPIRIT, AND THEIR UNION WITH CHRIST IN HIS DEATH, BURIAL,
20 AND RESURRECTION.

OF BELIEVERS. Matt. xxviii. 19. "teach all nations, baptizing
them—." Mark xvi. 15, 16. "preach the gospel . . . he
that believeth and is baptized, shall be saved." Acts viii. 36,
37. "what doth hinder me to be baptized? . . . if thou be-
25 lievest with all thine heart, thou mayest." Eph. v. 26. "that
he might cleanse it with the washing of water by the word."
1 Pet. iii. 21. "the like figure whereunto even baptism doth
also now save us (not the putting away of the filth of the flesh,

servat (non quo carnis sordes abiiciuntur, sed stipulatio bonæ conscientiæ apud Deum) per resurrectionem Iesu Christi.

Hinc sequitur infantes ut qui neque doceri, neque credere, neque stipulari, nec vel spondere vel respondere, ne audire 5 quidem verbum possunt, baptismi capaces non esse. Quo enim pacto per verbum purificantur infantes qui verbum non intelligunt? eodem certe quo ædificantur adulti qui linguam ignotam audiunt. Neque enim servat nos baptismus ille externus, quo carnis duntaxat sordes abluuntur, sed *stipulatio* 10 *illa bonæ conscientiæ,* teste Petro: conscientia autem non est infantium. Quid quod baptismus non solum fœdus est, in quo si stipulatio expressa sponsio quoque versatur, quæ infantis non est, verum etiam votum est quod ab infante neque nuncupari neque exigi potest. de quo infra l. 2. c. iv. ubi de 15 voto.

Qui contrarium statuunt Theologi, mirum est quam futilibus nitantur argumentis: Matt. xix. 14. *sinite puerulos, et ne prohibete eos ad me venire; talium est enim regnum cœlorum.* At neque eos attulit quisquam ut baptizarentur, v. 13. 20 *oblati sunt, ut manus iis imponeret et oraret,* nec eos Christus baptizavit, sed duntaxat manus iis imposuit, v. 15. *et cum accepisset eos in ulnas impositis super eos manibus, benedixit iis,* Marc. x. 16. Qui autem et adducti ad Christum sunt non

but the answer of a good conscience towards God) by the resurrection of Jesus Christ."

Hence it follows that infants are not to be baptized, inasmuch as they are incompetent to receive instruction, or to
5 believe, or to enter into a covenant, or to promise or answer for themselves, or even to hear the word. For how can infants, who understand not the word, be purified thereby; any more than adults can receive edification by hearing an unknown language? For it is not that outward baptism, which purifies
10 only the filth of the flesh, that saves us, but "the answer of a good conscience," as Peter testifies; of which infants are incapable. Besides, baptism is not merely a covenant, containing a certain stipulation on one side, with a corresponding engagement on the other, which in the case of an infant is
15 impossible; but it is also a vow, and as such can neither be pronounced by infants, nor required of them. See Book II. Chap. iv. under the head of vows.

It is remarkable to what futile arguments those divines have recourse, who maintain the contrary opinion. They allege
20 Matt. xix. 14. "suffer little children, and forbid them not to come unto me, for of such is the kingdom of heaven." It appears however that they were not brought to him for the purpose of being baptized; v. 13. "then were there brought unto him little children, that he should put his hands on them
25 and pray"; neither did Christ baptize them, but only put his hands on them, v. 15. Mark x. 16. "he took them up in his arms, put his hands upon them, and blessed them." Seeing then that they were neither brought to Christ to be baptized,

ut baptizarentur, et recepti ab eo, baptizati non sunt, quis ferat qui hinc argumentetur, baptizandos eos fuisse? vel, quod aliquanto plus est, infantes etiam baptismo idoneos esse? nam si idcirco baptizari poterunt, poterunt et cœnæ Domini eadem 5 ratione participes fieri. Sic itaque recipiat infantes ad se venientes ecclesia, quemadmodum Christus recepit; manus imponat, benedicat, non baptizet. At *talium* inquiunt *est regnum cœlorum*. Omniumne dicent, an eorum solum qui credituri sunt? Utcunque Deus novit suos, ecclesia non novit: aliud est 10 quid sint apud Deum, aliud quid sint iure ecclesiastico. *Talium* deinde simplicitate et innocentia: verum infantibus qui rationis compotes nondum sunt, nec simplicitas nec innocentia proprie tribui potest: neque vero sequitur, ad quos regnum cœlorum, ad eos quodvis religionis sacramentum, nec 15 ad quos fœdus, ad eos quamlibet fœderis obsignationem, quæ adultæ ætatis rationem et fidem postulat, pertinere: etenim non minus res signata in cœna Domini ad infantes pertinet quam in baptismo, nec tamen ad infantes cœna Domini pertinebit, etiamsi paschatis, cuius in locum cœna Domini suc-

nor, when received, were actually baptized by him, it is impossible to admit the sophistical inference, that they were properly qualified for baptism; or, which is still more difficult to conceive, that not little children merely, but infants, are so

5 qualified. For if competent to be baptized, they are competent on the same grounds to be partakers of the Lord's Supper. Let the church therefore receive infants which come unto her, after the example of Christ, with imposition of hands and benediction, but not with baptism. Again, they remind us,

10 that "of such is the kingdom of heaven." Is this to be understood of all without distinction, or only of such as shall subsequently believe? How perfectly soever God may know them that are his, the church does not know them; what they are in the sight of God is one thing, and what they are by church

15 privilege is another. It must mean, therefore, "of such" in respect of simplicity and innocence; whereas neither simplicity nor innocence, although they may be predicated of little children, can properly be attributed to infants, who have not as yet the faculty of reason: neither does it follow, that

20 because any one is an inheritor of the kingdom of heaven, he is therefore admissible to every religious sacrament; or that, because he is included in the covenant, he has therefore the right of participating in such signs and seals of that covenant as demand the exercise of mature faith and reason. For the

25 thing signified in the Supper of the Lord appertains no less to infants than the thing signified in baptism; and yet infants are not admitted to the former rite, although they were admitted to the passover, which held the same place in the

cessit, infantes expertes non fuerint. Unde perspicias licet, quam sit infirmum sic disputare; circumcisionis in locum successit baptismus; circumcidebantur infantes, ergo nunc baptizabuntur, cum non minus constet paschatis in locum successisse cœnam Dominicam: infantes tamen participes cum fuerint paschatis, expertes cœnæ Dominicæ sunt.

At inquiunt, *omnes baptizati sumus nube et mari,* I Cor. x. 2. ergo et infantes. Et inquam, *omnes eandem escam spiritualem comederunt, et omnes eundem potum spiritualem biberunt,* v. 3, 4. nec tamen eam ob causam infantes participes cœnæ Domini fiunt.

Urgent illo Gen. xvii. 7. *stabilio fœdus meum inter me et te ac semen tuum post te per ætates suas.* Quis sanus hoc de infantibus intelligi affirmet? et non de posteris adultis, per ætates videlicet suas? Non enim infantibus terram daturus erat, v. 8. non infantes servare fœdus iubentur, v. 9. Sic Act. ii. 39. *vobis facta est promissio et liberis vestris et omnibus longe post futuris; quoscunque advocaverit Dominus Deus noster. Liberis vestris,* id est, infantibus, ut volunt illi: eos nempe vocat Deus qui non intelligunt, eos alloquitur qui non audiunt. Quem non pudeat interpretum tam infantium? qui

former dispensation as the Lord's Supper in the present.
Hence, by the way, we may perceive how weak it is to reason
as follows: baptism has succeeded to circumcision; but infants
were circumcised, therefore infants are to be baptized: seeing
5 that it is equally certain that the Lord's Supper has succeeded
to the passover, notwithstanding which, infants, who were
admitted to the latter rite, are not admitted to the former.

They argue, again, that as it is said "we were all baptized
unto Moses in the cloud and in the sea," 1 Cor. x. 2. infants
10 must be included in the general expression. I answer, that
"all did eat the same spiritual meat, and did all drink the same
spiritual drink," iii. 4. yet that infants are not on this ground
admitted to partake of the Lord's Supper.

They lay much stress likewise on Gen. xvii. 7. "I will
15 establish my covenant between me and thee and thy seed after
thee . . . in their generations." No one, however, will seri-
ously affirm that this is to be understood of infants, and not of
the adult posterity of Abraham "in their generations," that is,
successively. Otherwise, we must suppose that God intended
20 to give the land also to infants, v. 8. and that infants are commanded to keep the covenant, v. 9. Again, Acts ii. 39. "the
promise is unto you and to your children, and to all that are
afar off, even as many as the Lord our God shall call." "Your
children," that is, as they understand it, your infants: in other
25 words, God calls those who cannot understand, and addresses
those who cannot hear; an interpretation which can only have
proceeded from the infancy of reasoning. Had these com-
mentators but read two verses farther, they would have found

si duos porro versiculos duntaxat legissent, clare audissent, v. 41. *qui libenter receperunt sermonem eius, baptizati sunt.* Hic et intellectus et voluntas ad baptizandum requiritur; quorum neutrius compotes infantes sunt. Unde et illud Act. viii. 5 37. *si credis ex toto corde, licet baptizari.* At certe infantes ne ex minima quidem cordis particula possunt credere. Quod autem toties inculcant, *vobis et semini vestro facta est promissio,* utinam satis attenderent quo pacto Paulus id explicet Rom. ix. 7, 8; intelligerent profecto factas esse promissiones 10 evangelicas, non cuivis suo semini, nam ne *Abrahami* quidem *secundum carnem,* sed *filiis* duntaxat *Dei,* id est, credentibus; qui soli sub evangelio et *filii promissionis sunt,* et *in semine reputantur.* Pro credentibus autem haberi ante non possunt ab ecclesia, quam se credere profitentur. Quibus igitur factas 15 esse promissiones nullo modo constat, iis ecclesia non debet baptismo promissiones obsignare.

   Deinde analogiam prædicant baptismi cum circumcisione, quæ infantium erat: Col. ii. 11. *in quo circumcisi estis circumcisione quæ fit sine manibus, exuendo corpus peccatorum* 20 *carnis per circumcisionem Christi: ei consepulti per baptismum*—. At vero ista primum analogia quæ tandem illic *circumcidi* et *consepeliri,* nisi quæ omnibus sacramentis idem

it expressly stated, "they that gladly received his word were baptized"; whence it appears that understanding and will were necessary qualifications for baptism, neither of which are possessed by infants. So also Acts viii. 37. "if thou be-
5 lievest with all thine heart, thou mayest be baptized"; where-as infants, so far from believing with all their heart, are in-capable of even the slightest degree of faith. With regard, however, to the text on which they insist so much, "the prom-ise is unto you and to your children," if they had attended
10 sufficiently to Paul's interpretation of this passage, Rom. ix. 7, 8. they would have understood that the promise was not to all seed indiscriminately, seeing that it was not even to the "seed of Abraham" according to the "flesh," but only to the "children of God," that is, to believers, who alone under the
15 gospel "are the children of the promise," and "are counted for the seed." But none can be considered believers by the church, till they have professed their belief. To those there-fore to whom it does not appear that the promise was ever made, the church cannot with propriety give the seal of the
20 promise of baptism.

Again, they allege the analogy between baptism and cir-cumcision, which latter was performed on infants. Col. ii. 11. "in whom also ye are circumcised with the circumcision made without hands, in putting off the body of the sins of the flesh
25 by the circumcision of Christ; buried with him in baptism—." In the first place, there is no other analogy between being "circumcised" and being "buried with him in baptism," than that which exists among all sacraments by which the same

fere, quamvis non eodem modo significantibus, inter se analogia est? Deinde analoga per omnia respondere, quis de-
fendat? Circumcisione carere sine periculo fœminæ potuerunt, baptismo non possunt; signo scilicet vel perfectiore vel
5 rei perfectioris. Circumcisio enim *sigillum* erat *iustitiæ* quidem *fidei,* Rom. iv. 11, 12. sed Abrahamo tantum qui in
præputio iam tum crediderat eiusque similibus qui sic credituri erant non itidem infantibus post eum circumcisis qui
in præputio credere non poterant; illis in carne sigillum erat
10 et quidem perobscurum gratiæ longo post tempore promul-
gandæ: baptismus est sigillum illius gratiæ iam exhibitæ, remissionis peccatorum, sanctificationis, signumque mortis
nostræ cum Christo et resurrectionis. Circumcisio sub lege et
sacrificiis data erat, et ad totam legem servandam obligabat,
15 Gal. v. 3. qui cultus erat servilis et pædagogicus: contra, per
baptismum evangelio initiamur; qui cultus est rationalis et
virilis et liberrimus: sub lege enim infantes et nascebantur et
senescebant; sub evangelio et baptismo nascimur viri. Itaque
in baptismo doctrina ac fides veluti conditiones ab adultis sus-
20 cipiendæ prius requiruntur; in circumcisione tanquam servis

thing is signified, the mode of signification being different. But, secondly, why is it necessary that things which are analogous should coincide in all points? Of circumcision, for instance, women were not partakers; in baptism they are
5 equally included with men, whether as being a more perfect sign, or a symbol of more perfect things. For circumcision, although "a seal of the righteousness of faith," Rom. iv. 11, 12. was such only to Abraham, who being uncircumcised had already believed, and to others who should believe in like
10 manner; not to his posterity, who in aftertimes were circumcised before they were of an age to exercise faith, and who, consequently, could not believe in the uncircumcision. To them it was a seal in the flesh, indistinctly and obscurely given, of that grace which was at some distant period to be revealed;
15 whereas baptism is a seal of grace already revealed, of the remission of sins, of sanctification; finally, a sign of our death and resurrection with Christ. Circumcision was given under the law and the sacrifices, and bound the individual to the observance of the whole law (Gal. v. 3.), which was a service
20 of bondage, and a schoolmaster to bring its followers to Christ; through baptism, on the other hand, we are initiated into the gospel, which is a reasonable, manly, and in the highest sense free service. For under the law men were not merely born, but grew up infants in a spiritual sense; under the gospel, in
25 baptism, we are born men. Hence baptism requires, as from adults, the previous conditions of knowledge and faith; whereas in circumcision all conditions are omitted, as unnecessary in the case of servants, and impracticable in that of in-

sub lege et infantibus conditiones feruntur nullæ. Circumcisio
denique fiebat non a sacerdotibus aut Levitis, sed vel a patre
familias, Gen. xvii. vel a matre, Exod. iv. 26. vel a quovis alio,
puta chirurgo: baptismus, ut ipsi volunt, non nisi ab evan-
5 gelico ministro, vel saltem, ut volunt omnes, a fideli quovis,
non rudi aut novitio: quo autem id, nisi ut is baptizandum
doctrina prius imbueret quam aqua demergeret? non ergo
infantem. Non ergo circumcisio et baptismus plane sunt
analoga. Nos certe in sacramentis non analogiam plane in-
10 certam, sed institutionem Domini attendere, eamque semper,
ut ipsi monent Theologi, ante omnia sequi debemus.

At inquiunt, circumcisio erat *sigillum iustitiæ fidei,* Rom.
iv. 11, 12. et tamen infantes circumcidebantur, qui credere
nequibant. Erat inquam ut et supra dictum est sigillum ius-
15 titiæ fidei, sed Abrahamo credenti, et qui eius exemplo in
præputio crediderunt; infantibus aliud quiddam erat, sanctificatio nempe Gentilitia et externa ad cultum Dei externum et
Mosaicum præsertim suo tempore secuturum.

Postremo, inquiunt, Apostoli integras familias baptizarunt.
20 ergo infantes. Verum huius argumenti inanitas refutatur aper-

fants. Lastly, circumcision was performed not by the priests
and Levites, but by the master of a family, Gen. xvii. by the
mother, Exod. iv. 26. or by any other person, a surgical opera-
tor for instance; whereas baptism, according to our opponents
5 themselves, can only be administered by a teacher of the
gospel; and even those who hold a wider opinion on the subject, allow that it can only be performed by a believer, and by
one who is neither a new convert, nor unlearned in the faith.
To what purpose is this, unless that the person to be baptized
10 may be previously instructed in the doctrines of the gospel?
which in the case of an infant is impossible. There is therefore
no necessary analogy between circumcision and baptism; and
it is our duty not to build our belief on vague parallels, but to
attend exclusively to the institution of the sacrament itself,
15 and regard its authority as paramount, according to the frequent admonition of our opponents themselves.

They contend, however, that circumcision was "the seal of
the righteousness of faith," Rom. iv. 11, 12. notwithstanding
which infants were circumcised, who were incapable of belief.
20 I answer, as above, that it was indeed the seal of the righteousness of faith, but only to Abraham, and to such as after his
example believed being yet uncircumcised; in the case of infants it was a thing of entirely different import, namely, an
outward and merely national consecration to the external ser-
25 vice of God, and, by implication, to the Mosaic form of worship, which was in due time to be ordained.

Lastly, it is urged that the apostles baptized whole families,
and consequently infants among the rest. The weakness of

tissime, Act. viii. 12. *cum credidissent—, baptizabantur et viri et mulieres.* non ergo infantes. et xvi. 31, 32, 33, 34. *crede in Dominum Iesum Christum, et servaberis, tu ac domus tua. et locuti sunt ei sermonem Domini et omnibus qui*
5 *erant domi ipsius. et baptizatus est ipse et omnes domestici eius illico. exultavit quod cum universa domo sua credidisset Deo.* universa igitur domus credentium dicitur, non infantium: ergo quibus locuti sunt sermonem Domini, quique crediderunt, illi soli baptizati sunt. Idem evincitur ex cap. xi. 17. *si*
10 *ergo æquale donum dedit illis Deus, sicut et nobis qui credimus—.* et xviii. 8. *credidit Domino cum tota domo sua. multique Corinthiorum audientes credebant et baptizabantur.* Ipsum denique Ioannis baptisma, quod quasi præludium sequentis fuit, *resipiscentiæ* dictus est, Marc. i. 4. quo qui bap-
15 tizati sunt *confitebantur* etiam *peccata sua,* Matt. iii. 6. resipiscere autem et confiteri infantes qui possunt? Itaque si Ioannis baptismo idonei non erant infantes, quo pacto erunt baptismo Christi, quem antequam suscipere possunt, et doceri et resipiscere et credere debebunt.
20 IMMERSIO. nam ut aspersionem significaret baptismus ex Marc. vii. 4. Luc. xi. 38. frustra contendunt qui aspersionem in baptismum pro immersione induxerunt: manus enim qui lavant immergere solent non aspergere.

this argument is clearly shown by Acts viii. 12. "when they believed . . . they were baptized, both men and women," infants not being included. xvi. 31–34. "believe on the Lord Jesus Christ, and thou shalt be saved, and thy house: and they
5 spake unto him the word of the Lord, and to all that were in his house: and he took them . . . and was baptized, he and all his, straightway . . . and he rejoiced, believing in God with all his house." Here the expression "all his house" obviously comprehends only those who believed in his house,
10 not infants; therefore those alone unto whom "they spake the word of the Lord," and who believed, were baptized. The same is evident from chap. xi. 17. "forasmuch then as God gave them the like gift as he did unto us who believe—." xviii. 8. "Crispus . . . believed on the Lord with all his
15 house: and many of the Corinthians hearing believed, and were baptized." Even the baptism of John, which was but the prelude to that of Christ, is called "the baptism of repentance," Mark i. 4. and those who came to it "were baptized, confessing their sins," Matt. iii. 6. whereas infants are incapable
20 either of repentance or confession. If then infants were not meet for the baptism of John, how can they be meet for the baptism of Christ, which requires knowledge, repentance, and faith, before it can be received?

IMMERSION. It is in vain alleged by those who, on the
25 authority of Mark vii. 4. Luke xi. 38. have introduced the practice of affusion in baptism instead of immersion, that to dip and to sprinkle mean the same thing; since in washing we do not sprinkle the hands, but immerse them.

AD REGENERATIONEM. Ioan. iii. 5. *nisi quis fuerit genitus ex aqua et spiritu, non potest introire in regnum Dei:* nempe si neglexisse reperietur. Act. xxii. 16. *quid cunctaris? surgens baptizator et abluitor a peccatis tuis, invocato nomine Domini.*
5 1 Cor. vi. 11. *sed abluti estis, sed sanctificati estis, sed iustificati estis in nomine Domini Iesu, et per Spiritum Dei nostri.* Eph. v. 26. *ut eam sanctificaret, ab eo purificatam lavacro aquæ per verbum.* Tit. iii. 5. *per lavacrum regenerationis.*

COALITIONEM PER MORTEM. 1 Cor. xii. 13. *per unum spiritum*
10 *nos omnes in unum corpus baptizati sumus.* Gal. iii. 27. *quicunque in Christum baptizati fuistis, Christo fuistis induti.* Rom. vi. 3. *an ignoratis, nos quotquot baptizati sumus in Iesum Christum, in mortem eius esse baptizatos? consepulti sumus igitur ei per baptismum in mortem.* Col. ii. 12. *ei*
15 *consepulti per baptismum.* Itaque baptismus figurate ærumnosam Christi vitam, mortem et sepulturam significat, in quam ipse ad tempus quasi immersus fuit: Marc. x. 38. *et baptismate quo ego baptizor baptizari.* Sic Luc. xii. 50. De administratione baptismi vide infra cap. xxix. de ecclesia
20 visibili, et cap. xxxi. de Ecclesiis particularibus.

Baptismus Ioannis idem reipsa cum baptismo Christi fuit: administrationis tamen formula et præsenti efficacia non

To SIGNIFY THEIR REGENERATION. John iii. 5. "except a man
be born of water and of the Spirit, he cannot enter into the
kingdom of God"; that is, if the omission proceed from neglect. Acts xxii. 16. "why tarriest thou? arise and be bap-
5 tized, and wash away thy sins, calling on the name of the
Lord." 1 Cor. vi. 11. "but ye are washed, but ye are sanctified,
but ye are justified in the name of the Lord Jesus, and by the
Spirit of our God." Eph. v. 26. "that he might sanctify and
cleanse it with the washing of water by the word." Tit. iii. 5.
10 "by the washing of regeneration."

UNION WITH CHRIST IN HIS DEATH, &c. 1 Cor. xii. 13. "by
one Spirit are we all baptized into one body." Gal. iii. 27. "as
many of you as have been baptized into Christ have put on
Christ." Rom. vi. 3. "know ye not that so many of us as were
15 baptized into Jesus Christ were baptized into his death? therefore we are buried with him by baptism into death." Col. ii.
12. "buried with him in baptism." Hence it appears that
baptism was intended to represent figuratively the painful
life of Christ, his death and burial, in which he was immersed,
20 as it were, for a season: Mark x. 38. "can ye be baptized with
the baptism that I am baptized with?" Compare also Luke
xii. 50. Respecting the administration of baptism, see chap.
xxix. on the visible church, and chap. xxxi. on particular
churches.

25 The baptism of John was essentially the same as the baptism of Christ; but it differed in the form of words used in its
administration, and in the comparative remoteness of its
efficacy. If it had not been really the same, it would follow

idem. Si idem reipsa non fuisset, sequeretur, non eundem nos cum Christo baptismum suscepisse; nostrum baptismum persona Christi sanctificatum non fuisse; Christum non omnem iustitiam implevisse, Matt. iii. 15. apostolos fuisse rursus bap-
5 tizandos, quod non legimus. Idem tamen per omnia non erat: etsi enim uterque baptismus divinitus fuit, Luc. iii. 2, 3. et vii. 29, 30. et resipiscentiam et fidem uterque requirebat, Act. xix. 4, 5. alter tamen subobscurius in Christum nondum satis manifestum, alter clarius in Christum iam cognitum; et
10 formula quidem solenniore, *in nomen patris, filii et spiritus sancti;* (quam tamen formulam ab Apostolis postea observatam nusquam Legimus;) et efficacia, ut ante dixi, præsentiore; prior enim aqua tantum baptizabat, Matt. iii. 11. Ioan. i. 33. Act. i. 5. et xix. 2. si solum Christum excipias; et hoc
15 quidem ad testimonium potius Christo perhibendum, quam ad vim illius baptismi demonstrandam: itaque apostoli non nisi diu postea spiritum sanctum acceperunt, Act. i. 5. et Ephesini illi Ioannis baptismo baptizati, *essetne spiritus sanctus ne audiverant quidem,* cap. xix. 1, 2. at Christi baptismus
20 et aqua et spiritu baptizans, dona spiritus e vestigio fere conferebat.

Sed opponi solet non baptismum a baptismo ex aqua et

that we had not undergone the same baptism as Christ, that
our baptism had not been sanctified by the person of Christ,
that Christ had not fulfilled all righteousness, Matt. iii. 15.
finally, that the apostles would have needed to be rebaptized,
5 which we do not read to have been the case. In some respects,
however, there was a difference; for although both baptisms
were from God, Luke iii. 2, 3. vii. 29, 30. and both required
repentance and faith, Acts xix. 4, 5. these requisites were less
clearly propounded in the one case than in the other, and the
10 faith required in the former instance was an imperfect faith,
founded on a partial manifestation of Christ; in the latter, it
was faith in a fully revealed Savior. The baptism of Christ
was also administered with a more solemn form of words, "in
the name of the Father, and of the Son, and of the Holy
15 Ghost," although it is nowhere said that this form was ever
expressly used by the apostles, and attended, as above observed, with a more immediate efficacy; inasmuch as the
baptism of John was with water only, Matt. iii. 11. John i. 33.
Acts i. 5. xix. 2. except in the single instance of Christ, the
20 design of which exception was not to prove the virtue of
John's baptism, but to bear testimony to the Son of God.
Hence the apostles did not receive the Holy Ghost till a much
later period, Acts i. 5. and the Ephesians, who had been baptized with the baptism of John, "had not so much as heard
25 whether there was any Holy Ghost," xix. 1, 2. whereas the
baptism of Christ, which was with water and the Spirit, conferred the gifts of the Spirit from the very beginning.

It is usually replied, that in the places where the baptism of

spiritu distingui, sed comparari inter se partes ministri in baptismo et Christi. At hoc si verum esset, idem de cæteris baptismi ministris apostolis dictum reperiretur: quod nusquam reperitur; immo cæteros apostolos et aqua et spiritu
5 sancto baptizasse satis constat.

Qua ratione baptismus Ioannis, quatenus aut non omnino aut non statim spiritum conferebat, initiatio quædam sive lustratio ad doctrinam evangelii recipiendam, promulgata (ex antiquo ritu Hebræorum, quo omnes proselytæ baptiza-
10 bantur) potius, quam absoluta fœderis obsignatio, videtur fuisse: spiritus enim solus obsignat, 1 Cor. xii. 13.

Hinc baptismus Christi baptismo Ioannis, licet non necessario, superinduci tamen videtur potuisse: Act. xix. 5. *his auditis, baptizati sunt in nomine Domini Iesu.* nimirum qui
15 prius ab Ioanne baptizati fuerant, v. 3. Non necessario inquam: apostoli enim aliique plurimi Ioannis baptismo videntur stetisse: quorum exemplo qui olim infantes, et per omnia non rite baptizati sunt, iterare baptismum iam adulti necesse, opinor, non habent: immo baptismum ipsum prose-
20 lytis duntaxat necessarium esse ducerem, non alumnis eccle-

John is said to be with water only, it is not intended to oppose the baptism of John to baptism with water and the Spirit, but to distinguish between the part which Christ acts in baptism, and that of the mere minister of the rite. If however this were
5 true, the same distinction would be made with respect to other ministers of baptism, the apostles for instance; which is not the case: on the contrary, it is abundantly evident that the apostles baptized both with water and the Holy Spirit.

Considering, therefore, that the baptism of John either did
10 not confer the gifts of the Spirit at all, or not immediately, it would appear to have been rather a kind of initiatory measure, or purification preparatory to receiving the doctrine of the gospel, in conformity with the ancient Hebrew custom that all proselytes should be baptized, than an absolute sealing of
15 the covenant; for this latter is the province of the Spirit alone: 1 Cor. xii. 13.

Hence it appears that the baptism of Christ, although not indispensable, might without impropriety be superadded to the baptism of John. Acts xix. 5. "when they heard this,
20 they were baptized in the name of the Lord Jesus"; those, namely, who had been already baptized by John, v. 3. I have said, not indispensable, inasmuch as the apostles and many others appear to have rested in the baptism of John; according to which analogy, I should be inclined to conclude, that
25 those persons who have been baptized while yet infants, and perhaps in other respects irregularly, have no need of second baptism when arrived at maturity: indeed, I should be disposed to consider baptism itself as necessary for proselytes

siæ, nisi apostolus baptismum non initiationem tantum, sed etiam nostræ cum Christo et mortis, et sepulturæ, et resurrectionis repræsentationem quandam esse docuisset.

Typus baptismi ante legem Mosis fuit arca Noæ; 1 Pet. iii. 20, 21. *cum construeretur arca* &c. *cui rei nunc respondens typus baptismi—*. Sub lege nubes: 1 Cor. x 2. *omnes in Mosen baptizatos esse nube et mari.*

Cœna Dominica est in qua fracto pane vinoque effuso, et utroque ab omnibus degustato, mors Christi commemoratur; eiusque mortis beneficia credentibus obsignantur: Matt. xxvi. 26, 27, 28, 29. *edentibus autem iis, Iesus cum accepisset panem et benedixisset, fregit eum, deditque discipulis suis, et ait, Accipite, comedite, hoc est corpus meum; et accepto poculo, et gratiis actis, dedit iis, dicens, Bibite ex eo omnes; hoc est enim sanguis meus novi pacti, qui pro multis effunditur in remissionem peccatorum. Non bibam ab hoc tempore ex hoc fructu vitis usque—*. Marc. xiv. 22, 23, 24, 25. idem. Luc. xxii. 19, 20. *et acceptum panem, cum gratias egisset, fregit, et dedit iis, dicens, Hoc est corpus meum quod pro vobis datur, hoc facite ad mei commemorationem. Ibidem etiam dedit iis poculum postquam cœnasset, dicens, hoc poculum est novum illud pactum per sanguinem meum, qui pro vobis effunditur.* Ioan. vi. 33. *panis ille Dei is est qui de cœlo descendit, et dat vitam mundo.* et v. 35. *ego sum panis ille*

alone, and not for those born in the church, had not the apostle taught that baptism is not merely an initiatory rite, but a figurative representation of our death, burial, and resurrection with Christ.

5   Previously to the promulgation of the Mosaic law, Noah's ark was the type of baptism: 1 Pet. iii. 20, 21. "while the ark was a preparing," &c. "the like figure whereunto even baptism doth also now save us—." Under the law it was typified by the cloud. 1 Cor. x. 2. "all our fathers were baptized unto
10 Moses in the cloud and in the sea."

      THE LORD'S SUPPER is a solemnity in which the death of Christ is commemorated by the breaking of bread and pouring out of wine, both of which elements are tasted by each individual communicant, and the benefits of his death thereby
15 sealed to believers. Matt. xxvi. 26–29. "as they were eating, Jesus took bread, and blessed it, and brake it, and gave it to the disciples, and said, Take, eat, this is my body; and he took the cup, and gave thanks, and gave it to them, saying, Drink ye all of it: for this is my blood of the new testament, which
20 is shed for many for the remission of sins . . . I will not drink henceforth of this fruit of the vine until that day," &c. See also Mark xiv. 22–25. Luke xxii. 19, 20. "he took bread, and gave thanks, and brake it, and gave unto them, saying, This is my body which is given for you; this do in remem-
25 brance of me: likewise also the cup after supper, saying, This cup is the new testament in my blood, which is shed for you." John vi. 33. "the bread of God is he which cometh down from heaven, and giveth life unto the world." v. 35. "I am the

vitæ: qui venit ad me, nequaquam esuriet; et qui credit in
me, non sitiet unquam. et 50, 51. *hic est panis ille, qui e*
cœlo descendit; ut qui edit ex eo, non moriatur. Ego sum panis
ille vivus, qui e cœlo descendi: siquis ederit ex hoc pane, vivet
5 *in æternum: panis autem quem ego dabo, caro mea est, quam*
ego dabo pro mundi vita. et v. 53, idem. et 54, 55, 56, 57.
qui edit carnem meam, et bibit meum sanguinem, in me
manet, et ego in eo. Sicut misit me vivens ille pater, et ego
vivo per patrem, ita etiam qui ederit me, vivet ipse quoque per
10 *me.* et 58, idem. et 63. *spiritus est id quod vivificat; caro*
non prodest quicquam: verba quæ ego loquor vobis, spiritus
sunt et vita sunt. Hoc caput Ioannis, tametsi non solum de
cœna Domini verba facit, sed de quacunque beneficiorum
Christi hominis facti receptione per fidem, quod enim *edere*
15 et *bibere* toties dicitur a versu 50, &c. id. v. 35. *venire* et
credere prius dicebatur, quemadmodum cap. iv. v. 10, 14.
aqua illa viva, de qua qui biberit, nunquam sitiet, neque ad
baptismum neque ad cœnam referri potest, cœnam tamen Dominicam postmodum statim instituendam, (*prope* enim *erat*
20 *pascha,* v. 4.) sermo iste Christi quam maxime illustrabat,
carnemque non illic magis quam hic prodesse, dilucide os-

bread of life; he that cometh to me shall never hunger, and he that believeth on me shall never thirst." v. 50, 51. "this is the bread which cometh down from heaven, that a man may eat thereof, and not die: I am the living bread which came down from heaven; if any man eat of this bread he shall live for ever: and the bread that I give is my flesh, which I will give for the life of the world." v. 53–58. "he that eateth my flesh and drinketh my blood, dwelleth in me, and I in him: as the living Father hath sent me, and I live by the Father, so he that eateth me, even he shall live by me." v. 63. "it is the Spirit that quickeneth, the flesh profiteth nothing; the words that I speak unto you, they are spirit, and they are life." It is true that this chapter of John does not relate exclusively to the Lord's Supper, but to the participation in general, through faith, of any of the benefits of Christ's incarnation: for what is called so repeatedly, v. 50, &c. "eating the flesh of Christ" and "drinking his blood," is described in v. 35. as "coming to Christ" and "believing in him"; in the same manner as the phrase in chap. iv. 10, 14. "that living water, of which whosoever drinketh he shall never thirst," cannot be referred in a primary sense either to baptism, or to the Lord's Supper, but must be considered as an expression purely metaphorical. Nevertheless, the words of Christ to his disciples in this chapter throw a strong light, by anticipation, on the nature of the sacrament which was to be so shortly afterwards instituted: for "the passover was nigh," v. 4. They teach us, by an obvious inference, that "flesh," or the mere bodily food received, has no more spiritual efficacy in the

tendit, immo carnem eius non quam dentes cuiusquam, sed quam sola fides manducat; panem cœlestem et spiritualem qui cœlo descenderat, dari, non terrenum ex virgine; qualem tum dedit, si carnem dedit, sed ipso manna, ut ita dicam, cœles-
5 tiorem, quem *qui ederit, vivet in æternum,* v. 58. Hæc si caro eius vera esset et ab omnibus in missa comederetur, ut volunt Pontificii, eorum profecto nemo vel improbissimus, ne mures dicam et vermes qui sæpe comedunt, non æternam vitam ex illo cœlesti pane assequeretur. Panis igitur ille vivus quem
10 Christus carnem esse suam, eiusque sanguis quem verum esse potum dicit, quid aliud esse potest, quam doctrina de Christo homine facto, ut pro nobis sanguinem profunderet? quam doctrinam qui vera fide percipit, non minus certo in æternum vivet, quam qui apud nos comedunt et bibunt vitam hanc
15 mortalem diutule sustentant, immo vero multo certius. sic enim Christus in nobis manebit et nos in eo, ut supra citatum est. quod contra, si carnem comedimus, non in nobis mane-bit, sed, ut dicam quod honestissimum est, in ventriculo coctus tandem exudabitur.
20 A Paulo *cœna Dominica* vocatur, 1 Cor. xi. 20. et sic a Domino instituta traditur et explicatur a v. 23. ad 30. *ego enim accepi a Domino, quod et tradidi vobis; Dominum*

sacrament than it had in the miracle of the loaves there recorded; and that the flesh which he verily and indeed gives
is not that which can be eaten with the teeth, and by any one
indiscriminately, but the food of faith alone; a heavenly and
5 spiritual bread, "which came down from heaven," not earthly,
as it must be, if we suppose that what he gave on that occasion was his literal flesh born of the Virgin, but heavenly in a
higher sense than manna itself, and of which "he that eateth
shall live for ever," v. 58. Were it, as the Papists hold, his
10 literal flesh, and eaten by all in the Mass, the consequence
would be that the very worst of the communicants, to say
nothing of the mice and worms by which the eucharist is
occasionally devoured, would through the virtue of this heavenly bread attain eternal life. That "living bread" therefore
15 which Christ calls "his flesh," and that "blood" which is
"drink indeed," can be nothing but the doctrine of Christ's
having become man in order to shed his blood for us; a doctrine which whosoever receives by faith, shall as surely attain
eternal life, as the partaking of meats and drinks supports our
20 brief term of bodily existence: nay, more surely; for thus, as
above quoted, "Christ dwells in us, and we in him"; whereas
the food which is received into the body does not dwell there,
being carried off partly by natural transpiration, and partly
in other ways, as soon as the process of digestion is completed.
25   This solemnity is called by St. Paul "the Lord's Supper,"
1 Cor. xi. 20. and its original institution by Christ, together
with an explanation of the rite, is given v. 23–30. "I have
received of the Lord that which also I delivered unto you,

*Iesum ea nocte qua proditus est, accepisse panem; et gratiis
actis, fregisse, ac dixisse, accipite, comedite; hoc est corpus
meum, quod pro vobis frangitur; hoc facite ad mei commemorationem: itidem et poculum postquam coenasset, dicendo,*
5 *hoc poculum est novum illud pactum per sanguinem meum;
hoc facite quotiescunque biberitis ad mei commemorationem:
quotiescunque enim ederitis panem hunc, et poculum hoc
biberitis, mortem Domini annuntiatis quoad venerit.* Explicatur etiam obiter cap. x. 16, 17, 21. *poculum benedictionis*
10 *cui benedicimus, nonne communio sanguinis Christi est?
panem quem frangimus, nonne communio corporis Christi
est? Quoniam unus est panis, unum corpus nos multi sumus;
nos enim omnes ex uno illo pane participamus.*

Typus coenæ Dominicæ sub lege erat manna et ex rupe
15 profluens aqua: 1 Cor. x. 3, 4. *et omnes eandem escam spiritualem edisse, et omnes eundem potum spiritualem bibisse;
bibebant enim ex sequente spirituali petra: petra vero illa
erat Christus.* Si sub fœdere carnali spiritualem Christum illi
comederunt, nos certe sub fœdere spirituali carnalem non
20 comedimus.

Hæc loca omnia quæ integra idcirco protuli, quia totam
coenæ Dominicæ doctrinam complectuntur, quisquis cum illa
simplicitate cordis qua primi Christiani solebant, prout verba
ipsa præ se ferunt, intellexerit, miretur sane unde tot doctri-
25 narum portenta hac de re ecclesiam Dei conturbaverint, quæ
coenam Dominicam in coenam prope dixerem cyclopeam
converterunt.

that the Lord Jesus the same night in which he was betrayed took bread, and when he had given thanks, he brake it, and said, Take, eat; this is my body which is broken for you; this do in remembrance of me: after the same manner also he
5 took the cup, when he had supped, saying, This cup is the new testament in my blood; this do ye, as oft as ye drink it, in remembrance of me: for as often as ye eat this bread, and drink this cup, ye do show the Lord's death till he come." It is also incidentally explained x. 16, 17, 21. "the cup of bless-
10 ing which we bless, is it not the communion of the blood of Christ? the bread which we break, is it not the communion of the body of Christ? for we being many are one bread, and one body; for we are all partakers of that one bread."

Under the law, the Lord's Supper was typified by the
15 manna, and the water flowing from the rock. 1 Cor. x. 3, 4. "our fathers did all eat the same spiritual meat, and did all drink the same spiritual drink: for they drank of that spiritual rock that followed them, and that rock was Christ." If they under a carnal covenant partook spiritually of the body of
20 Christ, surely we do not partake of it carnally under a spiritual covenant.

I have quoted the above passages at length, inasmuch as in them is comprised the whole Scripture doctrine relative to the Lord's Supper. Whosoever interprets these with true Chris-
25 tian simplicity of heart according to their plain and obvious meaning, will be at a loss to account for the numberless absurd speculations on this subject, by which the peace of the church has been destroyed, and which have well nigh converted the Supper of the Lord into a banquet of cannibals.

Consubstantiatio certe et præsertim transubstantiatio illa
et ἀνθρωποφαγία papistica non solum ab omni ratione, sensu
ac moribus humanis, sed etiam a doctrina sacra, a natura et
fructu sacramenti, ab analogia baptismi, a communi more
5 loquendi, ab humana natura Christi eiusque statu in cœlis
glorioso in quo ad diem iudicii mansurus est alienissimæ sunt.

Notandus enim erat in sacramentis, quæ vocantur, idem
qui in omnibus fere rebus, inter quas ulla ratio est, adhiberi
sæpissime solet tropus sive usus loquendi figuratus, quo ea
10 res quæ quoquo modo illustrat rem aliquam aut significat,
poni solet non tam pro eo quod revera est quam pro eo quod
illustrat aut significat; qui mos loquendi, in sacramentis ubi
inter signum et rem signatam summa ratio est, non animad-
versus, multis olim imposuit, hodieque imponit: sic Gen.
15 xvii. 10. circumcisio *fœdus* nominatur: et, v. 11. *signum
fœderis:* Exod. xii. 11. agnus *pascha* appellatur, quem locum
ab adversariorum exceptionibus vindicant similia loca; Luc.
xxii. 7. *mactari pascha.* et v. 8. *parate nobis pascham.* et
11. *ubi pascha edam,* et 12. *illic parate pascham.* Huiusmodi
20 est illud 2 Sam. xxiii. 17. *an sanguinem istorum hominum,
qui iniverunt periculum vitæ suæ biberem?* Idem occurrit de
baptismo: Eph. v. 26. *ab eo purificatam lavacro aquæ per
verbum.* Col. ii. 12. *ei consepulti per baptismum.* Et de cœna

Consubstantiation, and above all the papistical doctrine of transubstantiation, or rather anthropophagy, for it deserves no better name, are irreconcilable, not only with reason and common sense, and the habits of mankind, but with the tes-
5 timony of Scripture, with the nature and end of a sacrament, with the analogy of baptism, with the ordinary forms of language, with the human nature of Christ, and finally with the state of glory in which he is to remain till the day of judgment.

In speaking of sacraments, as of most other subjects be-
10 tween whose parts an analogy exists, a figure is frequently employed, by which whatever illustrates or signifies any particular thing is used to denote, not what it is in itself, but what it illustrates or signifies. In sacraments, on account of the peculiarly close relation between the sign and the thing sig-
15 nified, this kind of identification is not uncommon; an inattention to which peculiarity has been, and continues to be, a source of error to numbers. Thus circumcision is called "a covenant," Gen. xvii. 10. and "a token of the covenant," v. 11. Again, a lamb is called "the passover," Exod. xii. 11.
20 which text is defended against the exceptions of objectors by the similar passages, Luke xxii. 7. "the passover must be killed." v. 8. "prepare us the passover." v. 11. "where I shall eat the passover." v. 13. "they made ready the passover." A similar expression occurs 2 Sam. xxiii. 17. "is not this the
25 blood of the men that went in jeopardy of their lives?" Accordingly, the same form of speech is used in regard to baptism: Eph. v. 26. "that he might cleanse it with the washing of water by the word"; Col. ii. 12. "buried with him in bap-

Domini: Matt. xxvi. 26, 27. *edentibus autem iis—; accipite,*
comedite; hoc est corpus meum—; et apud Marcum; et
Lucam, cap. xxii. 20. *hoc poculum est novum testamentum;*
et 1 Cor. xi. 25. Sic 1 Cor. x. 4. *petra erat Christus.* Et hoc
5 loquendi more videtur usos esse sacros scriptores, cum ut
summam relationem inter signa resque signatas, tum ut certissimam rerum spiritualium obsignationem significarent.
Unde et ad alias res certissimas quasque significandas modus
idem loquendi traductus est: Gen. xli. 27. *septem vaccæ sunt*
10 *septem anni—.* Apoc. i. 20. et xvii. 9. *septem capita sunt*
septem montes. et v. 12. *decem cornua sunt decem reges.*

Postremo cum omne sacramentum obsignatio fœderis
gratiæ sit, hinc patet falli pontificios qui signo externo ex
opere, quod aiunt, operato vel salutis vel gratiæ conferendæ
15 vim tribuunt: sacramenta enim per se nec salutem conferunt
nec gratiam, sed utramque tantummodo credentibus vel ob-
signant vel repræsentant: 1 Pet. iii. 21. *non quo carnis sordes*
abiiciuntur, sed stipulatio bonæ conscientiæ—.

Itaque nec absolute necessaria sunt: 1. quia multi sine iis
20 ut fœminæ scilicet sine circumcisione: salutem sunt adepti,
latro in cruce sine baptismo, infantesque et catechumeni,
proculdubio multi; adepti etiam dona spiritus per verbum

tism"; and to the Lord's Supper: Matt. xxvi. 26, 27. "as they were eating, Jesus took bread," &c. "take, eat; this is my body." Compare also Mark xiv. 23. and Luke xxii. 20. "this cup is the new testament." See also 1 Cor. xi. 25. Again,
5 1 Cor. x. 4. "that rock was Christ." The object of the sacred writers, in thus expressing themselves, was probably to denote the close affinity between the sign and the thing signified, as well as, by a bold metaphor, to intimate the certainty with which the seal is thus set to spiritual blessings; the same form
10 of speech being used in other instances, where the certainty of a thing is to be emphatically expressed: Gen. xli. 27. "the seven kine are seven years." Rev. i. 20. xvii. 9. "the seven heads are seven mountains," and v. 12. "the ten horns are ten kings."
15   Lastly, since every sacrament is, by its very definition, a seal of the covenant of grace, it is evident that the Papists err, when they attribute to the outward sign the power of bestowing salvation or grace by virtue of the mere *opus operatum;* seeing that sacraments can neither impart salvation nor grace
20 of themselves, but are given as a pledge or symbol to believers of the actual blessings. 1 Pet. iii. 21. "not the putting away of the filth of the flesh, but the answer of a good conscience."

Hence it follows, that sacraments are not absolutely indispensable: first, because many have been saved without par-
25 taking of them; thus circumcision was dispensed with in the case of women, baptism in that of the thief on the cross, and doubtless of many infants and catechumens. Thus also many have obtained the gifts of the Spirit through the word and faith

solum et fidem, Act. x. 44, &c. *illapsus est spiritus sanctus in omnes qui audiebant hunc sermonem—*. Ne ipse quidem baptizatus est Ioannes, baptismi primus minister, etiamsi baptismo sibi quoque opus esse testaretur, Matt. iii. 14. For-
5 tasse etiam ne Apollos quidem qui Alexandriæ natus, diu post Baptistæ tempora, Ephesum inde primum venit, et baptismum tantum Ioannis cognoverat, ex quo suscepisse unquam non necessario arguitur; hunc tamen Aquilas et Priscilla, nullo intercedente baptismo quod quidem legitur, tantum-
10 modo plenius erudierunt, Act. xviii. 24, 25, 26. 2. sigilla fœdus non faciunt, sed declarant: unde et Abrahamo iam ante credenti et iustificato sigillum iustitiæ circumcisio data est. Quod autem dicitur Ioan. iii. 5. *nisi quis renatus fuerit ex aqua et spiritu, non potest introire in regnum Dei,* intelli-
15 gendum est, si fieri hoc potest rite, et neglectio omnis abest. Idem de isto Eph. v. 26. erit dicendum; *purificatam lavacro aquæ per verbum.* et Tit. iii. 5. *per lavacrum regenerationis:* nam et evangelium dicitur *potentia Dei ad salutem,* Rom. i. 16. et *regenerari per verbum dicimur,* 1 Pet. i. 23. et tamen
20 qui infantes moriuntur, aut sine externo evangelio et verbo, solo spiritu, regenerantur, aut omnino pereunt. Similiter qui

alone. Acts x. 44. "the Holy Ghost fell on all them which heard the word." Nor was John himself, the first who administered the rite, baptized, although he testified that he also had need of baptism, Matt. iii. 14. The same was not improbably the
5 case with Apollos, inasmuch as he does not appear to have left his native city of Alexandria for Ephesus till long after the death of John; nor can it be inferred with certainty, from its being said of him that he "knew only the baptism of John," that he had actually undergone the ceremony. Yet, as far as
10 appears, Aquila and Priscilla considered a more thorough initiation in the gospel all that was wanting to him, without requiring that he should be baptized, Acts xviii. 24–26. Secondly, the seal does not constitute the covenant, but is only an evidence of it; whence Abraham, after that he had already
15 believed and was justified, received circumcision as the seal of his righteousness. When therefore it is said John iii. 5. "except a man be born of water and of the Spirit, he cannot enter into the kingdom of God," this must be understood in a conditional sense, assuming that a fit opportunity has been offered,
20 and that it has not been lost through neglect. The same may be said of Eph. v. 26. "that he might cleanse it with the washing of water by the word," and Tit. iii. 5. "by the washing of regeneration"; for the gospel is also called "the power of God unto salvation," Rom. i. 16. and we are said "to be born again
25 by the word," 1 Pet. i. 23. although those who die in infancy must either be regenerated by the Spirit alone, without any outward reception of the gospel or word, or they must perish altogether. In the same manner, he who believes only, drinks

tantummodo credit, is et aquam illam vivam et sanguinem
Christi bibit, et panem illum cœlestem et carnem Christi
comedit; et vitam habet æternam, Ioan. iv. et vi. ut supra.
Ad necessitatem ergo sacramentorum si spectas, vere hoc
5 quoque dici potest; spiritus vivificat, fides manducat, oris
manducatio neque fieri commode semper potest, neque est
absolute necessaria. Profecto, si sacramentum nihil aliud nisi
obsignatio, vel potius repræsentatio quædam est, quid peccat
is qui Deo non minus credit etiam sine ea prorsus obsigna-
10 tione, quam habere rite et commode, non potest; præsertim
cum Deo gratus esse, Christique mortem commemorare, si
non eo modo ac ritu conceditur quo Deus instituit, at multis
aliis modis per omnem vitam possit.

Administratio cœnæ Dominicæ nulla usquam legitur in
15 scriptura, sed participatio tantum, eaque assidua atque domes-
tica apud primos Christianos: Act. ii. 42. *perdurabant in*
doctrina apostolorum et communicatione et fractione panis et
orationibus. et v. 46. *quotidie perdurantes concorditer in*
templo, ac frangentes donatim panem, capiebant cibum cum
20 *exultatione et simplicitate cordis.* et xx. 7. *primo die heb-*
domadis congregatis discipulis ad frangendum panem, Pau-

of that living water which is the blood of Christ, and eats of
that heavenly bread which is the flesh of Christ, and has
eternal life: John iv. and vi. as above. When therefore the
necessity of the sacraments is under discussion, it may in like
5 manner be urged, that it is the Spirit which quickens, and that
it is faith which feeds upon the body of Christ; that on the
other hand the outward feeding of the body, as it cannot
always take place conveniently, so neither is it absolutely
necessary. Assuredly, if a sacrament be nothing more than
10 what it is defined to be, a seal, or rather visible representation
of God's benefits to us, he cannot be wrong, who reposes the
same faith in God's promises without this confirmation as
with it, in cases where it is not possible for him to receive it
duly and conveniently; especially as so many opportunities
15 are open to him through life of evincing his gratitude to God,
and commemorating the death of Christ, though not in the
precise mode and form which God has instituted.

We nowhere read in Scripture of the Lord's Supper being
distributed to the first Christians by an appointed minister;
20 we are only told that they partook of it in common, and that
frequently, and in private houses. Acts ii. 42. "they continued
stedfastly in the apostles' doctrine and fellowship, and in
breaking of bread, and in prayers." v. 46. "they continuing
daily with one accord in the temple, and breaking bread from
25 house to house, did eat their meat with gladness and single-
ness of heart." xx. 7. "upon the first day of the week, when
the disciples came together to break bread, Paul preached
unto them——." I know no reason therefore why ministers

lus—. Cur itaque ministri celebrationem cœnæ Dominicæ, nisi se ministrantibus, nemini concedant, nescio: nam quod Christus et panem et poculum discipulis suis dedit, sane neque singulis dedisse legitur, et institutoris tunc partes, non mini-
5 stri, egit. Et quod scriptum est 1 Cor. iv. 1. *sic de nobis reputet homo ut de ministris Christi et dispensatoribus mysteriorum Dei,* id Paulus de se reliquisque ministris sui ordinis loquitur, qui soli mysteriorum Dei, id est, doctrinæ evangelicæ tunc primum divinitus traditæ dispensatores erant, non
10 panis et vini; neque enim ministrabant mensis, Act. vi. 2. ne illis quidem ubi synaxin assiduam probabile est fuisse; quemadmodum nec Paulus ut baptizaret, sed ut evangelizaret se esse missum testatur, 1 Cor. i. 17. et *mysteria illa* doctrinam duntaxat significare sequens versus ostendit: *illud requiritur*
15 *in dispensatoribus, ut quisque fidus inveniatur.* At hoc profecto tenuius est, quam ut in tanto dispensatore dignum sit requiri, ut fidus reperiatur in dispensando pane et vino, elementis, non mysteriis. Et cap. x. 16, 17. benedictio poculi et fractio panis iisdem omnibus tribuitur quibus corporis et
20 sanguinis Christi communio non adimitur. Etenim novi testamenti sacerdos unicus est Christus, Heb. vii. 23, 24. non

refuse to permit the celebration of the Lord's Supper, except where they themselves are allowed to administer it; for if it be alleged that Christ gave the bread and wine to his disciples, it may be replied, first, that we nowhere read of his giving them to each individually, and secondly, that he was then acting in the character, not of a minister, but of the founder of a new institution. With regard to the expression in 1 Cor. iv. 1. "let a man so account of us, as of the ministers of Christ, and stewards of the mysteries of God," it is evident that Paul is there speaking of himself and the other ministers of his own order, who were the exclusive stewards of the divine mysteries, that is, of the doctrine of the Gospel, before hidden, but then first revealed from God; not of bread and wine, for they did not "serve tables," Acts vi. 2. not even those at which we may suppose them to have met constantly for the celebration of the sacrament; in like manner as Paul himself was not sent "to baptize, but to preach the gospel," 1 Cor. i. 17. That the "mysteries" in question are to be understood of doctrine, is evident from the verse following, "it is required in stewards that a man be found faithful"; for it would be derogating from the dignity of such a steward as Paul to consider faithfulness in administering bread and wine, which are mere elements, and not mysteries, as of sufficient importance to be specified in his case among the requisite qualifications for his office. So also chap. x. 16, 17. the cup of blessing and the breaking of bread is spoken of as common to all, who are qualified to participate in the communion itself. For Christ is the sole priest of the new covenant, Heb. vii. 23, 24. nor is

est igitur ullus ordo hominum qui munus hoc sacra dandi ac
dispensandi, sibi præ aliis vindicare iure possit; cum in Christo
æque omnes sacerdotes simus, 1 Pet. ii. 9. Apoc. i. 6. Aut si
non essemus, quod tantum est paschatis et cœnæ Dominicæ
5 discrimen, ut paschatis dispensatio sub lege, ubi sacra nemini
nisi sacerdotibus aut Levitis attingere fas erat, eorum tamen
nemini attributa aut mandata sit, cœnæ Dominicæ sub evangelio, ubi illa tactionis cæremonia obsolevit, ius fidelium atque
libertas latius patet, nemini præter cæteros dispensatio attri-
10 buta, solis ministris ecclesiasticis attribuenda videatur, ita ut
patrifamilias aut eius permissu cuivis alteri non æque nunc
liceat donatim cœnam Dominicam atque olim licuit cœnam
paschalem suis dispensare, si modo ulla omnino dispensatione
vel hic vel illic fuisse opus aut nunc esse arbitramur?
15   Ad sacramenta accedere non nisi explorata conscientia eiec-
tisque peccatis debemus: 2 Chron. xxx. 13, 14, 15. *surgentes*
amoverunt altaria quæ erant Hierosolymis, et omnes aras
thurarias amoventes, proiecerunt in torrentem Chidronis;
deinde iugularunt pascha. Ezræ vi. 21. *quod comederunt*
20 *Israelitæ—, et quisquis separatus ab immunditia gentium re-*
gionis adiunxerat se illis; quærendo Iehovam Deum Israelis.
1 Cor. xi. 28. *exploret se quisque—.*

there any order of men which can claim to itself either the right of distributing or the power of withholding the sacred elements, seeing that in Christ we are all alike priests, 1 Pet. ii. 9. Rev. i. 6. Even were it otherwise, however, it is not con-
5 ceivable that there should be any such essential distinction between the passover and the Lord's Supper, that whereas under the law, when it was forbidden to all but the priests and Levites even to touch the sacred things, there was no ordinance restricting the celebration of the passover to the members of
10 that body, under the gospel, by which these ceremonial sanctities have been abolished, and a wider scope given to the rights and liberties of believers, the dispensing of the elements, which in Scripture is committed to no one in particular, should be considered as an unfit office for any but the
15 ministers of the church; so that the master of a family, or any one appointed by him, is not at liberty to celebrate the Lord's Supper from house to house, as was done in the dispensation of the passover: if indeed we are to suppose that any distribution of the elements by an individual officiator was then, or
20 is now, requisite.

The sacraments are not to be approached without self-examination and renunciation of sin. 2 Chron. xxx. 13–15. "they arose and took away the altars that were in Jerusalem, and all the altars for incense took they away, and cast them
25 into the brook Kidron: then they killed the passover." Ezra vi. 21. "all such as had separated themselves unto them from the filthiness of the heathen of the land, to seek Jehovah, God of Israel, did eat." 1 Cor. xi. 28. "let a man examine himself."

Neglecta enim aut indigne suscepta æque iram numinis irritant: Exod. iv. 24, 25, 26. *velut quærens morte afficere eum: sed accipiens Zippora cultrum—; sic destitit Iehova.* I Cor. xi. 29, &c. *nam qui edit ac bibit indigne, ipse sibi* 5 *iudicium edit ac bibit, non discernens corpus Domini: propterea inter vos multi sunt ægroti—.*

Differri igitur possunt ac debent quoad temporis et loci opportunitas, mensque pura, vitæ sanctitas, fidelium denique iusta communio ferat. Exod. xiii. 5. *futurum est, cum intro-* 10 *duxerit te Iehova in regionem Chananæi—, ut obeas istum cultum hoc mense.* Num. ix. 10, 11. *si ullus e vobis erit immundus propter cadaver, aut ullus e vobis aut ex generationibus vestris in via remota fuerit, tamen celebrabit Iehovæ pascha; mense secundo—.* Sic 2 Chron. xxx. 2, 3. Ios. v. 4. 15 *qui nati fuerant in deserto, in ipso itinere, postquam exivissent ex Ægypto, eos non circumciderant.* Missa Papistica a cœna Dominica longe discrepat. 1. hæc instituta est a Domino, illa a pontifice. 2. hæc in memoriam Christi semel, idque a semetipso unico sacerdote oblati, Heb. vii. 24, 25, 27. et ix. 20 15, 25, 26. et x. 10, 12, 14; at missa est oblatio ipsa quotidie,

The neglect, or the improper celebration of the sacraments, equally provokes the indignation of the Deity. Exod. iv. 24–26. "Jehovah met him and sought to kill him: then Zipporah took a sharp stone, and cut off the foreskin of her son 5 . . . so he let him go." 1 Cor. xi. 29, &c. "he that eateth and drinketh unworthily, eateth and drinketh damnation to himself, not discerning the Lord's body: for this cause many are weak and sickly among you—." Hence it is not only allowable, but necessary to defer partaking in them, till such time 10 as a proper place and season, purity of heart and life, and a regular communion of believers, concur to warrant their celebration. Exod xiii. 5. "it shall be when Jehovah shall bring thee into the land of the Canaanites . . . that thou shalt keep this service in this month." Num. ix. 10, 11. "if any man 15 of you or of your posterity shall be unclean by reason of a dead body, or be in a journey afar off, yet he shall keep the passover unto Jehovah; the fourteenth day of the second month at even they shall keep it." Compare also 2 Chron. iii. 2, 3. Josh. v. 5. "all the people that were born in the wilderness, by the 20 way as they came forth out of Egypt, them they had not circumcised."

The Mass of the Papists differs from the Lord's Supper in several respects. In the first place, the one is an ordinance of our Lord, the other an institution of the Pope. Secondly, the 25 Lord's Supper is celebrated in remembrance of Christ once offered, which offering he himself made by virtue of his own peculiar priesthood. Heb. vii. 24, 25, 27. ix. 15, 25, 26. x. 10, 12, 14. whereas in the Mass the offering itself is supposed to

idque a sacrificulis innumeris facta. 3. Christus se non in sacra
cœna, sed in cruce obtulit; in missa Christus quotidie a sacerdote sacrificatur. 4. in cœna Dominica adfuit ipsum corpus
Domini vivi factum ex Maria virgine; in missa creari repente
5 ex pane fingitur a sacrificulo quatuor verborum demurmu-
ratione, *hoc est corpus meum,* et creatum statim frangi. 5.
in sacra cœna vera substantia panis et vini, sicut et nomen,
post consecrationem manet; in missa, si credimus, externa
tantum species manet, nova utriusque metamorphosi in cor-
10 pus Domini conficta. 6. in sacra cœna, Christi mandato, e
poculo biberunt omnes; in missa poculum negatur laicis.
Missa denique Sanctum Christi corpus perpessionibus ac mise-
riis omnibus perfunctum a summo exaltationis gradu, a
dextera Dei patris ad statum humiliationis multo quam antea
15 miseriorem atque indigniorem in terras retrahit, rursus frangendum, comminuendum, commolendum etiam brutorum
morsibus exponit; per omnes denique viscerum meatus ac
fœditates excoctum, quod dictu horrendum est, in latrinam
extrudit.

20   Cætera quæ pontificii sacramenta nominant, CONFIRMATIO-

be repeated daily, and that by innumerable petty priests at the same point of time. Thirdly, Christ offered himself, not at the holy Supper, but on the cross; whereas it is in the Mass that the pretended daily sacrifice takes place. Fourthly, in the
5 Lord's Supper the real body of the living Lord, made of the Virgin Mary, was personally present; in the Mass, by the mere muttering of the four mystical words "this is my body," it is supposed to be created out of the substance of the bread at some given moment, for the sole purpose of being broken in pieces
10 as soon as created. Fifthly, in the Lord's Supper the bread and wine, after consecration, remain unchanged in substance as in name; in the Mass, if we believe the Papists, although the outward appearance remains the same, they are converted by a sudden metamorphosis into the body of our Lord.
15 Sixthly, in the Lord's Supper, according to the original institution, all the communicants drink of the cup; in the Mass, the cup is refused to the laity. Lastly, in the Mass the sacred body of Christ, after having completed its appointed course of hardship and suffering, is dragged back from its state of
20 exaltation at the right hand of the Father to a condition even more wretched and degrading than before; it is again exposed to be broken, and crushed, and bruised by the teeth not only of men, but of brutes; till, having passed through the whole process of digestion, it is cast out at length into the draught;
25 a profanation too horrible to be even alluded to without shuddering.

It is manifest from the very definition of the word, that the other sacraments so called by the Papists, namely, CONFIRMA-

NEM, PŒNITENTIAM, EXTREMAM UNCTIONEM, ORDINATIONEM et
MATRIMONIUM, non esse vere ac proprie sacramenta ex ipsa
sacramenti definitione perspicimus; si nempe divinitus instituta non sunt; si signum non habent a Deo institutum ad
5 obsignandum fœdus gratiæ.

CONFIRMATIO sive MANUUM IMPOSITIO adhibita quidem est
a Christo, at non ut sacramentum, sed ut benedictionis quoddam symbolum, prout illius gentis mos ferebat, exemplo for-
sitan patriarcharum, qui benedicentes filiis suis manus im-
10 ponebant, ut et magistratus magistratui successuro, Moses
Iosuæ, Num. xxvii. 18; unde et electis fere ad munus aliquod
ecclesiasticum et baptizatis apostoli manus imponere solebant;
fere inquam, non semper; nam septem diaconis manus im-
positas legimus, Act. vi. 6. Matthiæ in apostolorum numerum
15 cooptato, Act. i. 26. non legimus. Et baptizatis quidem impositio illa manuum dona spiritus sancti miraculosa gratiamque mirificam, non salvificam, conferebat, Act. viii. 17, &c.
et xix. 6. et 1 Tim. iv. 14. et 2 Ep. i. 6. Itaque ut sacramentum improprie sane, ut benedictionis symbolum pie ac
20 salutariter in ecclesia retinetur: Heb. vi. 2. *baptismatum
doctrinæ ac manuum impositionis.*

Ad PŒNITENTIAM lapsi post baptismum (eam enim solam
pro sacramento habent Pontificii) et SACROS ORDINES quod
attinet, siquis ita sacramenta vult dici ut tantummodo res

TION, PENANCE, EXTREME UNCTION, ORDERS, and MARRIAGE, cannot be such in the proper sense of the term; inasmuch as they are not of divine institution, neither do they possess any sign appointed by God for the sealing of the covenant of grace.

5   CONFIRMATION or IMPOSITION OF HANDS was, it is true, administered by Christ, not however as a sacrament, but as a form of blessing, according to a common Jewish custom, derived probably from patriarchal times, when fathers were accustomed to lay their hands on their children in blessing
10 them, and magistrates on those whom they appointed their successors, as Moses on Joshua, Num. xxvii. 18. Hence the apostles usually laid hands on such as were baptized, or chosen to any ecclesiastical office; usually, I say, not always: for, although we read of imposition of hands on the seven
15 deacons, Acts vi. 6. we do not find that this ceremony was practised towards Matthias, when he was numbered with the eleven apostles, Acts i. 26. In the case of the baptized, imposition of hands conferred, not indeed saving grace, but miraculous powers, and the extraordinary gifts of the Spirit: Acts
20 viii. 17, &c. xix. 6. 1 Tim. iv. 14. 2 Tim. i. 6. Hence, although the church rejects this ceremony as a sacrament, she retains it with great propriety and advantage as a symbol of blessing. Heb. vi. 2. "the doctrine of baptisms, and of laying on of hands."
25   With respect to ORDERS, and to the act of PENANCE for sins committed subsequently to baptism (for to this penance alone the Papists apply the name of a sacrament) we have no objection to their being called sacraments, in the sense of reli-

sacras significent, ut pedum lotio antiqua et similia, nihil est
quod repugnemus. Quod enim vocabulum in scriptura non
extat, de eius accurata significatione cur magnopere laboran-
dum sit, non reperio. Certe pœnitentia nec signum habet pro-
5 prium, nec obsignat quicquam magis quam fides.

MATRIMONIUM autem cum omnium promiscue mortalium
communi iure gentium sit, nisi vere fidelium duntaxat matrimonium intelligatur, profecto non res sacra, sed civilis plane,
nedum sacramentum dicendum erit; tantum abest ut ad mi-
10 nistros ecclesiasticos celebratio eius ullo modo pertineat.

Quod ad UNCTIONEM ÆGROTORUM, Apostoli quidem *ægrotos*
unxerunt oleo, et sanarunt, Marc. vi. 13. et Iacobus idem
præcipit, cap. v. 14, 15. Verum hi ritus non fuerunt sacramenta, sed cum miraculis tantum adhibiti, qui una cum mi-
15 raculorum donis desiti sunt: nihil igitur similitudinis cum
illa antiqua habet extrema unctio Papistarum hodierna; apostoli enim non præcise morituros, ut nunc fit, sed quosvis
graviter modo ægrotantes ungebant, eosque sanabant. Marc.
vi. 13. Quid quod! sacramenta omnia, cum ad obsignandam

gious emblems, or symbols of things sacred, analogous to the ancient custom of washing the feet of the poor, and the like. It is unnecessary to be very scrupulous as to the sense of a word which nowhere occurs in Scripture. Penance however has no peculiar sign attached to it, neither is it a seal of the covenant, any more than faith.

With regard to MARRIAGE, inasmuch as it is not an institution peculiar to Christian nations, but common to them all by the universal law of mankind, unless it be meant to restrict the word to the union of believers properly so called, it is not even a religious ceremony, still less a sacrament, but a compact purely civil; nor does its celebration belong in any manner to the ministers of the church.

As to the UNCTION OF THE SICK, it is true that the apostles "anointed with oil many that were sick, and healed them," Mark vi. 13. and St. James enjoins the same custom, v. 14, 15. This rite, however, was not of the nature of a sacrament; and as it was employed solely in conjunction with miraculous powers, with the cessation of those powers its use must have also ceased. There is therefore no analogy between the anointing of the first Christians, and the extreme unction of the Papists in modern times; seeing that, in the first place, the apostles anointed not only those who were at the point of death, as is now the custom, but all, as many as were grievously sick; and that, secondly, this unction was attended with the cure of their disorder: Mark vi. 13.

To the above may be added, that sacraments, being instituted chiefly for purposes in which all are concerned, namely,

gratiam fidemque firmandam constituta potissimum sint, fidelibus æque omnibus debent impertiri: at vero ex quinque illis pontificiorum sacramentis quatuor non omnibus sed certis duntaxat hominibus, pœnitentia nempe lapsis, unctio ægrotis, 5 ordo ecclesiasticis, matrimonium laicis duntaxat impertitur.

CAPUT XXIX.

DE ECCLESIA VISIBILI.

D E VOCATIONE eamque sequente vel alteratione sola vel etiam regeneratione et auctione hominis regenerati, de fœderis denique quod vocatis propositum est manifestatione varia, obsignationeque hactenus 10 dictum est.

VOCATORUM CŒTUS est VISIBILIS ECCLESIA. Vocatorum, inquam, in communi, sive regeniti sint sive non: Matt. iii. 12. *cuius ventilabrum est in manu sua, et perpurgabit aream suam; et congregabit triticum suum in horreum, paleam au-* 15 *tem exuret igni inextincto.* et xiii. 24, 25. *simile est regnum cœlorum homini serenti bonum semen in agro suo: quum autem dormirent homines, venit eius inimicus, et sevit zizania inter triticum.* et v. 47. *simile est regnum cœlorum sagenæ iactæ in mare, et quæ res cuiusvis generis congregavit.* et cap.

as tokens of the sealing of the covenant of grace, and for the confirmation of our faith, ought to be imparted equally to all believers; whereas of the five papistical sacraments above mentioned, four are exclusively appropriated to particular classes
5 of individuals; penance to the lapsed, orders to the clergy, extreme unction to the sick, marriage to the lay members of the church alone.

CHAPTER XXIX.

OF THE VISIBLE CHURCH

WE HAVE hitherto treated of the vocation of man, and of the effects thereby produced, whether consisting in a mere outward change of character, or in actual regeneration; of the spiritual increase of the regenerate; of the various manifestations of the offered covenant; and, finally, of the sealing of that covenant by sacraments.

15   THE ASSEMBLY OF THOSE WHO ARE CALLED is termed THE VISIBLE CHURCH. By the CALLED, I mean those indiscriminately who have received the call, whether actually regenerate or otherwise. Matt. iii. 12. "whose fan is in his hand, and he will thoroughly purge his floor, and gather his wheat into
20 his garner; but he will burn up the chaff with unquenchable fire." xiii. 24, 25. "the kingdom of heaven is likened unto a man which sowed good seed in his field; but while men slept, his enemy came and sowed tares among the wheat." v. 47. "the kingdom of heaven is like unto a net that was

xxii. 9, 10. *ite ad compita—; et congregarunt malos pariter ac bonos* et xxv. 1, 2. *simile erit regnum cœlorum decem virginibus—; quinque autem ex iis erant prudentes, et quinque fatuæ.* 1 Ioan. ii. 19. *e nobis egressi sunt, sed non erant ex*
5 *nobis.*

Notæ visibilis ecclesiæ sunt pura doctrina, verus Dei cultus externus, vera charitas evangelica, quantum homines diiudicare possunt, et recta sigillorum administratio. Matt. xxviii. 19, 20. *profecti docete omnes gentes, baptizantes eas—; do-*
10 *centes eas observare omnia quæ præcepi vobis.* Act. ii. 42. *perdurantes in doctrina apostolorum, et communicatione, et fractione panis, et orationibus.* 1 Tim. iii. 15. *ecclesia Dei vivi, columna et stabilimentum veritatis.* Ecclesiæ Iudaicæ notas non absimiles recenset Paulus, Rom. ix. 4. *qui sunt*
15 *Israelitæ; quorum est adoptio et gloria et pacta et legis constitutio et cultus et promissiones.* Et contra ubi istæ notæ non fuissent, ostendit nullam fuisse ecclesiam: Eph. ii. 12. *vos illo tempore fuisse absque Christo, abalienatos a civitate Israelis, et extraneos quod ad pactorum promissiones, spem non ha-*
20 *bentes, et absque Deo in mundo.*

Quæ autem signa dicuntur, Marc. xvi. 16, 17, 18. *signa eos qui crediderint hæc consequentur, per nomen meum dæ-*

cast into the sea, and gathered of every kind." xxii. 9, 10. "go
ye therefore into the highways . . . and they gathered together all as many as they found, both bad and good." xxv. 1,
2. "then shall the kingdom of heaven be likened unto ten
5   virgins . . . and five of them were wise, and five were foolish." 1 John ii. 19. "they went out from us, but they were
not of us."

The tokens of the visible church are, pure doctrine; the
proper external worship of God; genuine evangelical love, so
10 far as it can be distinguished from the fictitious by mere human perception; and a right administration of the seals of the
covenant. Matt. xxviii. 19, 20. "go ye therefore and teach all
nations, baptizing them . . . teaching them to observe all
things whatsoever I have commanded you." Acts ii. 42. "they
15 continued stedfastly in the apostles' doctrine and fellowship,
and in breaking of bread, and in prayers." 1 Tim. iii. 15. "the
church of the living God, the pillar and ground of the truth."
The tokens of the Jewish church enumerated by St. Paul are
not dissimilar: Rom. ix. 4. "who are Israelites; to whom
20 pertaineth the adoption, and the glory, and the covenants, and
the giving of the law, and the service of God, and the promises." On the other hand, he intimates, that where these
tokens are wanting, there is no church. Eph. ii. 12. "at that
time ye were without Christ, being aliens from the common-
25 wealth of Israel, and strangers from the covenant of promise,
having no hope, and without God in the world."

As to what are called signs, Mark xvi. 17, 18. "these signs
shall follow them that believe; in my name shall they cast out

monia eiicient, linguis loquentur novis, serpentes tollent, et
siquid lethale biberint nequaquam nocebit iis, male valentibus
manus imponent, et bene habebunt, hæ quidem notæ perpetuæ
non sunt, sed primis ecclesiæ temporibus, cum evangelium
5 res nova, inaudita prius et pene incredibilis Iudæorum et Eth-
nicorum auribus primo acciderat magis necessariæ fuerunt,
quam hodie cum iam homines in evangelica fide primitus
educantur, et a prima ætate credere incipiunt. Satis est eos
audire et legere quæ fuerint a Christo eiusque apostolis mira-
10 cula initio edita Deut. xxxi. 13. *Filii quoque ipsorum qui*
experti non fuerint, audientes discant timere Iehovam Deum
vestrum: quibuscunque diebus—. Itaque *linguæ,* 1 Cor. xiv.
22. *in signum sunt, non credentibus sed incredulis* et *cessa-*
bunt. 1 Cor. xiii. 8. Miracula impostoribus etiam et falsæ ec-
15 clesiæ concessa sunt: Deut. xiii. 1, 2, 3. *quum surgens in*
medio tui propheta aut somnians somnium, ediderit tibi sig-
num aut prodigium quamvis eveniat signum illud aut pro-
digium quod prædixerat tibi dicendo—, ne auscultato verbis
prophetæ istius aut isti somnianti somnium; quia tentat Iehova
20 *Deus vester vos ad cognoscendum an sitis amantes Dei vestri*
ex toto corde vestro et ex toto animo vestro. Matt. vii. 22, 23.
multi dicent, Domine, Domine, nonne per nomen tuum pro-
phetavimus, et in nomine tuo dæmonia eiecimus, et per nomen

devils; they shall speak with new tongues; they shall take up serpents; and if they drink any deadly thing, it shall not hurt them; they shall lay hands on the sick, and they shall recover"; these are not to be considered as tokens uniformly
5 attending the visible church, but as testimonies which, however necessary at the time of its first establishment, when the doctrines of Christianity were to Jews and Gentiles alike, new, unheard of, and all but incredible, are less requisite at the present period, when men are educated in the apostolic faith,
10 and begin their belief from their earliest childhood. Under these circumstances, the same end is answered by their hearing and reading of the miracles performed at the beginning by Christ and his apostles. Deut. xxxi. 13. "that their children, which have not known anything, may hear, and learn
15 to fear Jehovah your God, as long as ye live—." So also 1 Cor. xiv. 22. "tongues are for a sign, not to them that believe, but to them that believe not," and "they shall cease," 1 Cor. xiii. 8. The working of miracles was sometimes permitted even to impostors, and to a false church. Deut. xiii. 1–3. "if there
20 arise among you a prophet, or a dreamer of dreams, and giveth thee a sign or a wonder, and the sign or the wonder come to pass whereof he spake unto thee . . . thou shalt not hearken unto the words of that prophet, or that dreamer of dreams; for Jehovah your God proveth you, to know whether
25 ye love Jehovah your God with all your heart and with all your soul." Matt. vii. 22, 23. "many will say to me in that day, Lord, Lord, have we not prophesied in thy name, and in thy name have cast out devils, and in thy name have done

tuum multas virtutes edidimus? tunc profitebor iis, nunquam novi vos. et xxiv. 24. *excitabuntur pseudochristi et pseudoprophetæ, et edent signa magna et prodigia, ita ut seducant (si fieri possit) etiam electos.* Gal. i. 8. *etiamsi nos aut an-*
5 *gelus e cœlo evangelizet vobis præter id quod vobis evangelizavimus, anathema esto.* 2 Thess. ii. 9. *cuius adventus est ex efficacia satanæ, cum omni potentia et signis ac prodigiis mendacibus.* Apoc. xiii. 13. *editque signa magna.*

Nec semper ecclesiæ restaurationem comitantur miracula,
10 uti nec multos olim prophetas nec baptistam, Ioan. x. 41. nec ipsos apostolos: Matt. xvii. 16. *obtuli eum discipulis tuis, nec potuerunt eum sanare.* 2 Tim. iv. 20. *Trophimum reliqui Mileti ægrotantem.* ergo ne credentem quidem et inter fideles etiam insignem sanare potuit.

15 Nec magis perficiunt miracula ut quisquam credat quam doctrina per se sola, id est, nihil; nisi mentem utrobique det Deus: Deut. xxix. 2, 3, 4. *vos vidistis omnia quæ fecit Iehova ante oculos vestros in terra Ægypti—, sed nondum dederat vobis Iehova mentem ad cognoscendum et oculos ad viden-*
20 *dum, et aures ad audiendum usque in diem hunc.* Psal. lxxviii. 11, &c. *obliti mirabilium eius—.* et v. 32. *neque crediderunt, propter mirabilia eius opera.* Luc. xvi. 31. *si Mosen et prophetas non audiunt, ne si ex mortuis quidem quispiam resurgat,*

many wonderful works? and then will I profess unto them,
I never knew you." xxiv. 24. "there shall arise false Christs,
and false prophets, and shall show great signs and wonders,
insomuch that, if it were possible, they shall deceive the very
5 elect." Gal. i. 8. "though we, or an angel from heaven,
preach any other gospel unto you than that which we have
preached unto you, let him be accursed." 2 Thess. ii. 9.
"whose coming is after the working of Satan with all power
and signs and lying wonders." Rev. xiii. 13. "he doeth great
10 wonders."

Neither is the re-establishment of the church uniformly
attended by miracles; in like manner as this species of attes-
tation was not granted to several of the prophets, nor to the
Baptist, John x. 41. nor in all cases to the apostles themselves,
15 Matt. xvii. 16. "I brought him to thy disciples, and they
could not cure him." 2 Tim. iv. 20. "Trophimus have I left
at Miletum sick": whence it appears that Paul was unable to
heal, not only one who was a believer, but of note among
the believers.

20 Miracles have no inherent efficacy in producing belief, any
more than simple preaching; it is God that gives the right
heart in the one case as in the other. Deut. xxix. 2–4. "ye have
seen all that Jehovah did before your eyes in the land of Egypt
. . . yet Jehovah hath not given you an heart to perceive, and
25 eyes to see, and ears to hear, unto this day." Psal. lxxviii. 11.
"they forgat his wonders." v. 32. "they believed not his
wondrous works." Luke xvi. 31. "if they hear not Moses and
the prophets, neither will they be persuaded, though one rose

persuadebuntur. Act. iv. 16, 17. *conspicuum signum editum esse per eos, manifestum est omnibus habitantibus Hierosolymis, nec id possumus negare—.*

Et beati qui sine miraculis credunt. Ioan. xx. 29. *beati qui*
5 *non viderunt, et crediderunt.* Matt. xii. 39, &c. *gens improba et adulterina requirit signum, sed signum non dabitur ei, nisi—. Ninevitæ resurgent in iudicio cum gente ista, et condemnabunt eam, quod ipsi resipuerint ad præconium Ionæ—.* Luc. x. 20. *de eo ne gaudete, quod spiritus vobis subiiciantur;*
10 *gaudete vero potius quod nomina vestra scripta sunt in cœlis.*

Quamdiu itaque charitas donorum maxima et ubicunque manet, de veritate ecclesiæ visibilis dubitare non debemus. Ioan. xiii. 35. *ex hoc omnes cognoscent vos esse discipulos meos, si charitatem habueritis alii in alios.* 1 Cor. xii. 31.
15 *æmulamini dona potiora, et adhuc excellentiorem viam vobis demonstro.* et xiii. 1, &c. *si linguis—.* et v. 8. *charitas nunquam excidit; sed et prophetiæ evanescent—: et* 13. *nunc vero manet fides, spes, charitas, tria hæc; maxima autem harum charitas.*

20 Quemadmodum ecclesiæ mysticæ caput est Christus, ita et visibili ecclesiæ nemo iure præest aut præesse potest nisi ipse Christus. Matt. xviii. 20. *illic sum in medio eorum.* et xxviii. 20. *ego vobiscum sum omnibus diebus usque ad consummationem sæculi.* 1 Cor. v. 4. *vobis et meo spiritu in nomine*

from the dead." Acts. iv. 16, 17. "that a notable miracle hath been done by them is manifest to all them that dwell in Jerusalem, and we cannot deny it." Those also are declared blessed who believe without the testimony of miracles. John xx. 29. "blessed are they that have not seen, and yet have believed." Matt. xii. 39, &c. "an evil and adulterous generation seeketh after a sign, and there shall no sign be given it, but the sign of the prophet Jonas . . . the men of Nineveh shall rise in judgment with this generation, and shall condemn it, because they repented at the preaching of Jonas." Luke x. 20. "in this rejoice not, that the spirits are subject unto you, but rather rejoice because your names are written in heaven."

So long therefore as charity, the greatest of all gifts, exists, and wheresoever it is found, we cannot doubt that the visible church there established is a true church. John xiii. 35. "by this shall all men know that ye are my disciples, if ye have love one to another." 1 Cor. xii. 31. "covet earnestly the best gifts: and yet show I you a more excellent way." xiii. 1, &c. "though I speak with the tongue of men and of angels, and have not charity, I am become as sounding brass—." v. 8. "charity never faileth: but whether there be prophecies, they shall fail—." v. 13. "now abideth faith, hope, charity, these three; but the greatest of these is charity."

As Christ is the head of the mystical church, so no one besides Christ has the right or power of presiding over the visible church. Matt. xviii. 20. "there am I in the midst of them." xxviii. 20. "I am with you alway, even unto the end of the world." 1 Cor. v. 4. "in the name of our Lord Jesus Christ,

Domini nostri Iesu Christi congregatis cum potestate domini nostri Iesu Christi. Heb. iii. 6. *Christus ut filius domui suæ præest.* Apoc. ii. 1. *qui ambulat inter septem illa candelabra aurea.*

5   Errant igitur qui quenquam in terris et nominatim Petrum eiusque successores vulgo dictos, pontifices nempe Romanos, nulla auctoritate divina, ecclesiæ caput imponunt.

Petrus certe neque missione, Matt. x. 1. neque mandatis, Ioan. xx. 21, 22. neque sententiæ auctoritate in controversiis 10 dirimendis, Act. xv. 2, 6, 7, 19, 23, 25. neque scientia vel saltem constantia, primum insigniter lapsus in illa abnegatione, deinde levius, ob idque a Paulo reprehensus, Gal. ii. 11. et *una presbyter,* 1 Pet. v. 1. nec honoris gradu, Matt. xix. 28. cæteris apostolis prælatus videtur, immo nihilo plus Petro 15 quam Iacobo, quam Ioanni, quam Paulo et Barnabæ tribuitur, Gal. ii. 9. immo circumcisorum duntaxat apostolus fuit, sicut Paulus gentium, v. 8, 9. qui *summis apostolis nihilo fuit inferior,* 2 Cor. xi. 5. quinetiam Petrus Ioannis collega Samariam mittitur, Act. viii. 14. et ad disceptantes contra se aposto- 20 latus sui rationem reddit, cap. xi. 2. quin et ecclesia *apostolorum* non Petri solius *fundamento superstructa* dicitur, Eph. ii. 20. Apoc. xxi. 14. Utcunque, fundamenti quæ potest esse

when ye are gathered together, and my spirit, with the power of our Lord Jesus Christ." Heb. iii. 6. "Christ as a son over his own house." Rev. ii. 1. "who walketh in the midst of the seven golden candlesticks." They are therefore in error, who would set up an earthly head over the church in the person of the apostle Peter, and his successors commonly so called, the Roman pontiffs; for which no authority can be found in Scripture. As to Peter, it does not appear that any preference was given to him over the other apostles, either with regard to his mission, Matt. x. 1. or to any special command assigned to him, John xx. 21, 22. or to any authority reposed in him for the deciding of controversies, Acts xv. 2, 6, 7, 19, 23, 25. or to his knowledge of the faith, at least to his constancy in professing it, since he fell grievously in his denial of Christ, and was afterwards reprehensible, though in a less degree, in the matter for which he was reproved by Paul, Gal. ii. 11. He was "also an elder" like the others, 1 Pet. v. 1. neither is he promised any distinction of honors hereafter, Matt. xix. 28. nor is superiority of any kind attributed to him rather than to James, or John, or Paul and Barnabas, Gal. ii. 9. Nay, he was the apostle of the circumcision only, as was Paul of the Gentiles, v. 8, 9. who was "not a whit behind the very chiefest apostles," 2 Cor. xi. 5. He was likewise sent as the colleague of John into Samaria, Acts viii. 14. and gave an account of his apostleship to those who contended with him, xi. 2. Lastly, the church is not said to be "built upon the foundation" of Peter alone, but "of the apostles," Eph. ii. 20. Rev. xxi. 14. Even supposing, however, that it were otherwise,

successio? neque vero celebratus ille locus, Matt. xvi. 18, 19. quo Papa sibi pro diplomate sui papatus abutitur, quicquam in Petrum confert quod non cum aliis eandem fidem profitentibus, communicetur, quemadmodum enim alii multi, ut

5 ex evangelistis liquet, Christum esse Dei filium non minus clare sunt confessi, ita responsum est, non *super te Petrum,* sed *super hanc Petram,* id est, super hanc fidem tibi cum cæteris fidelibus communem; vera enim petra est Christus, 1 Cor. x. 4. et unicum fundamentum, cap. iii. 11. adeoque

10 in Christum fides, Iudæ 20. *sanctissimæ vestræ fidei super-struentes vos ipsos;* et præter cæteros imprimis apostoli, ut supra Eph. ii. 20. nec soli petro claves regni cœlorum traduntur, siquidem ius clavium ligandi nempe et solvendi non soli traditur Petro, Matt. xviii. 18, 19. *quicquid ligaveritis—.*

15 Ioan. xx. 23. *si quorum remiseritis peccata—,* in illo autem Ioan. xxi. 15, &c. grex Christi pascendus non Petro præ cæteris mandatur, sed ipse Petrus triplici negatione lapsus, per confessionem ter repetitam, in eum unde lapsus est locum

how can a "foundation" have any succession? Nor does the celebrated text, Matt. xvi. 18, 19. which is perverted by the Pope to form the charter of his authority, confer any distinction on Peter beyond what is enjoyed by other professors
5 of the same faith. For inasmuch as many others confessed no less explicitly than Peter that Christ was the Son of God, as is clear from the narrative of the evangelists, the answer of Christ is not, "upon thee Peter," but "upon this rock I will build my church," that is, upon this faith which thou hast in
10 common with other believers, not upon thee as an individual; seeing that, in the personal sense of the word, the true rock is Christ, 1 Cor. x. 4. nor is there any other foundation, iii. 11. whence also faith in Christ is called the foundation, Jude 20. "building up yourselves on your most holy faith"; and the
15 same term is applied to the apostles as the original teachers of that faith, though not to the exclusion of others, Eph. ii. 20. "ye are built upon the foundation of the apostles and prophets." Nor is it to Peter exclusively that the keys of the kingdom of heaven are committed, inasmuch as the power of the
20 keys, as it is called, or the right of binding and loosing, is not entrusted to him alone, Matt. xviii. 18, 19. "whatsoever ye shall bind on earth, shall be bound in heaven," &c. John xx. 23. "whosesoever sins ye remit, they are remitted unto them." Nor does the passage of St. John, xxi. 15, &c. imply that the
25 office of feeding the flock of Christ was committed to Peter in any higher sense than to the others; the meaning of the repetition is, that he who had fallen by denying his master thrice, is here, by a confession as often repeated, restored to

restituitur; et qui se amare Christum plus quam cæteri omnes
nimium sibi fidens affirmaverat, Matt. xxvi. 33. nunc et
nimiæ fiduciæ suæ, experimento convictus, arguitur, et siquidem Christum plusquam reliqui discipuli dilexisset, id ut in
5 pascendis Christi ovibus, et præsertim agnis ostenderet, mo-
netur; idem nimirum quod antea monebatur, Luc. xxii. 32.
tu conversus, confirma fratres tuos: nam pascere oves Christi,
id est, docere omnes gentes, commune cæterorum munus
apostolorum fuit, Matt. xxviii. 19.

10   Verum ut Petro omnia concedamus, quis doceat successo-
ribus Petri eadem esse concessa; quis successores Petri esse
pontifices Romanos?

ECCLESIA VISIBILIS est UNIVERSALIS aut PARTICULARIS.

UNIVERSALIS est UNIVERSA MULTITUDO VOCATORUM TOTO ORBE
15 TERRARUM QUOVIS LOCO VEL SEPARATIM VEL UNA CUM ALIIS
DEUM PATREM IN CHRISTO PALAM COLENTIUM.

QUOVIS LOCO. Ioan. iv. 21. *neque in monte hoc, neque Hierosolymis.* 1 Cor. i. 2. *cum omnibus qui invocant nomen
Domini nostri Iesu Christi, quovis loco.*

20   VEL SEPARATIM. tametsi cuiusque est fidelium se ecclesiæ
recte institutæ, si fieri potest, aggregare, Heb. x. 25. *non
deserentes aggregationem nostri mutuam, sicuti mos est quibusdam, sed adhortantes alii alios—,* tamen qui id commode

the place from whence he fell; and that he who in his over-weening self-confidence had maintained that he loved Christ more than all the rest, is at once reminded of the event by which his weakness had been manifested, and admonished
5 that if he really loved Christ more than the other disciples, he should show his love by a greater assiduity in feeding Christ's flock, and more particularly his lambs; being in effect a repetition of the charge he had shortly before received, Luke xxii. 32. "when thou art converted, strengthen thy brethren."
10 For to feed the sheep of Christ, that is, to teach all nations, was the common office of all the apostles. Matt. xxviii. 19.

Granting, however, to Peter all that is claimed for him, what proof have we that the same privileges are continued to his successors? or that these successors are the Roman pontiffs?
15 THE VISIBLE CHURCH is either UNIVERSAL or PARTICULAR.

THE UNIVERSAL VISIBLE CHURCH is THE WHOLE MULTITUDE OF THOSE WHO ARE CALLED IN EVERY PART OF THE WORLD, AND WHO OPENLY WORSHIP GOD THE FATHER THROUGH CHRIST IN ANY PLACE WHATEVER, EITHER INDIVIDUALLY, OR IN CONJUNC-
20 TION WITH OTHERS.

IN ANY PLACE WHATEVER. John iv. 21. "the hour cometh, when ye shall neither in this mountain, nor yet at Jerusalem, worship the Father." 1 Cor. i. 2. "with all that in every place call upon the name of Jesus Christ our Lord."
25 EITHER INDIVIDUALLY, &c. for although it is the duty of believers to join themselves, if possible, to a church duly con-stituted, Heb. x. 25. "not forsaking the assembling of our-selves together, as the manner of some is, but exhorting one

aut informata plene conscientia facere nequeunt, non idcirco benedictione ecclesiis impertita excluduntur aut expertes sunt. I Reg. xix. 10, 14. *ego relictus sum solus.* et v. 18. *reliquos feci ex Israele septies mille.* Ioan. iv. 23. *venit tempus, et nunc est, quum veri adoratores adorabunt patrem spiritu ac veritate; etenim pater tales quærit qui ipsum adorent.* I Cor. i. 2. *ecclesiæ Dei quæ est Corinthi, sanctificatis in Christo Iesu, vocatis sanctis, cum omnibus qui invocant nomen Domini nostri Iesu Christi, quovis loco, tum ipsorum tum nostri.* et 2 Ep. i. 1. *ecclesiæ Dei quæ est Corinthi, una cum omnibus sanctis qui sunt in tota Achaia.*

Partes ecclesiæ universalis sunt MINISTRI et POPULUS. I Cor. iii. 9. *Dei sumus administri; Dei arvum, Dei ædificium estis.* et 2 Ep. iv. 5. *nos autem servos vestros propter Iesum.* Matt. xx. 25, &c. *sicut filius hominis non venit ut sibi ministretur, sed ut ministret.* Rom. x. 14. *quomodo autem audient absque prædicante?*

MINISTRI SUNT DIVINITUS MISSI AD ECCLESIAM CHRISTI VARIE ADMINISTRANDAM.

DIVINITUS MISSI. Ier. xxiii. 21. *me non mittente prophetas istos, ipsos cucurrisse; me non alloquendo, prophetasse ipsos.* Matt. xxviii. 19, 20. *profecti, docete omnes gentes.* Rom. x. 15. *quomodo prædicabunt, nisi missi fuerint?* I Cor. ii. 1. *veni non cum eminentia sermonis aut sapientiæ, annuntians vobis testimonium Dei.* et v. 4. *neque sermo meus neque*

another"; yet such as cannot do this conveniently, or with full satisfaction of conscience, are not to be considered as excluded from the blessing bestowed by God on the churches. 1 Kings xix. 10, 14. "I, even I only, am left." v. 18. "yet
5 I have left me seven thousand in Israel." John iv. 23. "the hour cometh, and now is, when the true worshippers shall worship the Father in spirit and in truth; for the Father seeketh such to worship him." 1 Cor. i. 2. "unto the church of God which is at Corinth, to them that are sanctified in Christ
10 Jesus, called to be saints, with all that in every place call upon the name of Jesus Christ our Lord, both theirs and ours." 2 Cor. i. 1. "unto the church of God which is at Corinth, with all the saints which are in all Achaia."

The universal church consists of MINISTERS and PEOPLE.
15 1 Cor. iii. 9. "we are laborers together with God; ye are God's husbandry, ye are God's building." 2 Cor. iv. 5. "ourselves your servants for Jesus' sake." Matt. xx. 25–28. "even as the Son of man came not to be ministered unto, but to minister." Rom. x. 14. "how shall they hear without a preacher?"
20 MINISTERS are PERSONS APPOINTED BY DIVINE COMMISSION TO PERFORM VARIOUS OFFICES IN THE CHURCH OF CHRIST.

By DIVINE COMMISSION. Jer. xxiii. 21. "I have not sent these prophets, yet they ran; I have not spoken to them, yet they prophesied." Matt. xxviii. 19, 20. "go ye therefore, and
25 teach all nations—." Rom. x. 15. "how shall they preach, except they be sent?" 1 Cor. ii. 1. "I came not with excellency of speech or of wisdom, declaring unto you the testimony of God." v. 4. "my speech and my preaching was not with

præconium meum versatum est in persuasoriis humanæ sapi-
entiæ verbis, sed in demonstratione spirituali et potente. et
13. *quæ loquimur, non sermonibus quos docet humana sa-*
pientia, sed quos docet spiritus sanctus, spiritualibus spiri-
5 *tualia comparantes.* 1 Tim. iv. 6. *hoc si subieceris fratribus,*
bonus eris minister Iesu Christi innutritus in sermonibus fidei,
et præclaræ illius doctrinæ, quam affectatus es.

VARIE. 1 Cor. xii. 28. *alios quidem constituit Deus in eccle-*
sia, primum apostolos, deinde prophetas, tertio doctores:
10 *deinde constituit virtutes, deinde dona sanationum, opitula-*
tiones, gubernationes, genera linguarum. Act. xx. 20, 21. *ut*
nihil subterfugerim eorum quæ vobis conducerent, quominus
ea vobis annuntiarem, et docerem vos publice ac domatim:
etiam atque etiam testificans Iudæis simul et Græcis conver-
15 *sionem ad Deum, et fidem quæ est in Dominum nostrum*
Iesum Christum. 2 Tim. iv. 2. *prædica sermonem illum, insta*
tempestive, intempestive; argue, obiurga; exhortare cum omni
animi patientia et doctrina. 2 Pet. i. 12. *non negligam vos*
de istis semper commonefacere, quamvis peritos et stabilitos
20 *in præsenti veritate.*

Ministrorum opera ad gratiam conferendam per se non
valet: 1 Cor. iii. 7. *neque is qui plantat, est aliquid; neque*
qui rigat; sed Deus, qui dat crescendi vim.

Merces tamen eorum apud Deum reposita est: Isa. xlix. 4.
25 *ego vero dixi, Frustra laboro, inaniter et vane vires meas con-*
sumo: veruntamen officium meum penes Iehovam est, et

enticing words of man's wisdom, but in demonstration of the
Spirit and of power." v. 13. "which things also we speak, not
in the words which man's wisdom teacheth, but which the
Holy Ghost teacheth; comparing spiritual things with spir-
5 itual." 1 Tim. iv. 6. "if thou put the brethren in remembrance of these things, thou shalt be a good minister of Jesus
Christ, nourished up in the words of faith and of good doctrine, whereunto thou hast attained."

VARIOUS OFFICES. 1 Cor. xii. 28. "God hath set some in the
10 church, first apostles, secondarily prophets, thirdly teachers,
after that miracles, then gifts of healings, helps, governments,
diversities of tongues." Acts xx. 20, 21. "I kept back nothing
that was profitable unto you, but have showed you, and have
taught you publicly, and from house to house, testifying both
15 to the Jews, and also to the Greeks, repentance towards God,
and faith towards our Lord Jesus Christ." 2 Tim. iv. 2.
"preach the word, be instant in season, out of season, reprove, rebuke, exhort with all long-suffering and doctrine."
2 Pet. i. 12. "I will not be negligent to put you always in
20 remembrance of these things, though ye know them, and be
established in the present truth."

Ministerial labors are of no efficacy in themselves, inde-
pendently of divine grace. 1 Cor. iii. 7. "neither is he that
planteth anything, neither he that watereth, but God that
25 giveth the increase." A reward, however, is laid up for such
as are faithful in the ministry. Isa. xlix. 4. "then I said, I
have labored in vain, I have spent my strength for nought,
and in vain; yet surely my judgment is with Jehovah, and my

opus meum penes Deum meum. Dan. xii. 3. *erudientes splendebunt quasi splendore expansi, et iustificantes multos, ut stellæ, in sempiterna sæcula.*

MINISTRI ecclesiæ universalis sunt EXTRAORDINARII vel ORDI-
5 NARII: 1 Cor. xii. 28. ut supra. Eph. iv. 11, 12, 13. *is igitur dedit alios quidem apostolos, alios vero prophetas, alios autem evangelistas, alios autem pastores et doctores; ad concinnationem integram sanctorum, ad opus ministerii, ad ædificationem corporis Christi; donec deveniamus nos omnes in unitatem*
10 *fidei, in agnitionem filii Dei.* ubi notandum, *pastores* et *doctores* eosdem esse: neque enim dicit, *alios dedit pastores, alios doctores,* sed vocem priorem tropicam posteriore propria interpretatur: unde doctoratus Academici vanitas hodierna redarguitur. Nam et doctor et pastor et docet et exhortatur,
15 facultate quidem diversa, muneris eiusdem atque hominis. etsi alius alium alterutro officio præstat et nonnunquam distinguitur: Rom. xii. 7, 8.

MINISTRI EXTRAORDINARII sunt divinitus missi et inspirati ad ecclesiam et viva voce et scriptis vel instituendam vel refor-
20 mandam.

Tales fuere prophetæ, apostoli, evangelistæ, et similes: 1 Cor. iv. 1. *sic de nobis reputet homo, ut de ministris Christi,*

work with my God." Dan. xii. 3. "they that be wise shall shine as the brightness of the firmament, and they that turn many to righteousness as the stars for ever and ever."

THE MINISTERS of the universal church are either EXTRA-
5 ORDINARY or ORDINARY. 1 Cor. xii. 28. as above. Eph. iv. 11–13. "he gave some, apostles; and some, prophets; and some, evangelists; and some, pastors and teachers; for the perfecting of the saints, for the work of the ministry, for the edifying of the body of Christ; till we all come in the unity of the faith and
10 of the knowledge of the Son of God—": where it is observable that pastors and teachers are used synonymously; for the apostle does not say, "he gave some, pastors, some, teachers," but merely adds the second or proper title as an explanation of the figurative term; whereby is evinced the futility of the
15 modern academical title of doctor, as distinguishing its possessor from other ministers of the word. For the provinces of teaching and of exhortation are nowhere separated, but are both alike assigned to the pastor, no less than to the teacher so called; the functions are twofold, but the office and the
20 agent are one; although individuals may possess peculiar powers either of teaching or of exhortation, and may be distinguished as such, Rom. xii. 7, 8.

EXTRAORDINARY MINISTERS are persons inspired and sent on a special mission by God, for the purpose of planting the
25 church where it did not before exist, or of reforming its corruptions, either through the medium of preaching or of writing. To this class belong the prophets, apostles, evangelists, and the like. 1 Cor. iv. 1. "let a man so account of us as of

et dispensatoribus mysteriorum Dei. Gal. i. 1. *Paulus apostolus, non ab hominibus, neque per hominem; sed per Iesum Christum, ac Deum patrem qui suscitavit eum ex mortuis.* et v. 17. *neque redii Hierosolymam ad eos qui ante me fuerant*
5 *apostoli.* et cap. ii. 6. *ab iis qui existimantur esse aliquid, quales olim fuerint, nihil mea refert. personam hominis Deus non accipit: nam qui sunt in pretio, nihil mecum præterea contulerunt.* Act. xiii. 2. *dixit spiritus sanctus, Separate mihi Barnabam et Saulum ad opus ad quod eos advocavi.*
10 2 Tim. iv. 5. *opus perage evangelistæ.*

ORDINARII MINISTRI esse possunt quilibet fideles, donis modo instructi (quæ eorum missio est) quoties opportunum erit.

Sic ante legem fuerunt patresfamilias et primogeniti, Abelus, Noachus, Abrahamus &c. et Iethro, Exod. xviii. 12. et
15 xix. 22. *ipsi sacrorum ministri, qui ad Iehovam appropinquant, seipsos sanctificanto—.* et xxiv. 5. *misit pueros filiorum Israelis, qui obtulerunt holocausta, sacrificarunt sacrificia eucharistica Iehovæ.*

Sub lege Aaron cum posteris et tota tribus Levitica: pro-
20 phetæ denique; et Quisquis idoneus videbatur, tametsi neque sacerdos neque Levita esset, potuit in synagoga palam docere; quod et Christo permissum est in synagoga, et Paulo Act. xiii. 15. *Post lectionem Legis et Prophetarum miserunt,—dicen-*

the ministers of Christ, and stewards of the mysteries of God."
Gal. i. 1. "Paul, an apostle, not of men, neither by man, but
by Jesus Christ, and God the Father, who raised him from the
dead." v. 17. "neither went I up to Jerusalem to them which
5 were apostles before me." ii. 6. "of those who seemed to be
somewhat, whatsoever they were, it maketh no matter to me;
God accepeth no man's person: for they who seemed to be
somewhat, in conference added nothing unto me." Acts xiii.
2. "the Holy Ghost said, Separate me Barnabas and Saul for
10 the work whereunto I have called them." 2 Tim. iv. 5. "do
the work of an evangelist."

Any believer is competent to act as an ORDINARY MINISTER,
according as convenience may require, supposing him to be
endowed with the necessary gifts; these gifts constituting his
15 mission. Such were, before the law, the fathers or eldest sons
of families, as Abel, Noah, Abraham, &c. Jethro, Exod. xviii.
12. xix. 22. "let the priests also, which come near to Jehovah,
sanctify themselves—." xxiv. 5. "he sent young men of the
children of Israel, which offered burnt-offerings, and sacri-
20 ficed peace-offerings of oxen unto Jehovah." Such were,
under the law, Aaron and his posterity, the whole tribe of
Levi, and lastly the prophets. In like manner, any one appearing to be in other respects qualified, was allowed to
teach openly in the synagogue, though he were neither priest
25 nor Levite; a permission which was granted to Christ, and
subsequently to Paul at Antioch. Acts xiii. 15. "after the
reading of the law and the prophets, the rulers of the synagogue sent unto them, saying, Ye men and brethren, if ye

tes, viri fratres si quis est in vobis sermo exhortationis ad popu-
lum, dicite. quanto magis fideli cuique iisdem donis prædito
idem sub evangelio licebit? ut sane licuit, Marc. ix. 38, 39.
vidimus quendam per nomen tuum eiicientem dæmonia, qui
5 *non sequitur nos; et prohibuimus eum—. Ne prohibete.* Act.
viii. 4. *qui dispersi fuerant, peragrabant regionem, evangeli-*
zantes sermonem Dei. et xi. 19, &c. *qui dispersi fuerant ex*
afflictione orta ob Stephanum, transierunt usque in Phœni-
ciam—: qui locuti sunt Græcis, evangelizantes Dominum
10 *Iesum. Fuit autem manus Domini cum iis: multusque*
numerus, fide ipsis habita, conversus est ad Dominum—.
miserunt igitur Barnabam—. Qui cum advenisset et vidisset
gratiam Dei, gavisus est; et hortatus est omnes, ut proposito
cordis permanerent cum Domino. At noster, si diis placet,
15 clerus hodiernus, qui hanc evangelizandi provinciam sibi soli
vindicat, eam si vidisset gratiam laicis, quos vocant, imper-
titam, non gavisus, sed oblocutus potius fuisset. Et cap. xviii.
24, 25. *Iudæus quidam, Apollos nomine, Alexandrinus na-*
tione, vir eloquens, pervenit Ephesum potens in scripturis:
20 *hic erat initiatus via Domini, et fervens spiritu loquebatur et*
docebat diligenter ea quæ sunt Domini, sciens tantum bap-
tisma Ioannis. 2 Tim. ii. 2. *quæ audisti a me inter multos*
testes, hæc committe fidis hominibus, qui sunt idonei ad alios

have any word of exhortation for the people, say on." How
much more then must every believer endowed with similar
gifts enjoy the same liberty under the gospel? Accordingly,
this liberty is expressly conceded: Mark ix. 38, 39. "we saw
5 one casting out devils in thy name, and he followeth not us;
and we forbad him, because he followeth not us: but Jesus
said, Forbid him not." Acts viii. 4. "they that were scattered
abroad went everywhere preaching the word." xi. 19, &c.
"they which were scattered abroad upon the persecution that
10 arose about Stephen, travelled as far as Phenice, and Cyprus,
and Antioch . . . which spake unto the Grecians, preaching the Lord Jesus; and the hand of the Lord was with them,
and a great number believed, and turned unto the Lord . . .
they sent forth Barnabas . . . who when he came, and had
15 seen the grace of God, was glad, and exhorted them all that
with purpose of heart they would cleave unto the Lord." If
our modern clergy, as they are called by way of distinction,
who claim to themselves the exclusive right of preaching the
gospel, had seen this grace imparted to those whom they are
20 pleased to denominate the laity, it would have been to them
a subject, not of rejoicing, but of censure and obloquy. xviii.
24, 25. "a certain Jew named Apollos, born at Alexandria,
an eloquent man and mighty in the Scriptures, came to Ephesus: this man was instructed in the way of the Lord, and being
25 fervent in the spirit, he spake and taught diligently the things
of the Lord, knowing only the baptism of John." 2 Tim. ii.
2. "the things that thou hast heard of me among many witnesses, the same commit thou to faithful men, who shall be

quoque docendos. Exod. xix. 6. cum Isa. lxi. 6. *vos vero sacerdotes Iehovæ vocabimini, ministri Dei nostri dicemini.* et cum 1 Pet. ii. 9. *vos estis genus electum, regale sacerdotium, gens sancta, populus quem sibi Deus ut proprium vindicat, ut virtutes prædicetis illius qui nos vocavit e tenebris in admirabilem suam lucem.* Apoc. i. 6. *qui fecit nos reges et sacerdotes Deo et patri suo.* Rursus 1 Pet. v. 2, 3. *neque ut dominantes cleris.* hic si quid in eo est *cleri* nomine quod postea ecclesiastici sibi solis tribui voluerunt, tota ecclesia est clerus. Propheta etiam non tantum is qui futura prædicit, sed is etiam qui eximia pietate et sapientia ad docendum instructus est, nominatur: Gen. xx. 7. de Abrahamo, *propheta est; cumque oraverit pro te, vivito.* Sic Miriam prophetissa, Exod. xv. 20. et Debora, Iudic. iv. 4. et omnes fideles, Psal. cv. 15. *ne attingitote unctos meos, et prophetas meos ne afficitote malo.* Hinc simplex donum docendi, præsertim publice, *prophetia* quoque dicitur sub evangelio: 1 Cor. xiv. 1. *maxime ut prophetetis.* v. 3. *qui prophetat, hominibus loquitur ædificationem—* toto capite. 1 Cor. iii. 8, &c. *is qui plantat et is qui rigat, unum sunt: unusquisque vero suam mercedem accipiet secundum suum laborem. Etenim Dei*

able to teach others also." Exod. xix. 6. compared with Isa.
lxi. 6. "ye shall be named the priests of Jehovah; men shall
call you the ministers of our God." 1 Pet. ii. 9. "ye are a
chosen generation, a royal priesthood, an holy nation, a pecu-
5 liar people; that ye should show forth the praises of him who
hath called you out of darkness into his marvellous light."
Rev. i. 6. "who hath made us kings and priests unto God and
his Father." Again, 1 Pet. v. 3. "neither as being lords over
God's heritage." If in this passage the word "heritage,"
10 Latin *clerus,* whence the term clergy, appropriated by the
ecclesiastics to themselves, has any meaning at all, it must
designate the whole body of the church. Nor is the name of
prophet applied exclusively to such as foretell future events,
but to any one endowed with extraordinary piety and wisdom
15 for the purposes of teaching. Thus it was said of Abraham,
Gen. xx. 7. "he is a prophet, and he shall pray for thee, and
thou shalt live." So also Miriam is called a prophetess, Exod.
xv. 20. and Deborah, Judges iv. 4. and the same title is applied to believers in general, Psal. cv. 15. "touch not mine
20 anointed, and do my prophets no harm." Hence under the
gospel likewise, the simple gift of teaching, especially of
gospel teaching, is called "prophecy." 1 Cor. xiv. 1. "desire
spiritual gifts, but rather that ye may prophesy." v. 3. "he
that prophesieth, speaketh unto men to edification"; and so
25 through the remainder of the chapter. 1 Cor. iii. 8, &c. "he
that planteth and he that watereth are one; and every man
shall receive his own reward according to his own labor: for
we are laborers together with God." Pastors and teachers,

sumus administri—. Qui enim dedit apostolos, et prophetas, is etiam dedit pastores et doctores; non Academiæ. 1 Pet. iv. 10, 11. *prout quisque accepit donum, ita alter alteri illud subministrantes, ut boni dispensatores variæ Dei gratiæ: si* 5 *quis loquitur, loquatur ut eloquia Dei*—.

Quodsi fidelis quilibet, donis modo instructus, potest evangelizare, potest idem et baptizare: illud enim maius, hoc minus est: Ioan. iv. 2. *Iesus ipse non baptizabat, sed discipuli eius.* 1 Cor. i. 17. *non enim misit me Christus ut baptizarem,* 10 *sed ut evangelizarem.* Sic Ananias, discipulus duntaxat, baptizavit Paulum, Act. ix. 10, 18. Et cap. x. 48. *præcepit eos baptizari in nomen Domini.* præcepit autem iis qui una venerant; qui *fratres* duntaxat et *fideles* nominantur, v. 23, 45. Nam si, baptismus circumcisioni successit, ut vulgo vo- 15 lunt, tamque similis est, quid est, cum Iudæus quivis circumcidere potuerit, quod non Christianus quivis, modo idoneus, id est, non rudis, possit baptizare?

Cœnæ etiam Dominicæ communionem quidem esse omnium, administrationem vero nullius ordinis aut hominis 20 egregie præter cæteros propriam, superiore capite ostendimus.

therefore, are the gift of the same God who gave apostles and
prophets, and not of any human institution whatever. 1 Pet.
iv. 10, 11. "as every man hath received the gift, even so let
him minister the same one to another, as good stewards of
5 the manifold grace of God: if any man speak, let him speak
as the oracles of God."

If therefore it be competent to any believer whatever to
preach the gospel, provided he be furnished with the requisite gifts, it is also competent to him to administer the rite of
10 baptism; inasmuch as the latter office is inferior to the former.
John iv. 2. "Jesus himself baptized not, but his disciples."
1 Cor. i. 17. "Christ sent me not to baptize, but to preach the
gospel." Hence Ananias, who was only a disciple, baptized
Paul. Acts ix. 10, 18. x. 48. "he commanded them to be bap-
15 tized in the name of the Lord"; which command was given
to the companions of Peter, who are only called "brethren,"
v. 23. and "they which believed," v. 45. And if it be true that
baptism has succeeded to the place of circumcision, and bears
the analogy to it which is commonly supposed, why should
20 not any Christian whatever, provided he be not a mere novice,
and therefore otherwise incompetent, be qualified to administer baptism, in the same manner as any Jew was qualified
to perform the rite of circumcision?

With regard to the Lord's Supper also, it has been shown
25 in the preceding chapter that all are entitled to participate in
that rite, but that the privilege of dispensing the elements is
confined to no particular man, or order of men. There can be
still less shadow of reason for assigning to the ministers of

Quanto minus nuptiarum auι funerum celebratio ad ecclesiasticos ministros pertinebit; quam nullo iuris divini vestigio
ne a sacerdotibus quidem et Levitis translatitio mercenarii
vulgo sibi vindicant.

5 POPULUS universalis ecclesiæ sunt *omnes gentes.* Matt. xxviii.
19, 20. *profecti, docete omnes gentes.* Quarum conversionem
procurare quantum in se est et promovere unusquisque debet:
Rom. i. 14. *et Græcis et Barbaris tum sapientibus tum insi-
pientibus debitor sum.*

CAPUT XXX.

DE SCRIPTURA SACRA.

SCRIPTA prophetarum, apostolorum, evangelistarum,
utpote divinitus inspirata, SCRIPTURA SACRA dicitur. 2
Sam. xxiii. 2. *spiritus Iehovæ locutus est in me, et
sermo eius per linguam meam.* Matt. xxii. 43. *David per
spiritum vocat eum Dominum, dicens——.* 2 Cor. xiii. 3.
15 *quandoquidem experimentum quæritis in me loquentis
Christi.* 2 Tim. iii. 16. *omnis scriptura divinitus inspirata est.*

De libris tam veteris quam novi testamenti, qui CANONICI
vocantur, id est, qui pro veris prophetarum, apostolorum,
evangelistarum scriptis sunt, recepti, inter orthodoxos fere
20 convenit, ut in bibliis vulgo editis videre est.

the church the celebration of marriages or funerals, offices which hirelings are wont to assume to themselves exclusively, without even the feeble semblance of prescription derived from the Levitical law.

5   THE PEOPLE of the universal church comprise "all nations": Matt. xxviii. 19, 20. "go ye and teach all nations"; whose conversion it is the duty of all men to promote to the utmost of their power. Rom. i. 14. "I am debtor both to the Greeks and to the barbarians; both to the wise and to the unwise."

CHAPTER XXX.

OF THE HOLY SCRIPTURES.

THE writings of the prophets, apostles, and evangelists, composed under divine inspiration, are called THE HOLY SCRIPTURES. 2 Sam. xxiii. 2. "the Spirit of Jehovah spake by me, and his word was in my tongue." Matt. xxii. 43. "how then doth David in spirit call him Lord, saying
15 —?" 2 Cor. xiii. 3. "since ye seek a proof of Christ speaking in me." 2 Tim. iii. 16. "all scripture is given by inspiration of God."

With regard to the question, what books of the Old and New Testament are to be considered as CANONICAL, that is to
20 say, as the genuine writings of the prophets, apostles, and evangelists, there is little or no difference of opinion among the orthodox, as may be seen in the common editions of the Bible.

The books usually subjoined to these under the name of

Libri vero adiungi soliti, qui APOCRYPHI nominantur, neutiquam eandem habent cum canonicis auctoritatem, nec in probandis fidei articulis recipiuntur.

Rationes sunt: 1. quia cum sub vetere testamento sint
5 scripti, Hebraice tamen scripti non sunt, quod certe oportuit, quandoquidem ecclesia apud Hebræos adhuc solos erat, gentibus nondum vocatis, Rom. iii. 2. et ix. 4. eorum itaque lingua scripsisse ad quos res scribendæ nihildum attinebant, absurdum pene fuisset. 2. quia in novo testamento nusquam
10 citantur, non immerito eorum fides in dubium vocatur. 3. quia multa scripturæ canonicæ contraria, quædam fabulosa, demissa, frivola, et a vera sapientia ac religione aliena continent.

Scriptura sacra non ex occasione tantum, ut Pontificii do-
15 cent scripta fuit; sed ut omnibus postea ecclesiæ sæculis usui esse possit: non sub lege solum, verum etiam sub evangelio. Exod. xxxiv. 27. *scribo tibi verba hæc; quia ex præstituto horum verborum pangam tecum fœdus et cum Israele.* Deut. xxxi. 19. *scribe vobis—, ut sit mihi hoc ipsum canticum loco*
20 *testis—.* Isa. viii. 20. *legem et contestationem consulunto: annon loquuntur in sententiam illam cui nulla est lucis scintilla? et* xxx. 8. *inscribe hoc—, ut sit temporibus sequentibus in sempiternum—.* Abac. ii. 2. *scribe—, nam adhuc visio ad constitutum tempus reiecta est.* Luc. xvi. 29. *habent*
25 *Mosen et prophetas; audiant eos: si Mosen et prophetas non audient—.* Ioan. v. 39. *scrutamini scripturas, quia vos vide-*

APOCRYPHAL, are by no means of equal authority with the canonical, neither can they be adduced as evidence in matters of faith.

The reasons for their rejection are, first, because, although written under the old dispensation, they are not in the Hebrew language, which they would undoubtedly be if genuine; for as the Gentiles were not then called, and the church consisted wholly of Hebrews, Rom. iii. 2. ix. 4. it would have been preposterous to write in the language of a people who had no concern in the things discoursed of. Secondly, their authority is deservedly called in question, inasmuch as they are never quoted in the New Testament. Lastly, they contain much that is at variance with the acknowledged parts of Scripture, besides some things fabulous, low, trifling, and contrary to true religion and wisdom.

The Holy Scriptures were not written for occasional purposes only, as is the doctrine of the Papists, but for the use of the church throughout all ages, as well under the gospel as under the law. Exod. xxxiv. 27. "write thou these words; for after the tenor of these words I have made a covenant with thee and with Israel." Deut. xxxi. 19. "write ye this song for you . . . that this song may be a witness for me." Isa. viii. 20. "to the law and to the testimony; if they speak not according to this word, it is because there is no light in them." xxx. 8. "write it . . . that it may be for the time to come for ever and ever." Hab. ii. 2. "write . . . for the vision is yet for an appointed time." Luke xvi. 29. "they have Moses and the prophets; let them hear them." John v. 39. "search

mini vobis in ipsis vitam æternam habere. Rom. xv. 4. *quæ*
antea scripta sunt ad nos docendos scripta sunt, ut per tole-
rantiam et consolationem scripturarum spem retineamus. 1
Cor. x. 11. *scripta sunt ad nostri admonitionem, in quos fines*
5 *sæculorum devenerunt.*

In novo autem testamento omnia fere ex veteri probantur:
librorum etiam novi testamenti usus declaratur. Ioan. xx. 31.
hæc scripta sunt ut credatis—. Eph. ii. 20. *superstructi super*
fundamentum apostolorum ac prophetarum. Philipp. iii. 1.
10 *eadem scribere vobis me quidem haud piget, vobis autem*
tutum est. 1 Thess. v. 27. *adiuro vos per Dominum ut reci-*
tetur hæc epistola omnibus sanctis fratribus. 1 Tim. iii. 15.
sin autem tardavero, ut noris quomodo oporteat in domo Dei
versari. 2 Ep. iii. 15, 16, 17. *teque a puero sacras literas*
15 *novisse, quæ te possunt sapientem reddere ad salutem per*
fidem quæ est in Christo Iesu. Omnis scriptura divinitus in-
spirata est, et utilis ad doctrinam, ad redargutionem, ad cor-
rectionem, ad disciplinam quæ est in iustitia. ut perfectus sit
homo Dei, ad omne opus bonum instructus. Hic etsi scrip-
20 turæ quas Timotheus *a puero novisse* dicitur, quæ et ipsæ
sapientem possunt reddere per fidem in Christo, veteris testamenti fuisse duntaxat videntur, nam novi testamenti librum
nullum, Timotheo adhuc puero, videtur fuisse scriptum,
tamen sequenti versu de omni scriptura divinitus inspirata

the scriptures, for in them ye think ye have eternal life."
Rom. xv. 4. "whatsoever things were written aforetime were
written for our learning, that we through patience and comfort of the scriptures might have hope." 1 Cor. x. 11. "they
5 are written for our admonition, upon whom the ends of the
world are come."

Almost every thing advanced in the New Testament is
proved by citations from the Old. The use of the New Testament writings themselves is declared John xx. 31. "these are
10 written that ye might believe—." Eph. ii. 20. "built upon
the foundation of the apostles and prophets." Philipp. iii. 1.
"to write the same things to you, to me indeed is not grievous,
but for you it is safe." 1 Thess. v. 27. "I charge you by the
Lord, that this epistle be read unto all the holy brethren."
15 1 Tim. iii. 15. "if I tarry long, that thou mayest know how
thou oughtest to behave thyself in the house of God." 2 Tim.
iii. 15–17. "from a child thou hast known the holy scriptures,
which are able to make thee wise unto salvation through faith
which is in Christ Jesus: all scripture is given by inspiration
20 of God, and is profitable for doctrine, for reproof, for correc-
tion, for instruction in righteousness." It is true that the
Scriptures which Timothy is here said to have "known from
a child," and which were of themselves "able to make him
wise unto salvation through faith in Christ," were probably
25 those of the Old Testament alone, since no part of the New
Testament appears to have existed during the infancy of
Timothy; the same is, however, predicated of the whole of
Scripture in the succeeding verse, namely, that it is "profit-

idem dicitur; *utilem* nempe *esse ad doctrinam*—: etiam iam
doctis et sapientibus, 1 Cor. x. 15. *ut intelligentibus hoc dico,*
iudicate vos quod aio: et perfectis sive adultis, Philipp. iii. 15.
quotquot adulti sumus, hoc sentiamus; veluti Timotheo ipsi
5 et Tito, ad quos scripsit Paulus: et fortibus, 1 Ioan. ii. 14.
scripsi vobis adolescentes, quia fortes estis et verbum Dei
habitat in vobis. 2 Pet. i. 12, 15. *quapropter non negligam*
vos de istis semper commonefacere, quamvis peritos et sta-
bilitos—: *sed et studebo subinde ut vos possitis post exitum*
10 *meum facere horum mentionem.* et iii. 15, 16. *sicut et charus*
frater noster Paulus pro sibi data sapientia scripsit vobis.
Scripsit quidem Paulus Romanis, cap. i. 7, 15. scripsisse
tamen non illis solum, sed omnibus fidelibus hic ait Petrus.
2 Pet. iii. 1, 2. *hasce iam alteras vobis litteras scribo, dilecti,*
15 *quibus sinceram mentem vestram per submonitionem ex-*
pergefacio—. 1 Ioan. ii. 21. *non scripsi vobis quod veritatem*
nesciatis, sed quoniam eam scitis. Apoc. i. 19. *scribe quæ*
vidisti, et quae sunt, et quæ posthæc sunt futura.

Hæc omnia evincunt, lectione scripturæ neminem esse pro-
20 hibendum; immo potius ab omni hominum genere atque
ordine scripturas assidue vel audiri vel perlegi convenire: a
rege, Deut. xvii. 19. a magistratibus, Ios. i. 8. et a qui-

able for doctrine"; even to such as are already wise and learned, 1 Cor. x. 15. "I speak as unto wise men, judge ye what I say," to men arrived at Christian maturity, Philipp. iii. 15. "let us therefore, as many as be perfect, be thus minded,"
5 such as Timothy himself, and Titus, to whom Paul wrote; and to the strong in faith, 1 John ii. 14. "I have written unto you, young men, because ye are strong, and the word of God abideth in you." 2 Pet. i. 12, 15. "wherefore I will not be negligent to put you always in remembrance of these things,
10 though ye know them, and be established in the present truth: moreover I will endeavor that ye may be able after my decease to have these things always in remembrance." iii. 15, 16. "even as our beloved brother Paul also, according unto the wisdom given unto him, hath written unto you." For
15 although the epistle of Paul here alluded to was more immediately directed to the Romans, Rom. i. 7. 15. Peter in the above passage expressly intimates that it was addressed not to that church alone, but to believers generally. 2 Pet. iii. 1, 2. "this second epistle, beloved, I now write unto you; in both
20 which I stir up your pure minds by way of remembrance." 1 John ii. 21. "I have not written unto you, because ye know not the truth, but because ye know it." Rev. i. 19. "write the things which thou hast seen, and the things which are, and the things which shall be hereafter."
25   From all these passages it is evident, that the use of the Scriptures is prohibited to no one; but that, on the contrary, they are adapted for the daily hearing or reading of all classes and orders of men; of princes, Deut. xvii. 19. of magistrates,

busvis, Deut. xxxi. 9, 10, 11, &c. *cumque Moses scripta hac lege dedisset eam sacerdotibus filiis Levi, et omnibus senioribus Israelis præcepit iis, dicendo, legito legem hanc coram toto Israele.* et c[ap]. xi. 18, 19, 20. *reponetis hæc*
5 *verba mea in corde vestro et in animo vestro, et alligabitis ea in signum manui vestræ—: etiam inscribes ea postibus domus tuæ et portis tuis.* et xxix. 29. *hæc nobis et filiis nostris sunt revelata, ut faciamus—.* et xxx. 11. *nam hoc præceptum non est occultum a te neque longinquum.* 2
10 Chron. xxxiv. 30. *legit ipsis audientibus omnia verba libri fœderis.* Isa. viii. 20. *legem et contestationem consulunto.* Nehem. ix. 3. *Et surrexerunt in statione sua, et legerunt in libro legis* &c. cunctus nimirum populus ex ver. secundo. Et quem auctorem adversarii pro canonico habent: 1 Macab. i.
15 59, 60. *ubicunque inveniebatur apud aliquem liber fœderis.*

In novo testamento clarius: Luc. x. 26. *in lege quid scriptum est? quomodo legis?* Hæc Christus interrogavit quendam legis interpretem, quorum extitisse multos eo tempore, Pharisæos nempe et alios qui neque sacerdotes erant
20 neque Levitæ, satis constat; et Christo ipsi, qui minime ab iis habitus est doctus, ne interpretatio quidem in synagoga, non

Josh. i. 8. of men of all descriptions, Deut. xxxi. 9–11. "Moses
wrote this law, and delivered it unto the priests the sons of
Levi . . . and unto all the elders of Israel: and Moses commanded them, saying . . . Thou shalt read this law before
5 all Israel." xi. 18–20. "therefore shall ye lay up these my
words in your heart, and in your soul, and bind them for a
sign upon your hand . . . and thou shalt write them upon
the door-posts of thine house." xxix. 29. "those things which
are revealed belong unto us and to our children for ever, that
10 we may do all the words—." xxx. 11. "for this commandment which I command thee this day, it is not hidden from
thee, neither is it far off." 2 Chron. xxxiv. 30. "he read in
their ears all the words of the book of the covenant." Isa. viii.
20. "to the law and to the testimony." Neh. ix. 3. "they
15 stood up in their place, and read in the book of the law of
Jehovah"; that is, the whole people, as appears from the
second verse of the chapter. To the same purpose may be adduced the testimony of a writer whom the opponents of this
opinion regard as canonical. 1 Macc. i. 56, 57. "wheresoever
20 was found with any the book of the testament, the king's
commandment was that they should put him to death."

The New Testament is still more explicit. Luke x. 26.
"what is written in the law? how readest thou?" This was
the question of Christ to one of the interpreters of the law, of
25 whom there were many at that time, Pharisees and others,
confessedly neither priests nor Levites; neither was expound-
ing in the synagogue forbidden to Christ himself, whom we
cannot suppose to have been considered as particularly learned

ergo lectio certe scripturæ domi interdicta est. Et cap. xvi. 29. *habent Mosen et prophetas; audiant eos.* Ioan. v. 39. *scrutamini scripturas.* Act. viii. 28. *legebat Isaiam prophetam.* Et xvii. 11. *quotidie examinantes scripturas, an—.* Et xviii. 5 24. *potens in scripturis.* 2 Tim. iii. 15. *teque a puero sacras litteras novisse.* Apoc. i. 3. *beatus qui legit.*

Perspicuæ itaque sunt scripturæ, vel per se, vel Deo illuminante; in iis quæ maxime ad salutem pertinent, et ad imperitos per diligentiam lectionemque assiduam erudiendos 10 accommodatæ. Psal. xix. 8. *doctrina Iehovæ integra est, restituens animam; testimonium Iehovæ verax, sapientiam afferens imperito—.* Et cxix. 105. *lucerna pedi meo verbum tuum est, et lux itineri meo.* Et v. 130. *aditus verborum tuorum illuminat, prudentia instruit simplices.* Ex quo rursum 15 sequitur, scripturas a quibusvis esse perscrutandas. v. 18. *retege oculos meos, ut intuear mirabilia ex lege tua—.* Luc. xxiv. 45. *aperuit eorum mentem, ut intelligerent scripturas.* Act. xviii. 28. *Iudæos magis ac magis redarguebat publice, ostendens per scripturas Iesum esse Christum illum.* 2 Pet. 20 i. 20, 21. *nullam prophetiam scripturæ esse propriæ explicationis: non enim libitu hominis allata est olim prophetia—.* adeoque nec interpretanda proprio ingenio, id est, humano,

in the law; much less therefore could it have been unlawful to read the Scriptures at home. xvi. 29. "they have Moses and the prophets; let them hear them." John v. 39. "search the scriptures." Acts viii. 28. "he read Esaias the prophet." xvii.
5 11. "they searched the scriptures daily." xviii. 24. "mighty in the scriptures." 2 Tim. iii. 15. "from a child thou hast known the holy scriptures." Rev. i. 3. "blessed is he that readeth."

The Scriptures, therefore, partly by reason of their own
10 simplicity, and partly through the divine illumination, are plain and perspicuous in all things necessary to salvation, and adapted to the instruction even of the most unlearned, through the medium of diligent and constant reading. Psal. xix. 7. "the law of Jehovah is perfect, converting the soul; the testi-
15 mony of Jehovah is sure, making wise the simple." cxix. 105. "thy word is a lamp unto my feet, and a light unto my path." v. 130. "the entrance of thy words giveth light, it giveth understanding unto the simple"; whence it follows that the liberty of investigating Scripture thoroughly is granted to all.
20 v. 18. "open thou mine eyes, that I may behold wondrous things out of thy law." Luke xxiv. 45. "then opened he their understanding, that they might understand the scriptures." Acts xviii. 28. "he mightily convinced the Jews, and that publicly, showing by the scriptures that Jesus was Christ."
25 2 Pet. i. 20, 21. "no prophecy of the scripture is of any private interpretation; for the prophecy came not in the old time by the will of man"; neither therefore is it to be interpreted by the judgment of man, that is, by our own unassisted judg-

sed ope sancti spiritus, qui singulis credentibus promissus est. hinc prophetiæ donum, 1 Cor. xiv.

Quod si scripturæ per se perspicuæ sunt, atque in se integræ, ut *quæ possint sapientem reddere ad salutem per fidem, ut ex* 5 *iis perfectus sit homo Dei, et ad omne opus bonum perfecte instructus;* quid hoc insaniæ est, reformatos etiam, sanctissima religionis capita quasi in sacris libris obscurius tradita, ex metaphysicorum densissimis tenebris explanare, illustrare atque interpretari solere; adhibitis quibusdam ineptissimis 10 vocabulis ac distinctiunculis in media barbaria confictis ad scripturas scilicet, quarum ipsi summam claritatem aliis commendare non desinunt, planiores et clariores faciendas? Quasi vero, scriptura quæ summam in se lucem habet, sibique sufficit, ad fidem præsertim et sanctitatem, obscurissimis 15 hominum scientiis, falso ita dictis, extrinsecus indigeat ad lucidissimos veritatis divinæ sensus commodius ac disertius eliciendos et aliunde explicandos.

Difficiles autem et obscuræ sunt iis præsertim in rebus quæ ad salutem spectant, illis duntaxat qui pereunt: Luc. viii. 10. 20 *vobis datum est nosse mysteria regni Dei, reliquis autem per parabolas loquor, ut conspicientes non videant, et audientes non intelligant.* 1 Cor. i. 18. *sermo ille de cruce, iis quidem qui pereunt, stultitia est; iis autem qui servantur, id est, nobis, potentia Dei est.* Et ii. 14. *animalis homo non est capax eorum* 25 *quæ sunt spiritus Dei; sunt enim ei stultitia—.* Et 2 Ep. iv.

ment, but by means of that Holy Spirit promised to all believers. Hence the gift of prophecy, mentioned 1 Cor. i. 4.

If then the Scriptures be in themselves so perspicuous, and
sufficient of themselves "to make men wise unto salvation
5 through faith," that "the man of God may be perfect, thoroughly furnished unto all good works," through what infat-
uation is it, that even Protestant divines persist in darkening
the most momentous truths of religion by intricate meta-
physical comments, on the plea that such explanation is
10 necessary; stringing together all the useless technicalities and
empty distinctions of scholastic barbarism, for the purpose of
elucidating those Scriptures, which they are continually ex-
tolling as models of plainness? As if Scripture, which possesses
in itself the clearest light, and is sufficient for its own expla-
15 nation, especially in matters of faith and holiness, required
to have the simplicity of its divine truths more fully developed, and placed in a more distinct view, by illustrations
drawn from the abstrusest of human sciences, falsely so called.

It is only to those who perish that the Scriptures are obscure,
20 especially in things necessary for salvation. Luke viii. 10.
"unto you it is given to know the mysteries of the kingdom
of God, but to others in parables; that seeing they might not
see, and hearing they might not understand." 1 Cor. i. 18.
"the preaching of the cross is to them that perish foolishness;
25 but unto us which are saved, it is the power of God." ii. 14.
"the natural man receiveth not the things of the Spirit of
God, for they are foolishness unto him; neither can he know
them, because they are spiritually discerned." 2 Cor. iv. 2, 3.

2, 3. *manifestatione veritatis commendantes nos ipsos apud omnem conscientiam hominum in conspectu Dei. Quod si opertum est evangelium nostrum, iis qui pereunt opertum est.* 2 Pet. iii. 16. de epistolis Paulinis: *in quibus sunt nonnulla*
5 *difficilia intellectu, quæ indocti parumque stabiles detorquent, ut et reliquas scripturas suo ipsorum exitio.*

Sensus cuiusque scripturæ unicus est; in veteri tamen testamento sæpe est compositus ex historia et typo: exempli gratia in his Hoseæ verbis, cap. xi. 1. cum Matt. ii. 15. *ex Ægypto*
10 *vocavi filium meum.* ubi et de populo Israelitico et de Christo puero sensus duplex constare potest.

Mos in ecclesia scripturas interpretandi extat Neh. viii. 8, 9. *legebant librum illum Dei explanate; et exponendo sensum, dabant intelligentiam per scripturam ipsam: deinde*
15 *dixit Nehemia (is est legatus regis) et Ezra, sacerdos, legis peritus, ac Levitæ docentes populum—.* 2 Chron. xvii. 9, 10. *docuerunt in Iehuda, habentes secum librum legis Iehovæ; et obiverunt omnes civitates Iehudæ, docentes populum—.* Luc. iv. 17. *tunc datus est ei liber Isaiæ prophetæ—.* 1 Cor.
20 xiv. 1, &c. *ambite spiritualia; magis tamen ut prophetetis—.*

Ratio recte interpretandi scripturas utilius quidem a Theologis traditur, quam diligentius aut fidelius observatur; lin-

"by manifestation of the truth commending ourselves to every man's conscience in the sight of God: but if our gospel be hid, it is hid to them that are lost." 2 Pet. iii. 16. speaking of the epistles of St. Paul, "in which are some things hard to
5 be understood, which they that are unlearned and unstable wrest, as they do also the other scriptures, unto their own destruction."

No passage of Scripture is to be interpreted in more than one sense; in the Old Testament, however, this sense is
10 sometimes a compound of the historical and typical, as in Hosea xi. 1. compared with Matt. ii. 15. "out of Egypt have I called my son," which may be explained in a double sense, as referring partly to the people of Israel, and partly to Christ in his infancy.

15   The custom of interpreting Scripture in the church is mentioned Neh. viii. 8. 9. "they read in the book in the law of God distinctly, and gave the sense, and caused them to understand the reading: and Nehemiah, which is the Tirshatha, and Ezra the priest the scribe, and the Levites that
20 taught the people—." 2 Chron. xvii. 9. "they taught in Judah, and had the book of the law of Jehovah with them, and went about throughout all the cities of Judah, and taught the people." Luke iv. 17. "then was delivered unto him the book of the prophet Esaias." 1 Cor. xiv. 1. "desire spiritual
25 gifts, but rather that ye may prophesy."

The requisites for the public interpretation of Scripture have been laid down by divines with much attention to usefulness, although they have not been observed with equal

guarum peritia; fontium inspectio; scopi animadversio; locu-
tionis propriæ et figuratæ distinctio; causarum, circumstan-
tiarum, antecedentium, consequentium consideratio; locorum
cum aliis locis comparatio; fidei quoque analogia ubique spec-
5 tanda est; syntaxeos denique haud raro anomalia non omit-
tenda: exempli gratia ubi relativum non ad proximum ante-
cedens, sed ad principalius, quamvis remotius, referendum
est; 2 Reg. xvi. 2. cum v. 1. *natus viginti annos erat Acha,
cum ille* (id est, pater eius Iothamus) *regnare inciperet,* si
10 ætatem Ezechiæ, qua is regnum iniit, perpendas, cap. xviii. 2.
Sic 2 Chron. xxxvi. 9. *cum ille regnare inciperet,* cum 2 Reg.
xxiv. 10. Psal. xcix. 6. *Mosem, et Aharonem cum sacerdotibus ipsius.* Ioan. viii. 44. *mendax est, et pater eius.* Postremo, ex iis quæ scripta sunt, nulla consectaria, nisi neces-
15 sario plane deducta sunt admittenda; ne pro iis quæ scripta
sunt, ea quæ scripta non sunt, credere cogamur, et pro divina
doctrina humanas rationes plerumque fallaces, nubem pro
vero corpore amplectamur: iis enim quæ scripta sunt in sacris
libris, non iis quæ disputata sunt in scholis, fides obligatur.
20 Ius interpretandi scripturas, sibimet inquam interpretandi,
habet unusquisque fidelium: habet enim spiritum, veritatis
ducem; habet mentem Christi: immo alius nemo interpretari
cum fructu potest, nisi ipse quoque sibi conscientiæque suæ

fidelity. They consist in knowledge of languages; inspection of the originals; examination of the context; care in distinguishing between literal and figurative expressions; consideration of cause and circumstance, of antecedents and conse-
5 quents; mutual comparison of texts; and regard to the analogy of faith. Attention must also be paid to the frequent anomalies of syntax; as for example, where the relative does not refer to the immediate antecedent, but to the principal word in the sentence, though more remote. See 2 Kings xvi. 2.
10 compared with v. 1. "twenty years old was Ahaz when he began to reign," that is, Jotham the father of Ahaz, as appears by considering the age at which Hezekiah began his reign, xviii. 2. See also 2 Chron. xxxvi. 9. "when he began to reign," compared with 2 Kings xxiv. 8. Psal. xcix. 6. "Moses and
15 Aaron among his priests." John viii. 44. "he is a liar, and the father of it." Lastly, no inferences from the text are to be admitted, but such as follow necessarily and plainly from the words themselves; lest we should be constrained to receive what is not written for what is written, the shadow for
20 the substance, the fallacies of human reasoning for the doctrines of God: for it is by the declarations of Scripture, and not by the conclusions of the schools, that our consciences are bound.

Every believer has a right to interpret the Scriptures for
25 himself, inasmuch as he has the Spirit for his guide, and the mind of Christ is in him; nay, the expositions of the public interpreter can be of no use to him, except so far as they are confirmed by his own conscience. More will be added on this

idem interpretetur. Hac de re plura sequens caput adiiciet, ubi de populo Ecclesiæ particularis agetur. Aliis interpretandi publice ius habet is quemcunque Deus constituit vel apostolum, vel prophetam, vel evangelistam, vel pastorem, vel doc
5 torem, 1 Cor. xii. 8, 9. Eph. iv. 11, 12, 13. id est, dono docendi quicunque est præditus; *omnis scriba, cœlorum ad regnum instructus,* Matt. xiii. 52. Non quem solum homines aut academiæ constituerunt, et cathedra donarunt; de quibus illud vere dici haud raro queat, Luc. xi. 52, *væ vobis legis*
10 *interpretibus; quoniam sustulistis clavem cognitionis: ipsi non introistis; et eos qui introibant, prohibuistis.*

Nullum itaque ius habet vel ecclesia ulla visibilis, nedum magistratus, interpretamenta sua conscientiis hominum pro legibus, id est, fidem implicitam imponere.

15 Quod si inter eos qui fideles videntur esse, de scripturæ sensu non convenit, tolerare alii alios debebunt, donec Deus, quod verum sit, omnibus revelaverit: Philipp. iii. 15, 16. *quotquot itaque adulti sumus, hoc sentiamus: quod siquid aliter sentitis, hoc quoque vobis Deus revelabit. attamen in*
20 *eo ad quod usque pervenimus, eadem incedamus regula, et idem sentiamus.* Sic Rom. xiv. 4. *proprio domino perstat, aut cadit: stabilietur autem.*

Regula itaque fidei et canon, scriptura sola est; Psal. xix. 10. *iudicia Iehovæ sunt ipsa veritas;* controversiarum etiam

subject in the next chapter, which treats of the members of
particular churches. The right of public interpretation for the
benefit of others is possessed by all whom God has appointed
apostles, or prophets, or evangelists, or pastors, or teachers,
5 1 Cor. xii. 8, 9. Eph. iv. 11–13. that is, by all who are
endowed with the gift of teaching, "every scribe which is
instructed unto the kingdom of heaven," Matt. xiii. 52. not
by those whose sole commission is derived from human authority, or academical appointment; of whom it may too
10 often be said in the words of Scripture, "woe unto you, law-
yers, for ye have taken away the key of knowledge; ye enter
not yourselves, and them that were entering in ye hindered,"
Luke xi. 52.

It is not therefore within the province of any visible church,
15 much less of the civil magistrate, to impose their own inter-
pretations on us as laws, or as binding on the conscience; in
other words, as matter of implicit faith.

If however there be any difference among professed believers as to the sense of Scripture, it is their duty to tolerate
20 such difference in each other, until God shall have revealed
the truth to all. Philipp. iii. 15, 16. "let us therefore, as many
as be perfect, be thus minded; and if in anything ye be otherwise minded, God shall reveal even this unto you: nevertheless, whereto we have already attained, let us walk by the
25 same rule, let us mind the same thing." Rom. xiv. 4. "to his
own master he standeth or falleth: yea, he shall be holden up."

The rule and canon of faith, therefore, is Scripture alone.
Psal. xix. 9. "the judgments of Jehovah are true and right-

iudex nisi ea, nemo; aut saltem ex ea sibimet quisque cum spiritu Dei. Nam qui illis Pauli verbis, 1 Tim. iii. 15. *ecclesia Dei viventis, columna et stabilimentum veritatis,* abutuntur ad asserendam visibili ecclesiæ, quoquo modo intellectæ, sum-
5 mam illam interpretandi et iudicandi auctoritatem; hoc toto et superiore versu simul inspecto, aberrare longissime a veritate comperiuntur. Scripsit hæc Paulus Timotheo, quæ illi pro sacra scriptura essent; *ut sciret,* ex ea scilicet, *quomodo oporteat in domo Dei versari, quæ est ecclesia.* id est conventus
10 quilibet fidelium. domus ergo Dei, sive ecclesia, regula non erat unde sciret, sed illa sacra scriptura, quam a Paulo acceperat. Et est quidem ecclesia, vel saltem esse debet (neque enim semper est) *columna et stabilimentum,* id est custos, et sedes, et confirmatrix *veritatis:* verum ut hæc omnia sit,
15 regulam tamen aut iudicem hinc esse veritatis et scripturæ, non sequitur: siquidem domus Dei non regula sui est, sed regulam a verbo Dei accipit; debetque saltem firmissime retinere. Quid quod scripta prophetarum et apostolorum, quæ sunt ipsæ scripturæ, fundamenta sunt ecclesiæ. Eph. ii. 20.
20 *superstructi* &c. Ecclesia autem superstructa non est regula aut iudex sui fundamenti.

eous altogether." Scripture is the sole judge of controversies; or rather, every man is to decide for himself through its aid, under the guidance of the Spirit of God. For they who, on the authority of 1 Tim. iii. 15. "the church of the living God,
5 the pillar and ground of the truth," claim for the visible church, however defined, the supreme right of interpreting Scripture and determining religious controversies, are confuted by a comparison of the words in question with the former part of the verse, and with the preceding verses. What
10 St. Paul here writes to Timothy, and which is intended to have the force of Scripture with him, is a direction by which he may know "how he ought to behave himself in the house of God, which is the church"; that is, in any assembly of believers. It was not therefore "the house of God," or "the church,"
15 which was to be a rule to him "that he might know," but the Scripture which he had received from the hands of Paul. The church indeed is, or rather ought to be, for it is not always such in fact, the "pillar and ground," that is, the guardian, and repository, and support "of the truth"; even where it is
20 all this, however, it is not on that account to be considered as the rule or arbiter of truth and the Scripture; inasmuch as the house of God is not a rule to itself, but receives its rule from the word of God, which it is bound, at least, to observe scrupulously. Besides, the writings of the prophets and apostles,
25 in other words the Scriptures themselves, are said to be the foundation of the church: Eph. ii. 20. "built upon the foundation of the apostles and prophets, Jesus Christ himself being the chief corner-stone." Now the church cannot be the rule or arbiter of that on which it is itself founded.

Non tamen scripta esse omnia quæ apostoli ecclesiis tradiderunt, aut, scripta si fuerunt, ad nos pervenisse, videtur ex 2 Ep. Ioan. 12. *cul multa haberem vobis scribenda, nolui per chartam et atramentum.* 3 Ep. 13. idem. Col. iv. 16. *scrip-*
5 *tam Laodicæa, vos quoque legatis.*

Ergo hæc cum ad salutem non necessaria, sed utilia tantum existimanda sint, vel ex aliis scripturæ locis. vel, si hoc incertum est utrum fieri possit, non ex pontificum decretis, aut conciliorum, multo minus ex magistratuum edictis, sed ex eodem
10 spiritu, in nobismetipsis per fidem et charitatem agente, petenda sunt: Ioan. xvi. 12, 13. *adhuc multa habeo quæ vobis dicam; sed nunc non potestis portare: cum autem venerit ille, spiritus veritatis, dux viæ vobis erit in omnem veritatem.* Sic etiam Petrus ipse monet, *sermoni prophetico attendendum*
15 *esse, usquedum dies illuxerit, et lucifer exoriatur in cordibus nostris,* 2 Ep. i. 19. id est, lux evangelii, non in charta magis, quam in corde quærenda: 2 Cor. iii. 3. *vos esse epistolam Christi subministratam a nobis; inscriptam non atramento, sed spiritu Dei vivi; non in tabulis lapideis, sed in carneis*
20 *tabulis cordis.* Eph. vi. 17. *machæram spiritus, qui est verbum Dei.* 1 Ioan. ii. 20. *at vos unctionem habetis a sancto illo profectam, et nostis omnia.* et v. 27. *nec necesse habetis ut quisquam doceat vos: verum sicut eadem unctio docet vos*

That some of the instructions of the apostles to the churches were not committed to writing, or that, if written, they have not come down to us, seems probable from 2 John 12. "having many things to write unto you, I would not write with
5 paper and ink." See also 3 John 13. Col. iv. 16. "that ye likewise read the epistle from Laodicea." Seeing then that the lost particulars cannot be supposed to have contained anything necessary to salvation, but only matters profitable for doctrine, they are either to be collected from other passages
10 of Scripture, or, if it be doubtful whether this is possible, they are to be supplied, not by the decrees of popes or councils, much less by the edicts of magistrates, but by the same Spirit which originally dictated them, enlightening us inwardly through the medium of faith and love. John xvi. 12, 13. "I
15 have yet many things to say unto you, but ye cannot bear them now; howbeit when he, the Spirit of truth, is come, he shall guide you into all truth." So also St. Peter admonishes us, 2 Ep. i. 19. "to take heed to the sure word of prophecy, until the day dawn, and the day-star arise in our hearts," that is
20 to say, the light of the gospel, which is not to be sought in written records alone, but in the heart. 2 Cor. iii. 3. "ye are manifestly declared to be the epistle of Christ ministered by us, written not with ink, but with the Spirit of the living God; not in tables of stone, but in fleshy tables of the heart." Eph.
25 vi. 17. "the sword of the Spirit, which is the word of God."
1 John ii. 20. "ye have an unction from the Holy One, and ye know all things." v. 27. "ye need not that any man teach you; but as the same anointing teacheth you of all things, and

de omnibus, et verax est, et non mendax, et sicut docuit vos,
manebitis in eo. Sic Paulus quærentibus ex se Corinthiis certis
de rebus in quibus scriptura nihil præscripserat, ex Christiano
sensu et unctione illa spiritus, quam acceperat, respondet:

5　1 Cor. vii. 12. *ego dico, non Dominus.* et v. 25, 26. *de vir-*
ginibus imperium Domini non habeo; sententiam vero meam
dico, ut cui Dominus per misericordiam dederit fidum esse.
Existimo igitur—. v. 40. *beatior est si ita maneat secundum*
meam sententiam: videor autem mihi et ego spiritum Dei

10　*habere:* unde et illos in eiusmodi quæstionibus posse etiam
sibimetipsis respondere monet, v. 15. *non est servituti sub-*
iectus frater aut soror in causis huiusmodi. et 36. *cæterum*
siquis sese existimat aliquid indecorum in virginem suam com-
mittere, si florem ætatis excedat, et ita debet fieri, quod vult

15　*faciat, non peccat.*

　　Duplicem enim habemus sub evangelio maxime scripturam; externam verbi scripti, et internam sancti spiritus, quam
is ex promissione Dei in cordibus credentium minime negli-
gendam exaravit; ut supra cap. xxvii. de Evangelio. Isa. lix.

20　21. *de me autem, hoc erit fœdus meum cum istis, ait Iehova;*
spiritus meus qui est in te, et verba mea quæ posui in ore tuo,
non recedent ex ore tuo, aut ex ore seminis tui, aut ex ore
seminis seminis tui, ait Iehova, ex hoc tempore usque in sæcu-

is truth, and is no lie, and even as it hath taught you, ye shall abide in him." Thus when the Corinthians had made inquiry of St. Paul on certain subjects with regard to which there was no specific direction in Scripture, he answers them according to the natural dictates of Christianity, and the unction of the Spirit which he had received: 1 Cor. vii. 12. "to the rest speak I, not the Lord." v. 25. "concerning virgins, I have no commandment of the Lord; yet I give my judgment as one that hath obtained mercy of the Lord to be faithful: I suppose therefore—." v. 40. "she is happier if she so abide after my judgment; and I think also that I have the Spirit of God"; whence he reminds them that they are also able to give answer to themselves in such questions, v. 15. "a brother or sister is not under bondage in such cases." v. 36. "if any man think that he behaveth himself uncomely toward his virgin, if she pass the flower of her age, and need so require, let him do what he will, he sinneth not."

Under the gospel we possess, as it were, a twofold Scripture; one external, which is the written word, and the other internal, which is the Holy Spirit, written in the hearts of believers, according to the promise of God, and with the intent that it should by no means be neglected; as was shown above, chap. xxvii. on the gospel. Isa. lix. 21. "as for me, this is my covenant with them, saith Jehovah; my Spirit which is upon thee, and my words which I have put in thy mouth, shall not depart out of thy mouth, nor out of the mouth of thy seed, nor out of the mouth of thy seed's seed, saith Jehovah, from henceforth and for ever." See also Jer.

lum. Ier. xxxi. 33, 34. Act. v. 32. *nos sumus ei testes horum quæ dicimus, atque etiam spiritus ille sanctus quem dedit Deus obedientibus ipsi.* 1 Cor. ii. 12. *nos non spiritum mundi accepimus, sed spiritum qui est ex Deo, ut sciamus quæ Deus*
5 *est nobis gratificatus.*

Itaque auctoritas fidei externa est in scripturis quidem hodie maxima, et fere prior tempore; interna vero cuique, adeoque summa atque suprema, est ipse spiritus.

Scriptura enim externa, præsertim novi testamenti, ut de
10 supposititiis nihil dicam, a quibus iam tum cavendum esse monuit ipse Paulus, 2 Thess. ii. 2. *per epistolam tanquam a nobis scriptam,* et iii. 17. *quod est signum—;* scriptura inquam novi testamenti, cum sub custodibus variis male fidendis, ex manuscriptis proinde variis et discrepantibus, varie
15 quoque descripta et excusa demum sit; sæpe corrumpi potuit, et corrupta est: at spiritum veritatis ducem nemo potest corrumpere, aut hominem spiritualem facile decipere; 1 Cor. ii. 15, 16. *spiritualis diiudicat quidem omnia, ipse vero a nemine diiudicatur. Quis enim novit mentem Domini, qui*
20 *instructurus sit eum? nos autem mentem Christi habemus.* et xii. 10. *alii vero discretio spirituum.* Textus corrupti etiam

xxxi. 33, 34. Acts v. 32. "we are his witnesses of those things, and so is also the Holy Ghost, whom God hath given to them that obey him." 1 Cor. ii. 12. "we have received, not the spirit of the world, but the Spirit which is of God, that we might
5 know the things that are freely given to us of God."

Hence, although the external ground which we possess for our belief at the present day in the written word is highly important, and, in most instances at least, prior in point of reception, that which is internal, and the peculiar possession
10 of each believer, is far superior to all, namely, the Spirit itself.

For the external Scripture, or written word, particularly of the New Testament, to say nothing of spurious books, with regard to which the apostle has long since cautioned us, 2 Thess. ii. 2. "that ye be not shaken in mind . . . by letter
15 as from us—"; iii. 17. "the salutation of Paul with mine own hand, which is the token in every epistle—": the written word, I say, of the New Testament, has been liable to frequent corruption, and in some instances has been corrupted, through the number, and occasionally the bad faith of those
20 by whom it has been handed down, the variety and discrepancy of the original manuscripts, and the additional diversity produced by subsequent transcripts and printed editions. But the Spirit which leads to truth cannot be corrupted, neither is it easy to deceive a man who is really spiritual: 1 Cor. ii.
25 15, 16. "he that is spiritual judgeth all things, yet he himself is judged of no man: for who hath known the mind of the Lord, that he may instruct him? but we have the mind of Christ." xii. 10. "to another, discerning of spirits." An

in omnibus fere codicibus exempla sunt: Matt. xxvii. 9. ubi
ex Ieremia citatur quod in solo Zacharia reperitur; aliaque
loca innumera, quæ singulis fere paginis apud editores novi
testamenti Erasmum, Bezam aliosque occurrunt.

5   Fuit quidem legis Mosaicæ sacrosancta olim custos arca
fœderis, et post Babylonicam statim captivitatem fideiussores
atque custodes sacerdotes, prophetæ aliique divinitus edocti
Ezra, Zacharia, Malachias, alii; qui sacros libros Dei sacrario
et sacerdotibus posteris incorruptos procul dubio tradiderunt;
10 quibus per omnes ætates et summa religio erat ne quid mu-
taretur, et nulla suspicio quamobrem id facerent. reliqui
etiam libri præsertim historici quamvis quo auctore quove
tempore sint scripti in dubio sit, quamvis in historia ratio
temporum claudicare sæpe videatur, eorum tamen doctrinæ
15 partem ullam vel nemo vel pauci admodum in dubium vocarunt. Novi autem testamenti multa per sæcula varii, ut ante
diximus, varieque corrupti custodes fuere; autographum exemplar præ cæteris nullum quod pro germano asserere pos-
simus. Itaque ex variis codicibus manuscriptis viri docti quod
20 sibi germanissimum est visum ediderunt Erasmus, Beza, et
alii. Quod nescio sane cur factum providentia Dei sit, ut novi

instance of a corrupted text pervading nearly all the manuscripts occurs in Matt. xxvii. 9. where a quotation is attributed to Jeremiah, which belongs only to Zechariah; and similar instances are to be found in almost every page of Erasmus,
5 Beza, and other editors of the New Testament.

Previously to the Babylonish captivity, the law of Moses was preserved in the sacred repository of the ark of the covenant; after that event, it was committed to the trust and guardianship of the priests and prophets, as Ezra, Zechariah,
10 Malachi, and other men taught of God. There can be no doubt that these handed down the sacred volumes in an uncorrupted state to be preserved in the temple by the priests their successors, who were in all ages most scrupulous in preventing alterations, and who had themselves no grounds of
15 suspicion to induce them to make any change. With regard to the remaining books, particularly the historical, although it be uncertain by whom and at what time they were written, and although they appear sometimes to contradict themselves on points of chronology, few or none have ever questioned the
20 integrity of their doctrinal parts. The New Testament, on the contrary, has come down to us as before observed through the hands of a multitude of persons, subject to various temptations; nor have we in any instance the original copy in the author's hand-writing, by which to correct the errors of the
25 others. Hence Erasmus, Beza, and other learned men, have edited from the different manuscripts what in their judgment appeared most likely to be the authentic readings. It is difficult to conjecture the purpose of Providence in committing

testamenti scriptura custodibus tam incertis tamque lubricis commissa fuerit, nisi ut hoc ipsum argumento esset, certiorem nobis propositum ducem spiritum quam scripturam, quem sequi debeamus.

5   Hoc enim constat etiam, ecclesiam visibilem non semper ab ascensu Christi *columnam* aut *stabilimentum veritatis* extitisse, sed corda fidelium; quæ proprie sunt *domus et ecclesia Dei vivi,* 1 Tim. iii. 15.

Editores certe video et interpretes novi testamenti Græci, 10 cuius prima auctoritas est, non ecclesiæ visibilis, sed manuscriptorum fide ac numero omnia fere ponderare: quorum fides codicum si variat aut vacillat, ipsos quoque editores ambigere necesse est, nec habere quid pro certissimo Dei verbo textuque incorrupto sequantur aut statuant; ut in historia 15 adulteræ, aliisque nonnullis locis.

Utcunque scripturis generatim et universim quidem creditur, primo propter auctoritatem sive ecclesiæ visibilis sive codicum manuscriptorum; postea vero ecclesiæ ipsisque codicibus eorumque singulis partibus propter auctoritatem totius 20 scripturæ secum collatæ; toti denique scripturæ propter ipsum spiritum unicuique fidelium intus persuadentem: quemadmodum et Christo creditum est a Samaritanis primo propter

the writings of the New Testament to such uncertain and variable guardianship, unless it were to teach us by this very circumstance that the Spirit which is given to us is a more certain guide than Scripture, whom therefore it is our duty
5 to follow.

For with regard to the visible church, which is also proposed as a criterion of faith, it is evident that, since the ascension of Christ, the "pillar and ground of the truth" has not uniformly been the church, but the hearts of believers, which
10 are properly "the house and church of the living God," 1 Tim. iii. 15. Certain it is, that the editors and interpreters of the New Testament, which is the chief authority for our faith, are accustomed to judge of the integrity of the text, not by its agreement with the visible church, but by the number and
15 integrity of the manuscripts. Hence, where the manuscripts differ, the editors must necessarily be at a loss what to consider as the genuine word of God; as in the story of the woman taken in adultery, and some other passages.

The process of our belief in the Scriptures is, however, as
20 follows: we set out with a general belief in their authenticity, founded on the testimony either of the visible church, or of the existing manuscripts; afterwards, by an inverse process, the authority of the church itself, and of the different books as contained in the manuscripts, is confirmed by the internal
25 evidence implied in the uniform tenor of Scripture, considered as a whole; and, lastly, the truth of the entire volume is established by the inward persuasion of the Spirit working in the hearts of individual believers. So the belief of the Samaritans

verba mulieris; deinde non tam propter mulieris quam propter ipsius Christi verba coram loquentis, Ioan. iv. 42. Sic omnia demum ad spiritum atque verbum non scriptum, scriptura ipsa teste referenda sunt.

5   Qui igitur fidelibus, quorum unusquisque Dei spiritu regitur, sanctiones quascunque suas et dogmata sive ecclesiæ, sive Christiani magistratus nomine invitis imposuerit, is non hominibus tantum, verum etiam ipso sancto spiritui iugum imponit. Quod si ipsi apostoli, concilio etiam convocato cui 10 spiritus ipse sanctus præsidebat, divinam ipsam legem velut iugum non ferendum fidelibus imponere noluerunt, Act. xv. 10, 19, 28. *quid tentatis Deum—,* multo minus poterit ecclesia ulla hodierna quæ præsentiam spiritus certissimam arrogare sibi non potest, minimeque omnium magistratus ea vel 15 credenda solum fidelibus imperare quæ in scriptura vel non reperiuntur, vel humanis duntaxat rationibus, quæ fidem non faciunt, exprimuntur.

  Humanæ autem traditiones sive scriptæ sive non scriptæ palam prohibentur. Deut. iv. 2. *Ne addite ad verbum illud* 20 *quod ego præcipio vobis, neque detrahite de eo,* &c. Prov. xxx. 6. *Ne adiicito ad verba eius, ut non corripiat te, et efficiaris mendax.* Apoc. xxii. 18, 19. *Si quis adiecerit ad hæc,*

in Christ, though founded in the first instance on the word of the woman, derived its permanent establishment, less from her saying, than from the presence and discourses of Christ himself, John iv. 42. Thus, even on the authority of Scrip-
5 ture itself, every thing is to be finally referred to the Spirit and the unwritten word.

Hence it follows, that when an acquiescence in human opinions or an obedience to human authority in matters of religion is exacted, in the name either of the church or of the
10 Christian magistrate, from those who are themselves led individually by the Spirit of God, this is in effect to impose a yoke, not on man, but on the Holy Spirit itself. Certainly, if the apostles themselves, in a council governed by the inspiration of the Holy Spirit, determined that even the divinely
15 instituted law was a yoke from which believers ought to be exempt, Acts xv. 10, 19, 28. "why tempt ye God?" much less is any modern church, which cannot allege a similar claim to the presence of the Spirit, and least of all is the magistrate entitled to impose on believers a creed nowhere found in Scrip-
20 ture, or which is merely inferred from thence by human reasons carrying with them no certain conviction.

We are expressly forbidden to pay any regard to human traditions, whether written or unwritten. Deut. iv. 2. "ye shall not add unto the word which I command you, neither
25 shall ye diminish ought from it." Prov. xxx. 6. "add thou not unto his words, lest he reprove thee, and thou be found a liar." Rev. xxii. 18, 19. "if any man shall add unto these things," &c. . . . "and if any man shall take away from

&c. *et siquis abstulerit aliquid ex verbis:* &c. Isa. xxix. 13, 14. *estque reverentia eorum erga me, quam præcepto hominum edocti sunt.* Matt. xv. 3, 9. Gal. i. 8. *etiam si nos aut angelus e cœlo—:* 1 Tim. vi. 3, &c. *siquis diversam docet*
5 *doctrinam, neque accedit sanis sermonibus Domini nostri Iesu Christi, et ei quæ secundum pietatem est doctrinæ, is inflatus est nihil sciens, sed insaniens circa quæstiones ac pugnas de verbis—.* Tit. i. 14. *non attenti Iudaicis fabulis et præceptis hominum aversantium veritatem.* 1 Tim. i. 4. *ne*
10 *attendat fabulis et genealogiis nunquam finiendis, quæ potius quæstiones præbent quam ædificationem Dei quæ est per fidem.* Col. ii. 8. *Videte ne quis sit qui vos deprædetur per Philosophiam et inanem seductionem. secundum traditionem hominum, secundum elementa mundi, et non secundum*
15 *Christum.*

Neque hoc in genere fidendum maioribus aut antiquitati omnino est. 2 Chron. xxix. 6, &c. *nam prævaricati sunt patres nostri—.* Psal. lxxviii. 8, &c. *ac non sint ut maiores eorum—.* Ezech. xx. 18. *in statutis patrum vestrorum ne ambuletis—.*
20 Amos. ii. 1. *eo quod spernunt legem Iehovæ et statuta eius non observant, seducuntque ipsos mendacia ipsorum, quæ secuti sunt maiores ipsorum.* Mal. iii. 7. *inde a diebus maiorum vestrorum recessistis a statutis meis—.* Eccles. vii. 10. *ne dixeris quid est cur dies priores fuerint meliores istis? nam*
25 *non ex sapientia rogares super hoc.* Et Ieremia quidem hortatur, ut *inquirant in vias antiquas,* sed tamen ut *quæ via bona*

the words," &c. Isa. xxix. 13, 14. "their fear toward me is
taught by the precept of men." See also Matt. xv. 3, 9. Gal.
i. 8. "though we, or an angel from heaven, preach any other
gospel unto you—." 1 Tim. vi. 3. "if any man teach other-
5 wise, and consent not to wholesome words, even the words
of our Lord Jesus Christ, and to the doctrine which is according to godliness, he is proud, knowing nothing, but doting
about questions and strifes of words." Tit. i. 4. "not giving
heed to Jewish fables and commandments of men, that turn
10 from the truth." 1 Tim. i. 4. "neither give heed to fables and
endless genealogies, which minister questions, rather than
godly edifying which is in faith." Col. ii. 8. "beware lest any
man spoil you through philosophy and vain deceit, after the
tradition of men, after the rudiments of the world, and not
15 after Christ."

Neither can we trust implicitly in matters of this nature to
the opinions of our forefathers, or of antiquity. 2 Chron.
xxix. 6. "our fathers have trespassed." Psal. lxxviii. 8, &c.
"that they might not be as their fathers." Ezek. xx. 18. "walk
20 ye not in the statutes of your fathers." Amos ii. 4. "because
they have despised the law of Jehovah, and have not kept his
commandments, and their lies caused them to err, after the
which their fathers have walked." Mal. iii. 7. "even from
the days of your fathers ye are gone away from mine ordi-
25 nances." Eccles. vii. 10. "say not thou, What is the cause that
the former days were better than these? for thou dost not
inquire wisely respecting this." Jeremiah also admonishes the
people "to ask for the old paths," in order to see "where is

sit, eam duntaxat eligant, cap. vi. 16. alioqui idololatricum plane argumentum hoc est et Pharisaicum et Samaritanum; Ier. xliv. 17, &c. *adolendo rebus cœlestibus, et libando iis libamina quemadmodum fecimus nos, reges nostri ac prin-*
5 *cipes nostri—.* Matt. xv. 2, &c. *quare discipuli tui transgrediuntur traditionem seniorum?* cui opponit Christus mandatum Dei, v. 3. *quare et vos transgredimini mandatum Dei per traditionem vestram—?* et Marc. vii. 8, 9, idem. Ioan. iv. 20. *patres nostri in hoc monte adoraverunt—.*

10 Immo ne matris quidem ecclesiæ venerando nomini attribuere nimium debemus. Hos. ii. 2. *contendite cum matre vestra, contendite, ipsam non esse uxorem meam, et me non esse virum ipsius; ut amoveat scortationes suas:* nisi mysticam duntaxat Ecclesiam intelligimus et cœlestem, Gal. iv. 26. *illa*
15 *vero quæ sursum est Hierusalem libera est, quæ est mater omnium nostrum.*

CAPUT XXXI.

DE ECCLESIIS PARTICULARIBUS.

DE UNIVERSALI VISIBILI ECCLESIA hactenus. PARTICULARIS ECCLESIA est societas fidem profitentium fraterno inter se vinculo speciali coniunctorum ad
20 ædificationem et communionem sanctorum inter se habendam potissimum accommodata. Act. ii. 42. *perdurabant in doc-*

the good way," and to choose that alone, vi. 16. for in any other sense the argument may be as justly employed to defend the idolatries of the heathen, and the errors of the Pharisees and Samaritans. Jer. xliv. 17. "to burn incense unto the
5   queen of heaven, and to pour out drink-offerings unto her, as we have done, we, and our fathers, our kings, and our princes——." Matt. xv. 2, &c. "why do thy disciples transgress the tradition of the elders?" where Christ opposes to their tradition the commandment of God, v. 3. "why do ye also
10   transgress the commandment of God by your tradition?" See also Mark vii. 8, 9. John iv. 20. "our fathers worshipped in this mountain."

Even to the venerable name of our mother church itself we are not to attach any undue authority. Hos. ii. 2. "plead with
15   your mother, plead; for she is not my wife, neither am I her husband; let her therefore put away her whoredoms out of her sight": unless by this expression we understand exclusively the mystical church in heaven; Gal. iv. 26. "Jerusalem which is above is free, which is the mother of us all."

CHAPTER XXXI.

OF PARTICULAR CHURCHES.

THUS far of the UNIVERSAL VISIBLE CHURCH. A PARTICULAR CHURCH is a society of persons professing the faith, united by a special bond of brotherhood, and so ordered as may best promote the ends of edification and mutual communion of the saints. Acts ii. 42. "they continued

*trina apostolorum, et communicatione, et fractione panis et
precationibus.*

Ecclesiæ particularis ministri ordinarii sunt PRESBYTERI et
DIACONI.

5 PRESBYTERI alio nomine EPISCOPI vocantur. Act. xx. 17. *accer-
sivit presbyteros ecclesiæ,* cum v. 28. *attendite igitur animum
ad vos ipsos et totum gregem in quo vos spiritus sanctus constituit episcopos ad pascendam ecclesiam Dei.* 1 Tim. iii. 1,
&c. idem episcopi et presbyteri munus describitur, nullius
10 præterea ministri nisi diaconi facta mentione. Sic Philipp. i. 1.
una cum episcopis et diaconis. et Tit. i. 5. *ut constituas oppi-
datim presbyteros, sicut ego tibi ordinavi,* cum v. 7. *oportet
episcopum inculpabilem esse.* et 1 Pet. v. 1. *presbyteros qui
inter vos sunt precor—pascite Dei gregem qui penes vos est,*
15 *illius inspectioni operam dantes;* sive *episcopantes.* In illo
denique primo concilio Hierosolymis apostolorum duntaxat
et presbyterorum fit mentio: episcoporum nulla, Act. xv. 6.
et xvi. 4. iidem igitur fuerint episcopi et presbyteri oportet.

Presbyterorum alii doctrinæ vacabant, alii disciplinæ præ-
20 erant, nonnulli utroque munere fungebantur. 1 Tim. iii. 2.
aptum ad docendum. et v. 5. *nam siquis—, quomodo ecclesiam Dei curabit?* et cap. v. 17. *qui bene præsunt presbyteri
duplici honore digni habentor; maxime qui laborant in ser-*

stedfastly in the apostles' doctrine and fellowship, and in breaking of bread, and in prayers."

The ordinary ministers of a particular church are PRESBYTERS and DEACONS.

5   PRESBYTERS are otherwise called BISHOPS. Acts xx. 17. compared with v. 28. "he called the elders of the church: take heed therefore unto yourselves and to all the flock, over the which the Holy Ghost hath made you overseers, to feed the church of God." The same office of bishop or presbyter is

10   described 1 Tim. iii. 1, &c. where no mention is made of any other minister except deacon. Philipp. i. 1. "with the bishops and deacons." Tit. i. 5. "that thou shouldest ordain elders in every city, as I had appointed thee," compared with v. 7. "a bishop must be blameless." 1 Pet. v. 1. "the elders which are

15   among you I exhort . . . feed the flock of God which is among you, taking the oversight thereof," that is, performing the office of bishops. Lastly, in the first council of the church, held at Jerusalem, the apostles and elders alone are spoken of as present, no mention being made of bishops, Acts

20   xv. 6. xvi. 4. Bishops and presbyters must therefore have been the same.

Of the presbyters, some were set apart for the office of teaching, others watched over the discipline of the church, while in particular instances both these functions were united. 1 Tim.

25   iii. 2. "apt to teach." v. 5. "if a man know not how to rule his own house, how shall he take care of the church of God?" v. 17. "let the elders that rule well be counted worthy of double honor, especially they who labor in the word and doc-

mone et doctrina. Rom. xii. 7, 8. *is qui docet in docendo, qui præest cum diligentia.* I Cor. xii. 28. *gubernationes.* I Pet. v. 1. ut supra. Hinc episcopus sîve presbyter *œconomus Dei* vocatur, Tit. i. 7.

5 DIACONI est proprie ministrare cum toti ecclesiæ, tum præsertim pauperibus, ægris, hospitibus. Act. vi. 3. *deligite— quos huic usui præficiamus.* I Tim. iii. 10. *deinde ministrent, si sint inculpati.* et v. 13. *qui bene ministraverint.* Etiam docere ac baptizare: exemplo Philippi diaconi, qui, manente

10 Hierosolymis Philippo apostolo, et Samaritanos ad fidem convertit, et primum conversos, deinde eunuchum Æthiopem auctoritate propria baptizavit, Act. vi. 5. et viii. 1. et v. 12. *quum credidissent Philippo evangelizanti quæ ad regnum Dei et nomen Iesu Christi pertinent, baptizabantur tum viri*

15 *tum mulieres.* et v. 38. *ille baptizavit eum.* Unde, ex docendi nempe munere *evangelista* vocatur Philippus *ex septem illis,* Act. xxi. 8. Itaque, I Tim. iii. 13. *qui bene ministraverint, gradum sibi bonum acquirunt et multam loquendi libertatem per fidem quæ est in Christo Iesu.*

20 Diaconis viduæ annumerantur. I Tim. v. 3, &c. *viduas honora, quæ vere viduæ sunt—* usque ad v. 16.

trine." Rom. xii. 7, 8. "he that teacheth, on teaching . . .
he that ruleth, with diligence." 1 Cor. xii. 28. "governments," 1 Pet. v. 1. as above. Hence a bishop or presbyter is
called "the steward of God," Tit. i. 7.

5   The office of a DEACON is properly to administer, in the
character of a public servant, to the temporal wants of the
church in general, and particularly of the poor, the sick, and
strangers. Acts vi. 3. "look ye out among you . . . whom
we may appoint over this business." 1 Tim. iii. 10. "let them
10 use the office of a deacon, being found blameless." v. 13.
"they that have used the office of a deacon well." Also to
teach and baptize; as appears from the example of Philip,
who in his capacity of deacon, the apostle of that name having
remained during the same period at Jerusalem, converted the
15 people of Samaria to the faith, and on his own authority baptized, first his new converts, and afterwards the Ethiopian
eunuch. Acts vi. 5. viii. 1, 12. "when they believed Philip
preaching the things concerning the kingdom of God, and
the name of Jesus Christ, they were baptized, both men and
20 women." v. 38. "he baptized him." In allusion to this his
office of preaching he is called "the evangelist," Acts xxi. 8.
where his identity is established by his being designated as
"one of the seven." Hence 1 Tim. iii. 13. "they that have
used the office of a deacon well, purchase to themselves a good
25 degree, and great boldness in the faith which is in Christ
Jesus."

The widows of the church are also associated with the deacons in the performance of their duty, 1 Tim. v. 3–16. "honor
widows that are widows indeed," &c.

Electio ministrorum penes populum est. Act. i. 23. *statuerunt igitur duos—. et vi. 5. placuit hic sermo toti præsenti multitudini; et elegerunt Stephanum et xiv. 23. quum per suffragia creassent per singulas ecclesias presbyteros—* et xv.

5 22. *visum est apostolis et presbyteris cum tota ecclesia delectos ex sese viros mittere Antiochiam cum Paulo et Barnaba.*

Probandi autem sunt prius ministri quam admittendi. 1 Tim. iii. 10. *hi etiam explorentur prius; deinde ministrent, si sint inculpati.*

10 Quales esse debeant cum presbyteri tum diaconi, in epistolis ad Timotheum et Titum copiose docetur; et præsertim 1 Tim. iii. 1, &c. Tit. i. 5, &c.

Comprobatis autem presbyterorum manus imponebantur. 1 Tim. iv. 14. *donum quod in te est, quod datum est tibi per*

15 *prophetiam cum impositione manuum ordinis seniorum.* et v. 22. *manus cito ne cui imponito.* Quanquam impositio manuum non solum recens admissis presbyteris sed iamdiu in officio versatis quoties grave aliquod munus suscipiebant, velut benedictio adhibebatur. Act. xiii. 2, 3. *illis sacram suam*

20 *functionem obeuntibus—: quum ieiunassent et orassent et imposuissent eis manus.*

Successionis itaque per se nulla vis est, nulla auctoritas. Act. xx. 29, 30. *ego istud scio, lupos graves, non parcentes gregi, ingressuros esse ad vos post discessum meum, et ex vobis*

The choice of ministers belongs to the people. Acts i. 23. "they appointed two." vi. 5. "the saying pleased the whole multitude, and they chose Stephen." xiv. 23. "when they had ordained them elders in every church." xv. 22. "then
5 pleased it the apostles and elders, with the whole church, to send chosen men of their own company to Antioch with Paul and Barnabas."

It is proper that ministers should undergo a certain trial previous to their admission. 1 Tim. iii. 10. "let these also first
10 be proved; then let them use the office of a deacon, being found blameless." The requisite qualifications of an elder, as well as of a deacon, are detailed at length in the epistles to Timothy and Titus, and particularly 1 Tim. iii. 1, &c. Tit. i. 5, &c.

15   On such as were approved the presbyters laid their hands. 1 Tim. iv. 14. "neglect not the gift that is in thee, which was given thee by prophecy, with the laying on of the hands of the presbytery." v. 22. "lay hands suddenly on no man." The imposition of hands, however, was not confined to the
20 election of presbyters, but was practised even towards veteran ministers, in the way of solemn benediction, on their engaging in any work of importance. Acts xiii. 2, 3. "as they ministered unto the Lord . . . when they had fasted and prayed and laid hands upon them, they sent them away."

25   The right of succession is consequently nugatory, and of no force. Acts xx. 29, 30. "I know this, that after my departing shall grievous wolves enter in among you, not sparing the flock: also of your own selves shall men arise, speaking per-

ipsis orituros qui loquantur perversa, ut discipulos post se abstrahant. 2 Cor. xi. 13. *nam istiusmodi pseudoapostoli operarii dolosi sunt, transfigurantes se in apostolos Christi.*

Ad remunerationem autem ministrorum tam universalis
5 quam particularis cuiusque ecclesiæ quod attinet, tametsi hoc par est, et cum per se iustum, tum lege Dei et auctoritate Christi eiusque apostoli sancitum, Matt. x. 10. *dignus est operarius alimento suo,* 1 Cor. ix. a v. 7. ad 13. *quis militat propriis stipendiis—?* Gal. vi. 6. *communicet catechumenus,*
10 sive *is qui instituitur in sermone, cum illo qui eum instituit, omnia bona,* 1 Tim. v. 17, 18. *qui bene præsunt—,* unde et fas est et ius et æquum, et 1 Cor. ix. 14. ab ipso Deo ita provisum *iis qui evangelium annuntiant, ut ex evangelio vivant;* præstabilius tamen est, et ad imitationem perfectius, et
15 ad offensionem omnem ac suspicionem evitandam et ad præclaram in Deo gloriationem illustrius atque pulchrius, ecclesiæ Dei gratuitam navare operam, gratuito etiam, exemplo Domini nostri, ministrare atque servire: Matt. xx. 28. *sicut filius hominis non venit ut sibi ministretur, sed ut ministret;*
20 et cap. x. 8. *dono accepistis, dono date.* Act. xx. 35. *meminisse verborum Domini Iesu; quia ipse dixit, Beatius est dare quam accipere.* Idemque suo exemplo Paulus imitandum omnibus ecclesiæ ministris proposuit et commendavit: v. 34, 35. *ipsi nostis, usibus meis et iis qui mecum sunt manus istas*

verse things, to draw away disciples after them." 2 Cor. xi.
13. "such are false apostles, deceitful workers, transforming
themselves into the apostles of Christ."

With regard to the remuneration to be allotted to the ministers of the universal church, as well as to those of particular
religious communities, it must be allowed that a certain recompense is both reasonable in itself, and sanctioned by the
law of God and the declarations of Christ and his apostle.
Matt. x. 10. "the workman is worthy of his meat." 1 Cor. ix.
7–13. "who goeth a warfare at any time at his own charges?"
Gal. vi. 6. "let him that is taught in the word, communicate
unto him that teacheth in all good things." 1 Tim. v. 17, 18.
"let the elders that rule well," &c. Hence it is lawful and
equitable, and the ordinance of God himself, 1 Cor. ix. 14.
"that they which preach the gospel, should live of the gospel."
It is however more desirable for example's sake, and for the
preventing of offence or suspicion, as well as more noble and
honorable in itself, and conducive to our more complete glorying in God, to render an unpaid service to the church in this
as well as in all other instances, and, after the example of our
Lord, to minister and serve gratuitously. Matt. xx. 28. "even
as the Son of man came not to be ministered unto, but to
minister." x. 8. "freely ye have received, freely give." Acts
xx. 35. "remember the words of the Lord Jesus, how he said,
It is more blessed to give than to receive." St. Paul proposed
the same to the imitation of ministers in general, and recom-
mended it by his example. v. 34, 35. "ye yourselves know, that
these hands have ministered unto my necessities, and to them

ministrasse. omnino ostendi vobis, oportere sic laborando sus-
cipere infirmos—: 2 Thess. iii. 7, 8, 9. ipsi scitis quomodo
oporteat nos imitari: quoniam non inordinate nos gessimus
inter vos: neque gratis panem edimus acceptum a quoquam;
5 *sed cum labore et ærumna nocte dieque operantes, ne cui*
vestrum oneri essemus. non quod nobis id non liceat, sed ut
nosmetipsos pro exemplo præbeamus vobis ad nos imitan-
dum. 1 Cor. ix. 15, 18. *ego tamen nullo istorum sum usus:*
neque vero hæc scripsi, ut ita fiat mihi: nam bonum est mihi
10 *mori potius quam ut gloriationem meam aliquis inanem red-*
dat. quæ igitur mihi est merces? ut evangelizando gratuitum
constituam evangelium Christi, ut ne abutar iure meo in evan-
gelio. et 2 Ep. xi. 8. *quum apud vos essem et egerem, non*
gravavi vos. et v. 9. *in omnibus me conservavi vobis minime*
15 *onerosum, et conservabo.* et 10. *hæc gloriatio non obstru-*
etur in me. et 12. *quod facio etiam faciam ut amputem occa-*
sionem iis qui exoptant occasionem, ut in eo de quo gloriantur
inveniantur quales et nos. et cap. xii. 14. *ecce tertio paratus*
sum venire ad vos, et non ero gravis vobis: non enim quæro
20 *vestra, sed vos; non enim debent filii parentibus thesauros*
congerere, sed parentes filiis. et v. 17. *num per quenquam*
eorum quos misi ad vos quæstui vos habui? et 18. *num aliqua*
in re vos quæstui habuit Titus? nonne eodem spiritu ambu-
lavimus. et 19. *omnia autem hæc, dilecti, propter vestram*
25 *ædificationem.* Quod si quo tempore in summis angustiis aliquid subsidii ab ecclesiis ultro largientibus accipere coactus

that were with me: I have showed you all things, how that
so laboring ye ought to support the weak." 2 Thess. iii. 7–9.
"yourselves know how ye ought to follow us; for we behaved
not ourselves disorderly among you; neither did we eat any
5 man's bread for nought; but wrought with labor and travail
night and day, that we might not be chargeable to any of you:
not because we have not power, but to make ourselves an example unto you to follow us." 1 Cor. ix. 15, 18. "I have used
none of these things; neither have I written these things that
10 it should be so done unto me; for it were better for me to die,
than that any man should make my glorying void: what is my
reward then? verily that, when I preach the gospel, I may
make the gospel of Christ without charge, that I abuse not my
power in the gospel." 2 Cor. xi. 9. "when I was present with
15 you, and wanted, I was chargeable to no man . . . in all
things I have kept myself from being burthensome unto you,
and so will I keep myself." v. 10. "no man shall stop me of
this boasting." v. 12. "what I do, that I will do, that I may
cut off occasion from them that desire occasion; that wherein
20 they glory, they may be found even as we are." xii. 14. "behold the third time I am ready to come unto you, and I will
not be burthensome to you; for I seek not yours, but you; for
the children ought not to lay up for the parents, but the parents for the children." v. 17. "did I make a gain of you by
25 any of them whom I sent unto you?" v. 18. "did Titus make
a gain of you? walked we not in the same spirit?" v. 19. "we
do all things, dearly beloved, for your edifying." And if at any
time extreme necessity compelled him to accept the voluntary

est, id ei adeo molestum et grave fuit, ut quasi spoliationis cuiusdam reum ipse se facere videatur. 2 Ep. xi. 8. *alias ecclesias spoliavi, accepto ab iis stipendio, ut vobis—.*

Sin ad hanc virtutis praestantiam hodierni ministri per-
5 venire non possunt, proximum sane est ut Dei vocantis divina providentia freti, a benevolentia ac liberalitate ecclesiae quam volentes volentem pascunt potius quam ab edictis magistra-tuum, ea quae ad vitam opus sunt expectent. Matt. x. 11. *ex-quirite quis in ea sit dignus, et illic manete.* Luc. x. 7, 8.
10 *manete in ea ipsa domo, edentes et bibentes quae ab ipsis apposita fuerint. et in quamcunque urbem ingressi fueritis, et acceperint vos, edite quae apponuntur vobis.* et xxii. 35. *dixit eis, quando misi vos absque crumena et pera et soleis, numquid defuit vobis? ipsi vero dixerunt, Nihil.* 2 Cor. xi. 9.
15 *quod mihi deerat, suppleverunt fratres quum venissent e Macedonia.* Philipp. iv. 15, &c. *nostis et vos Philippenses quum initio evangelii proficiscerer e Macedonia, nullam mihi ecclesiam communicasse in ratione dati et accepti, nisi vos solos. nam etiam Thessalonicae semel atque iterum quod mihi
20 opus erat misistis: non quod requiram donum; sed requiro fructum illum exuberantem qui in rationes vestras inducatur. accepi autem omnia et abundo; expletus sum acceptis ab Epaphrodito quae a vobis missa sunt, odorem bonae fragrantiae, hostiam Deo acceptam ac placentem.*

aid of the churches, such constraint was so grievous to him, that he accuses himself as if he were guilty of robbery. 2 Cor. xi. 8. "I robbed other churches, taking wages of them, to do you service."

5   If however such self-denial be thought too arduous for the ministers of the present day, they will most nearly approach to it, when, relying on the providence of God who called them, they shall look for the necessary support of life, not from the edicts of the civil power, but from the spontaneous
10 good-will and liberality of the church in requital of their voluntary service. Matt. x. 11. "enquire who in it is worthy, and there abide till ye go thence." Luke x. 7, 8. "in the same house remain, eating and drinking such things as they give . . . and into whatsoever city ye enter, and they receive you,
15 eat such things as are set before you." xxii. 35. "he said unto them, When I sent you without purse, and scrip, and shoes, lacked ye anything? and they said, Nothing." 2 Cor. xi. 9. "that which was lacking to me, the brethren which came from Macedonia supplied." Philipp. iv. 15, &c. "now, ye
20 Philippians, know also, that in the beginning of the gospel, when I departed from Macedonia, no church communicated with me as concerning giving and receiving, but ye only: for even in Thessalonica ye sent once and again unto my necessity: not because I desire a gift, but I desire fruit that may
25 abound to your account: but I have all, and abound; I am full, having received of Epaphroditus the things which were sent from you, an odor of a sweet smell, a sacrifice acceptable, well pleasing to God."

Quicquid autem iustum est per se et summa ratione debitum, Deique præcepto sancitum, non est continuo civili lege a magistratibus imperandum aut cogendum. Debitas fuisse Iudæis ab gentibus eleemosynas eodem argumento, iisdem pene verbis ostendit Paulus quibus ecclesiæ ministros docet esse alendos; 1 Cor. ix. 11. cum Rom. xv. 27. *libuit enim iis inquam, et debitores eorum sunt: nam si spiritualia eorum bona gentibus communicata sunt, debent etiam ipsæ in carnalibus iis ministerio suo adesse.* et tamen eleemosynas esse imperandas aut vi cogendas nemo dixerit. Etenim si moralis duntaxat et civilis gratitudo cogenda non est, quanto magis ab evangelica vis omnis et coactio remotissima esse debet? quemadmodum et in evangelio annuntiando pecuniæ ratio quam minime debet versari; Act. viii. 20. *pecunia tua tecum pereat, qui donum Dei existimaris pecuniis acquiri.* Quod si emere evangelium est nefas, quanto magis nefarium est vendere? O vos ergo exigua fide quorum incredulam vocem sæpius audivi, si ecclesiasticos tollis reditus, actum est de evangelio. Immo vero si vi et pecunia stat Christiana religio atque fulcitur, quid est quamobrem non æque ac Turcarum religio suspecta esse videatur?

For it does not necessarily follow, that because a thing is in itself just, a matter of duty and conscience, and sanctioned by the word of God, the performance of it is therefore to be enjoined and compelled by the authority of the magistrate.

5 The same argument, and nearly the same words, which are used by St. Paul to prove that provision should be made for the ministers of the church, are also used to prove that the Gentiles ought to contribute to the support of the poor saints at Jerusalem; 1 Cor. ix. 11. compared with Rom. xv. 27. "it

10 hath pleased them verily, and their debtors they are; for if the Gentiles have been made partakers of their spiritual things, their duty is also to minister unto them in carnal things"; yet no one contends that the giving of alms should be compelled by authority. If then in a case of merely moral and civil grati-

15 tude, force is not to be employed, how much more ought the gratitude which we owe for the benefits of the gospel to be exempt from the slightest shadow of force or constraint? On the same principle, pecuniary considerations ought by no means to enter into our motives for preaching the gospel:

20 Acts viii. 20. "thy money perish with thee, because thou hast thought that the gift of God may be purchased with money." If it be a crime to purchase the gospel, what must it be to sell it? or what are we to think of the faith of those, whom I have so often heard exclaiming in the language of unbelief, "If

25 you take away church revenues, you destroy the gospel?" If the Christian religion depends for its existence on no firmer supports than wealth and civil power, how is it more worthy of belief than the Mahometan superstition?

Itaque decimas aut stipendium evangelicum pacisci aut exigere, aut vi atque edictis magistratuum impositum gregi extorquere, aut de mercede ecclesiastica in ius civile ambulare, litemque in foro intendere, ministrorum evangelii non est, sed luporum; Act. xx. 29. *scio lupos graves non parcentes gregi, ingressuros ad vos post discessum meum.* et v. 33. *argentum vel aurum aut vestem nullius concupivi.* Non ergo exegit aut exigendum cuivis ministro evangelii censuit. 1 Tim. iii. 3. *non turpis lucri, non pecuniæ cupidum:* quanto minus exactorem? et iterum v. 8. Tit. i. 7. et 11. idem. 1 Pet. v. 2, 3. *pascite Dei gregem, qui penes vos est——. neque turpis lucri causa, sed prompto animo.* Certe si homini Christiano vix licet cum adversario de bonis propriis in foro contendere, Matt. v. 39, 40. 1 Cor. vi. 7. quam turpe est hominem ecclesiasticum de decimis, id est, de bonis alienis, quæ vel ex bello vel ex voto pro libitu cuiusque vel antiquata iam non solum lege verum etiam omnibus illius legis, agrariæ scilicet nobis alienissimæ, causis olim quidem, idque diverso ministrorum generi debebantur, nunc nemini debentur, cum grege (id quod apud reformatos nusquam nisi apud nos fieri solet) cum

Hence to exact or bargain for tithes or other stipendiary payments under the gospel, to extort them from the flock under the alleged authority of civil edicts, or to have recourse to civil actions and legal processes for the recovery of allow-
5 ances purely ecclesiastical, is the part of wolves rather than of ministers of the gospel. Acts xx. 29. "I know this that after my departing shall grievous wolves enter in among you, not sparing the flock." v. 33. "I have coveted no man's silver, or gold, or apparel"; whence it follows that the apostle neither
10 exacted these things himself, nor approved of their exaction by ministers of the gospel in general. 1 Tim. iii. 3. "not greedy of filthy lucre; not covetous"; far less therefore an exactor of lucre. Compare also v. 8. Tit. i. 7, 11. 1 Pet. v. 2, 3. "feed the flock of God which is among you . . . not
15 for filthy lucre, but of a ready mind." If it be scarcely allow-able for a Christian to go to law with his adversary in de-fence even of his own property, Matt. v. 39, 40. 1 Cor. vi. 7. what are we to think of an ecclesiastic, who for the sake of tithes, that is, of the property of others, which, either as an
20 offering made out of the spoils of war, or in pursuance of a vow voluntarily contracted by an individual, or from an imi-tation of that agrarian law established among the Jews, but altogether foreign to our habits, and which is not only abol-ished itself, but of which all the causes have ceased to operate,
25 were due indeed formerly, and to ministers of another sect, but are now due to no one; what are we to think of a pastor, who for the recovery of claims thus founded, an abuse un-known to any reformed church but our own, enters into liti-

grege inquam vel suo vel revera non suo litigare? si suo, quam avarum ex re sacra tam cupide quæstum facere? si non suo, quam iniustum? quam deinde importunum docere velle qui abs te doceri nolit? quam violentum, docendi mercedem
5 exigere ab eo, qui doctorem te respuat? quem tu discipulum quoque nisi lucri causa æque respueres? *mercenarius* enim, *cuius non sunt oves propriæ, fugit quia mercenarius est, et non est ipsi cura ovium,* Ioan. x. 12, 13. tales permulti hodie de grege in gregem per causas fere levissimas toties desultant
10 atque fugitant, non tam luporum metu quam ipsimet lupi quoties opimioris præda ministerii aliunde ostentatur; et contra atque pastores facere solent, non gregi suo, sed ipsi sibi lætiora subinde pascua sectantur.

Dices unde ergo vivemus? unde nam vivetis? unde
15 prophetæ olim atque apostoli, facultatibus propriis, artificio aliquo aut honesto studio prophetarum exemplo, qui nec ligna cædendi nec domum ipsi suam fabricandi rudes erant, 2 Reg. vi. 2. exemplo Christi, qui et ipse faber fuit, Marc. vi. 3. Pauli, Act. xviii. 3, 4. qui cum in optimis esset artibus ac
20 disciplinis proprio sumptu educatus, non tamen ex evangelio reficiendas esse impensas educationis suæ, ut ministri solent hodierni, clamitabat. Hactenus de ministris.

gation with his own flock, or, more properly speaking, with
a flock which is not his own? If his own, how avaricious in
him to be so eager in making a gain of his holy office! if not
his own, how iniquitous! Moreover, what a piece of officious-
5 ness, to force his instructions on such as are unwilling to
receive them; what extortion, to exact the price of teaching
from one who disclaims the teacher, and whom the teacher
himself would equally disclaim as a disciple, were it not for
the profit! For "he that is an hireling, whose own the sheep
10 are not . . . fleeth because he is an hireling, and careth not
for the sheep," John x. 12, 13. Many such there are in these
days, who abandon their charge on the slightest pretences, and
ramble from flock to flock, less through fear of the wolf than
to gratify their own wolfish propensities, wherever a richer
15 prey invites; who, unlike good shepherds, are for ever seeking
out new and more abundant pastures, not for their flock, but
for themselves.

"How then," ask they, "are we to live?" How ought they
to live, but as the prophets and apostles lived of old? on their
20 own private resources, by the exercise of some calling, by
some industry, after the example of the prophets, who accounted it no disgrace to be able to hew their own wood, and
build their own houses, 2 Kings vi. 2. of Christ, who wrought
with his own hands as a carpenter, Mark vi. 3. and of St. Paul,
25 Acts xviii. 3, 4. to whom the plea so importunately urged in
modern times, of the expensiveness of a liberal education, and
the necessity that it should be repaid out of the wages of the
gospel, seems never to have occurred. Thus far of the ministers of particular churches.

Pro POPULO autem ecclesiæ, particularis præsertim ubi disciplina viget, ii sunt habendi, qui neque ullius doctrinæ evangelicæ neque cuiusvis doctoris per scripturas et per spiritum explorandi sunt rudes; ne doctorum quidem omnium simul, etsi ecclesiæ se nomine venditabunt. Matt. vii. 15, 16. *cavete vobis a pseudoprophetis qui veniunt ad vos cum indumentis ovium, sed intrinsecus sunt lupi rapaces: a fructibus eorum agnoscetis eos.* et xvi. 6. *videte et cavete a fermento Pharisæorum et Sadducæorum,* cum v. 12. *a fermento doctrinæ.* Ioan. vii. 17, 18. *si quis voluerit quod ille vult facere, cognoscet de doctrina, utrum ex Deo sit, an ego a meipso loquar: qui a semetipso loquitur, gloriam propriam quærit.* Act. xvii. 11. *quotidie examinantes scripturas, an hæc ita se haberent.* 1 Cor. ii. 15. *spiritualis diiudicat quidem omnia.* et x. 15. *ut prudentibus loquor; iudicate vos quod dico.* Eph. iv. 14. *ut ne simus amplius pueri, qui fluctuemus et circumferamur quovis vento doctrinæ.* et vi. 14, &c. *state igitur lumbis circumcinctis veritate.* Philipp. iii. 2. *cavete canes, cavete malos operarios, cavete concisionem.* 1 Thess. v. 21. *omnia explorate; quod bonum fuerit retinete.* Heb. xiii. 9. *doctrinis variis et peregrinis ne circumferimini.* Plura vide supra cap. xxi. de Intelligentia rerum spiritualium.

With regard to the PEOPLE OF THE CHURCH, especially in those particular churches where discipline is maintained in strictness, such only are to be accounted of that number, as are well taught in Scripture doctrine, and capable of trying by the rule of Scripture and the Spirit any teacher whatever, or even the whole collective body of teachers, although arrogating to themselves the exclusive name of the church. Matt. vii. 15, 16. "beware of false prophets, which come to you in sheep's clothing, but inwardly they are ravening wolves: ye shall know them by their fruits." xvi. 6. "take heed and beware of the leaven of the Pharisees and Sadducees," compared with v. 12. "then understand they how that he bade them not beware of the leaven of bread, but of the doctrine—." John vii. 17, 18. "if any man will do his will, he shall know of the doctrine, whether it be of God, or whether I speak of myself: he that speaketh of himself, seeketh his own glory." Acts xvii. 11. "they searched the scriptures daily, whether these things were so." 1 Cor. ii. 15. "he that is spiritual, judgeth all things." x. 15. "I speak as to wise men; judge ye what I say." Eph. iv. 14. "that we henceforth be no more children, tossed to and fro, and carried about with every wind of doctrine." vi. 14, &c. "stand therefore, having your loins girt about with truth." Philipp. iii. 2. "beware of dogs; beware of evil workers; beware of the concision." 1 Thess. v. 21. "prove all things; hold fast that which is good." Heb. xiii. 9. "be not carried about with divers and strange doctrines." See more on this subject above, chap. xxi. on the discernment of spiritual things.

Itaque vanis doctoribus delectari non debent. 2 Tim. iv.
3. *erit tempus quum sanam doctrinam non tolerabunt; sed*
auribus prurientes, ipsi sibi secundum illas suas peculiares cu-
piditates coacervabunt doctores. 1 Pet. ii. 2. *ut modo geniti*
5 *infantes, lac illud sermonis sincerum expetite, ut per illud*
augescatis. Nec falsos ferre: Apoc. ii. 2. *novi opera tua et*
laborem tuum et patientiam, et quod non possis ferre malos;
et exploraris eos qui se dictitant apostolos esse et non sunt, et
comperisti eos esse mendaces, cum v. 7. *qui habet aurem*
10 *audiat quid spiritus dicat ecclesiis.*

Quæ constat his partibus ecclesia, licet membrorum numero paucorum, integra tamen in sese et perfecta ecclesia
existimanda est, quod ad ius summum in sacris attinet; neque
mortalium quenquam neque cœtum ullum aut conventum
15 supra se habet in terris cui iure subiiciatur, cum et scripturas
et promissiones, præsentem Christum et præsidem spiritum
et donorum gratiam apud se precibus impetrandam, æque ac
alius extra se quivis mortalium, aut quævis classis aut synodus,
sperare sibi possit. Matt. xviii. 20. *ubi duo vel tres congre-*
20 *gati sunt in nomine meo, illic sum in medio eorum.* Act. xiv.
23. *quum per suffragia creassent per singulas ecclesias pres-*
byteros, et orassent cum Ieiuniis, commendarunt eos Domino,
in quem crediderant.

Hinc particulares quæque ecclesiæ, sive in Iudæa, ubi na-

Hence the people are warned not to take delight in vain teachers. 2 Tim. iv. 3. "the time will come when they will not endure sound doctrine, but after their own lusts shall they heap to themselves teachers, having itching ears." 1 Pet.
5 ii. 2. "as new born babes, desire the sincere milk of the word, that ye may grow thereby." False teachers are not to be tolerated. Rev. ii. 2. "I know thy works, and thy labor, and thy patience, and how thou canst not bear them which are evil; and thou hast tried them which say they are apostles, and are
10 not, and hast found them liars." v. 7. "he that hath an ear, let him hear what the Spirit saith unto the churches."

Every church consisting of the above parts, however small its numbers, is to be considered as in itself an integral and perfect church, so far as regards its religious rights; nor has it
15 any superior on earth, whether individual, or assembly, or convention, to whom it can be lawfully required to render submission; inasmuch as no believer out of its pale, nor any order or council of men whatever, has a greater right than itself to expect a participation in the written word and the
20 promises, in the presence of Christ, in the presiding influence of the Spirit, and in those gracious gifts which are the reward of united prayer. Matt. xviii. 20. "where two or three are gathered together in my name, there am I in the midst of them." Acts xiv. 23. "when they had ordained them elders
25 in every church, and had prayed with fasting, they commended them to the Lord, on whom they believed."

Hence all particular churches, whether in Judea, where there was originally one church comprehending the whole

tionalis una prius fuit, sive quacunque in regione, merito ecclesiæ dicuntur. 2 Cor. viii. 1. *ecclesiis Macedonum.* Gal. i. 2. *ecclesiis Galatiæ.* et v. 22. *ecclesiis Iudææ.* 1 Thess. ii. 14. idem. Apoc. i. 4. *septem ecclesiis quæ sunt in Asia.* Immo 5 quamvis paucorum singulæ sint. Rom. xvi. 5. *ecclesiam quæ est in domo eorum;* 1 Cor. xvi. 19. idem. Col. iv. 15. *ecclesiam quæ in domo illius est.* Philem. 2. *ecclesia quæ domi tuæ est.*

In quo differt ecclesia particularis a synagoga Iudaica; 10 quæ quamquam cœtus particularis et religiosus quidem erat, ecclesia tamen particularis non erat; cultus enim Dei totus et integer non potuit in synagoga rite celebrari; propterea quod sacrificia et cæremoniæ in templo solo erant obeundæ: nunc autem quicquid ad cultum Dei et fidelium salutem, quicquid 15 denique ad constituendam ecclesiam pertinet, id omne potest in ecclesia particulari intra privatos parietes in cœtu fidelium non ita magno recte atque ordine fieri. Immo eiusmodi ecclesia iusto numerosior dum pastorum avaritiæ consulit, fructu conveniendi magna ex parte ipsa sese frustratur.

20 Quocirca Iudæos et proselytas ex toto orbe terrarum religionis causa Hierosolymas oportebat proficisci, Act. ii. 5, &c. et viii. 27. propterea quod eo tempore una duntaxat sive nationalis sive universalis ecclesia Iudaica erat, particulares vero nullæ: nunc nationalis nulla est, particulares vero sunt

nation, or in any other country whatever, are properly called churches: 2 Cor. viii. 1. "the churches of Macedonia"; Gal. i. 2. "the churches of Galatia"; v. 22. "the churches of Judea"; see also 1 Thess. ii. 14. Rev. i. 4. "the seven churches
5 which are in Asia": even where they consist of but few members: Rom. xvi. 5. "greet the church that is in their house." See also 1 Cor. xvi. 19. Col. iv. 15. "the church which is in his house." Philem. 2. "the church in thy house."

In this respect a particular church differs from the Jewish
10 synagogue, which, although a particular assembly, and convened for religious purposes, was not a particular church, inasmuch as the entire worship of God could not be there duly celebrated, by reason that the sacrifices and ceremonies of the law were to be performed in the temple alone. Under the
15 gospel, on the contrary, all that pertains to the worship of God and the salvation of believers, all, in short, that is necessary to constitute a church, may be duly and orderly transacted in a particular church, within the walls of a private house, and where the numbers assembled are inconsiderable. Nay, such
20 a church, when in compliance with the interested views of its pastor it allows of an increase of numbers beyond what is convenient, deprives itself in a great measure of the advantages to be derived from meeting in common.

It was indeed necessary for Jews and proselytes to meet
25 together at Jerusalem from all quarters of the world for religious purposes, Acts ii. 5, &c. viii. 27. because at that time there was only one national or universal Jewish church, and no particular churches; whereas at present there is no national

multæ, suis in se numeris omnes absolutæ, divino iure ac potestate pares, quæ quasi partes quædam similares et homogeneæ æquali inter se vinculo coniunctæ unam constituunt ecclesiam catholicam: neque necesse habet earum una ab
5 altera quicquam petere quod ipsa apud se non habeat.

Possunt tamen ecclesiæ particulares inter se fraterno more atque consensu consilia communicare et in commune agere quæ universæ ecclesiæ ex re fore crediderint. 2 Cor. viii. 19. *suffragiis delectus est ab ecclesiis socius peregrinationis nostræ.*
10 et cap. i. 24. *non quod dominemur vestræ fidei, sed quod adiutores simus gaudii vestri.* 1 Pet. v. 3. *neque ut dominantes cleris.*

Conciliorum vestigium in scriptura nullum reperio: nam quod extat Act. xv. 2, &c. oraculum potius dicendum est ab
15 inspiratis apostolis petitum, ad quos in re dubia recurrebatur tanquam ad summos controversiarum disceptatores, nulla dum existente evangelii scriptura. Aliud longe nunc est concilium hodiernum episcoporum aut presbyterorum, qui et inspirati præ aliis non sunt, et scripturis auctoritate minores,
20 nec præter cæteros erroribus immunes, ut qui pro certo dicere non possint, *visum est spiritui sancto ac nobis* sicut illi, Act. xv. 28. et tamen iura ecclesiis imponendi ius sibi sumere audent, suisque decretis ut pareant cæteri omnes postulare:

church, but a number of particular churches, each complete and perfect in itself, and all co-equal in divine right and power; which, like similar and homogeneous parts of the same body, connected by a bond of mutual equality, form in conjunction
5 one catholic church: nor need any one church have recourse to another for a grace or privilege which it does not possess in its independent capacity.

Particular churches, however, may communicate with each other in a spirit of brotherhood and agreement, and co-
10 operate for purposes connected with the general welfare. 2 Cor. viii. 19. "who was also chosen of the churches to travel with us." i. 24. "not for that we have dominion over your faith, but are helpers of your joy." 1 Pet. v. 3. "neither as being lords over God's heritage."
15 Of councils, properly so called, I find no trace in Scripture; for the decision recorded Acts xv. 2, &c. is rather to be considered as an oracular declaration obtained from the inspired apostles, to whom recourse was had in a doubtful matter, as to the supreme authority on controverted points, while there
20 was as yet no written word. This was very different from a modern council composed of bishops or elders, who have no gift of inspiration more than other men; whose authority is not, like that of the apostles, co-ordinate with the Scriptures; who are equally liable to error with their brethren, insomuch
25 that they cannot pronounce with certainty, like the apostles, Acts xv. 28. "it hath seemed good to the Holy Ghost and to us"; who nevertheless assume the right of imposing laws on the churches, and require the rest of mankind to obey their

et tamen in illa synodo Hierosolymitana fidelium tota multitudo interfuit suffragia contulit, Act. xv. 12, 22, 23. Quod
si fraternum admonendi officium præstitisse satis habent,
nemo aspernatur.

5   Adversantur ecclesiæ cum hæretici tum hostes profani.

Hæretici vel suopte ingenio pravo. Philipp. i. 16. *alii per
contentionem Christum non caste annuntiant*—: vel cum
ecclesiæ iugum aliquod non necessarium imponitur, Matt.
ix. 16. *illud enim ipsius supplementum tollit aliquid ex illo*
10 *vestimento, et fit peior fissura.*

Et tamen hæreticorum usus aliquis. 1 Cor. xi. 19. *oportet
enim etiam hæreses inter vos esse, ut qui probi sunt, manifesti fiant inter vos.*

Hostes ecclesiæ varii sunt, quibus tamen omnibus interitus
15 denuntiatur Psal. cxxxvii. 7, 8, 9. *Recordare Iehova contra
Edomæos.* et gens *Babylonica vastanda, Beatus sit qui Repen-
det sibi*—. Ier. xxx. 16. *quicunque consumunt te, consumen-
tur*—. et l. 29, 30. *promulgate convenire in Babyloniam
amplissimos, omnes qui tendunt arcum*—, et v. 34. *vindex*
20 *eorum fortis*—. et cap. li. 11. *ultio Iehovæ est ultio templi
eius*—. et v. 24. *iam rependam Babyloni*—. et 34. *exedit
me, quatit me Nebuchadnezzar*—. et 49. *Babyloni caden-
dum est, o confossi Israelis*—. Ezech. xxv. 3, &c. *eo quod*

mandates; forgetting that at the assembly in Jerusalem the whole multitude of believers were present, and gave their voices: Acts xv. 12, 22, 23. Where however they content themselves with the fraternal office of admonition, their coun-
5 sel is not to be despised.

The enemies of the church are partly heretics, and partly profane opponents.

The hostility of heretics originates either in their own evil dispositions, Philipp. i. 16. "the one preach Christ of con-
10 tention, not sincerely"; or in the imposition of some unnecessary yoke on the church, Matt. ix. 16. "that which is put in to fill it up taketh from the garment, and the rent is made worse." Yet even these are not without their use. 1 Cor. xi. 19. "there must be also heresies among you, that they which
15 are approved may be made manifest among you."

The enemies of the church are various, but the destruction of all is portended. Psal. cxxxvii. 7–9. "remember, O Jehovah, the children of Edom . . . O daughter of Babylon, who art to be destroyed, happy shall he be that rewardeth thee
20 as thou hast served us." Jer. xxx. 16. "all they that devour thee shall be devoured." l. 29, 30. "call together the archers against Babylon, all ye that bend the bow——." v. 34. "their Redeemer is strong." li. 11. "the vengeance of Jehovah, the vengeance of his temple." v. 24. "I will render unto Baby-
25 lon——." v. 34. "Nebuchadrezzar hath devoured me, he hath crushed me." v. 49. "as Babylon hath caused the slain of Israel to fall, so at Babylon shall fall the slain of all the earth." Ezek. xxv. 3, &c. "because thou saidst, Aha, against my sanc-

dicis, euge, de sanctuario meo—. et xxviii. 24. *ita non am-*
plius erit domui Israelis spinus dolorificus—. et xxxv. 5, &c.
eo quod tibi est inimicitia perpetua—. Ioel. iii. 2, &c. *dedu-*
cam eas in convallem Iehosaphati—. Amos. i. 3, &c. *propter*
5 *tres defectiones Damasci*—. Hobad. 10, &c. *propter vio-*
lentiam in fratrem tuum Iacobum—. Mic. iv. 13. *surge, et*
tritura filia Sionis—. Zech. xii. 3, &c. *disponam Hierosoly-*
mas velut lapidem onerosissimum omnibus populis—. Apoc.
xix. 2. *vindicavit sanguinem servorum suorum ex manu eius.*

10   Magnus ille ecclesiæ hostis *antichristus* dicitur; ex ecclesia
etiam oriundus: de quo 2 Thess. ii. 3, &c. *homo ille peccati,*
sese opponens et efferens supra quicquid dicitur Deus aut
numen: adeo ut in templo Dei tanquam Deus sedeat, præ se
ferens se esse Deum—. 1 Ioan. ii. 18, &c. *etiam nunc anti-*
15 *christi multi cœperunt esse. e nobis egressi sunt*—. et iv. 3.
quicunque spiritus non profitetur Iesum Christum in carnem
venisse ex Deo non est; sed hic est ille spiritus antichristi,
quem audistis venturum fuisse. et 2 Ep. 7. *multi impos-*
tores ingressi sunt in mundum, qui non profitentur Iesum
20 *Christum venisse in carne, hic ille est impostor et antichristus.*
et Apoc. pene tota a cap. xiii.

    Hostium ecclesiæ doli, et persecutionum genera varia sunt.
Num. xxxi. 16. *en ipsæ fuerunt filiis Israelis ex sermone*

tuary—." xxviii. 24. "there shall be no more a pricking brier unto the house of Israel." xxxv. 5, &c. "because thou hast had a perpetual hatred—." Joel iii. 2, &c. "I will bring them down into the valley of Jehoshaphat—." Amos i. 3, &c. "for three transgressions of Damascus—." Obad. 10, &c. "for thy violence against thy brother Jacob." Micah iv. 13. "arise and thresh, O daughter of Zion—." Zech. xii. 3, &c. "I will make Jerusalem a burthensome stone for all people—." Rev. xix. 2. "he hath avenged the blood of his servants at her hand."

The great enemy of the church is called "Antichrist," who according to prediction is to arise from the church itself. 2 Thess. ii. 3, &c. "that man of sin, the son of perdition, who opposeth and exalteth himself above all that is called God, or that is worshipped; so that he as God sitteth in the temple of God, showing himself that he is God." 1 John ii. 18, &c. "even now are there many antichrists . . . they went out from us." iv. 3. "every spirit that confesseth not that Jesus Christ is come in the flesh, is not of God; and this is that spirit of antichrist, whereof ye have heard that it should come." 2 John 7. "many deceivers are entered into the world, who confess not that Jesus Christ is come in the flesh: this is a deceiver and an antichrist." See also nearly the whole of the latter part of Revelation, from chap. xiii. to the end of the book.

The frauds and persecutions practised by the enemies of the church are of various kinds. Num. xxxi. 16. "behold, these caused the children of Israel, through the counsel of

Bileami, quæ suppeditarunt—, cum Apoc. ii. 14. Neh. vi. 6, &c. *istam prophetiam indixerat, mihi quia Tobia et Sanballat mercede conduxerant eum.* Ezræ iv. 12, &c. *urbem ipsam rebellem et malam—*. Neh. ii. 19. idem. Esth. iii.

5 8. *est populus quidam dispersus ac dissipatus inter populos, in omnibus provinciis regni tui: quorum iura diversa sunt a iure omnium populorum, iura autem regis non exsequuntur—*. Ier. xxvi. 8. *prehenderunt eum sacerdotes—*. et xxix. 26. *Iehova disposuit te sacerdotem in loco Iehoiadæ sacerdo-*

10 *tis—: ut ponas eum in cippo aut in scapha—*. Amos. vii. 10, 13. *tunc misit Amasia sacerdos—*. Matt. v. 10, 11. *beati quos persequuntur homines—*. et x. 25. *si ipsum patremfamilias Beelzebulem vocarunt; quanto magis domesticos eius.* Gal. iv. 29. *quemadmodum tunc is qui secundum car-*

15 *nem genitus fuerat, persequebatur—*. Heb. xi. 36, &c. *alii rursus ludibria et flagella sunt experti—*.

Itaque fuga persecutionis et præcipitur et exemplis comprobatur. Eliæ, 1 Reg. xix. 3. Iosephi, Matt. ii. 13. Et x. 16, 17. *ecce mitto vos ut oves in medium luporum—: cavete*

20 *vobis ab hominibus; tradent enim vos—*: et v. 23. *quum persequentur vos in ea urbe, fugite in aliam.* Christi, Matt. xii. 15. Luc. iv. 30. Ioan. viii. 59. et xi. 54. Discipulorum, Act. viii. 4. Pauli et Barnabæ, cap. xiv. 6. 2 Cor. xi. 32, 33. *Damasci—*. Apoc. xii. 6. *mulier vero fugit—*. et v. 14. *datæ*

25 *sunt mulieri alæ—*.

Balaam, to commit trespass against Jehovah—" compared with Rev. ii. 14. Neh. vi. 6, &c. "he pronounced this prophecy against me; for Tobiah and Sanballat had hired him." Ezra iv. 12. "the rebellious and the bad city." See also Neh. ii. 19. Esther iii. 8. "there is a certain people scattered abroad and dispersed among the people in all the provinces of thy kingdom; and their laws are diverse from all people, neither keep they the king's laws." Jer. xxvi. 8. "the priests took him." xxix. 26. "Jehovah hath made thee priest in the stead of Jehoiada the priest . . . that thou shouldest put him in prison and in the stocks." Amos vii. 10, 13. "then Amaziah the priest of Bethel sent—." Matt. v. 10, 11. "blessed are they which are persecuted—." x. 25. "if they have called the master Beelzebub, how much more shall they call them of his household?" Gal. iv. 29. "but as then he that was born after the flesh persecuted him that was born after the Spirit, even so it is now." Heb. xi. 36, &c. "others had trial of cruel mockings and scourgings—."

Hence we are enjoined to flee from persecution, and the precept is confirmed by the example of Elijah, 1 Kings xix. 3. of Joseph, Matt. ii. 13. and x. 16, 17. "behold, I send you forth as sheep in the midst of wolves . . . but beware of men, for they will deliver you up to the councils." v. 23. "when they persecute you in this city, flee ye into another"; of Christ, Matt. xii. 15. Luke iv. 30. John viii. 59. xi. 54. of the disciples, Acts viii. 4. of Paul and Barnabas, xiv. 6. 2 Cor. xi. 32, 33. Rev. xii. 6. "the woman fled into the wilderness." v. 14. "to the woman were given two wings—."

Nisi non fugisse gloriæ Dei magis conducat. Sic Paulus, Act. xxi. 13. *non solum vinciri, sed et mori paratus sum—.*

Persecutionum solatia sunt, Matt. x. 32. *quisquis agnoscet me coram hominibus, agnoscam et ego eum—.* Luc. xii. 4, 5, &c. *ne metuite vobis ab iis qui interimunt corpus—.* et xxi. 18, 19. *sed pilus capitis vestri non peribit—.* Ioan. xv. 18, 19, 20. *si mundus vos odit, scitis me prius quam vos illis odio habitum—.* Act. v. 41. *gaudentes— quod digni habiti sunt—.* Rom. viii. 35, &c. *num persecutio—?* 2 Cor. iv. 8, 9. *persecutionem patimur, at in ea non deserimur—.* Philipp. ii. 17. *si pro libamento offerar—.* 2 Tim. iii. 12. *omnes qui volunt pie vivere in Christo Iesu, persecutionem patientur.* 1 Pet. iv. 14. *si conviciis afficimini in nomine Christi, beati estis—.* et v. 16. *si ut Christianus, ne pudefiat.*

Et compensatio. Marc. x. 30. *centuplicia—.* Luc. vi. 23. *ecce enim merces vestra multa est in cœlis—.* Rom. viii. 18. *reor minime dignas esse præsentis temporis perpessiones—.* 2 Thess. i. 6, 7. *iis qui affligunt vos, afflictionem: vobis vero qui affligimini, relaxationem—.* Heb. x. 34. *ut qui sciretis vos habere apud vos potiorem substantiam in cœlis.* et 36. *ut reportetis promissionem illam.* et xi. 26. *intuebatur enim in præmii retributionem.*

Except where flight would not be conducive to the glory of God. Hence St. Paul declares Acts xxi. 13. "I am ready not to be bound only, but also to die."

There are appropriate consolations for the persecuted.
Matt. x. 32. "whosoever shall confess me before men, him will I confess also." Luke xii. 4, 5, &c. "be not afraid of them that kill the body." xxi. 18, 19. "there shall not an hair of your head perish." John xv. 18–20. "if the world hate you, ye know that it hated me before it hated you." Acts v. 41. "rejoicing that they were counted worthy to suffer shame for his name." Rom. viii. 35, &c. "who shall separate us . . . shall persecution?" 2 Cor. iv. 8, 9. "we are persecuted, but not forsaken." Philipp. ii. 17. "if I be offered upon the sacrifice of your faith, I joy." 2 Tim. iii. 12. "all that will live godly in Christ Jesus shall suffer persecution." 1 Pet. iv. 14. "if ye be reproached for the name of Christ, happy are ye." v. 16. "if any man suffer as a Christian, let him not be ashamed."

A compensation is also promised. Mark x. 30. "he shall receive an hundred-fold." Luke vi. 23. "behold, your reward is great in heaven." Rom. viii. 18. "I reckon that the sufferings of this present time are not worthy to be compared with the glory which shall be revealed in us." 2 Thess. i. 6, 7. "tribulation to them that trouble you; and to you who are troubled rest with us." Heb. x. 34. "knowing in yourselves that ye have in heaven a better and an enduring substance." v. 36. "that ye might receive the promise." xi. 26. "he had respect unto the recompense of the reward."

CAPUT XXXII.

DE DISCIPLINA ECCLESIASTICA.

ECCLESIÆ particularis commune vinculum est DISCI-
PLINA ECCLESIASTICA.

Ea est ecclesiæ consentio ad vitam ex doctrina
Christiana recte instituendam: omniaque in cœtibus decenter
5 atque ordine facienda. Rom. xii. a v. 4. ad finem capitis.
Eph. iv. 1, 2, 3. *precor vos ego vinctus in Domino, ut ambuletis sicuti convenit vocationi qua vocati estis: cum omni
animi submissione et lenitate, cum iræ cohibitione, sustinentes
alii alios per charitatem; studentes conservare unitatem spi-
10 ritus per connexum pacis.* Col. iii. 16. *sermo Christi inhabitet
in vobis copiose cum omni sapientia, docendo et commone-
faciendo vos mutuo psalmis et hymnis et cantionibus spiritualibus, cum gratia canendo in vestro corde Domino.* 1 Thess.
iv. 18. *consolamini alii alios istis sermonibus.* Heb. iii. 13.
15 *exhortamini alii alios quotidie, quoad appellatur dies hodiernus.* et x. 24. *observemus alii alios, ut nos acuamus ad charitatem et bona opera.* 1 Cor. xi. 17, 18. *ut vos non laudem
quod videlicet, non cum emolumento, sed cum detrimento
convenitis. primum enim cum convenitis in ecclesia, audio
20 dissidia inter vos esse—.* 1 Cor. xiv. 40. *omnia decenter et
ordine fiant.* Col. ii. 5. *etsi enim corpore absum, spiritu*

CHAPTER XXXII.

OF CHURCH DISCIPLINE.

THE bond by which a particular church is held together, is its DISCIPLINE.

CHURCH DISCIPLINE consists in a mutual agreement among the members of the church to fashion their lives according to Christian doctrine, and to regulate every thing in their public meetings decently and with order. Rom. xii. 4. to the end of the chapter. Eph. iv. 1–3. "I therefore, the prisoner of the Lord, beseech you that ye walk worthy of the vocation wherewith ye are called, with all lowliness and meekness, with longsuffering, forbearing one another in love; endeavoring to keep the unity of the Spirit in the bond of peace." Col. iii. 16. "let the word of Christ dwell in you richly in all wisdom, teaching and admonishing one another in psalms and hymns and spiritual songs, singing with grace in your hearts unto the Lord." 1 Thess. iv. 18. "comfort one another with these words." Heb. iii. 13. "exhort one another daily, while it is called to-day, lest any of you be hardened through the deceitfulness of sin." x. 24. "let us consider one another to provoke unto love and to good works." 1 Cor. xi. 17, 18. "I praise you not, that ye come together not for the better, but for the worse; for first of all, when ye come together in the church, I hear that there be divisions among you." xiv. 40. "let all things be done decently and in order." Col. ii. 5. "though I be absent in the flesh, yet am I with you

tamen sum vobiscum, gaudens et cernens vestrum ordinem et
soliditatem vestræ in Christum fidei.

In ecclesiis particularibus constituendis prudenter et pie
solennis renovatio fœderis fieri solet: quemadmodum et in
5 reformatione ecclesiæ antiquæ sæpe fieri solebat. Deut. xxix.
1. *hæc sunt verba fœderis quod præcepit Iehova Mosi ut pan-*
geret cum filiis Israelis in terra Moabitarum, præter fœdus
illud quod pepigerat cum illis in Chorebo. Sic sub Asa, Ezra,
Nehemia et aliis.

10 Necnon ut quisque se particulari ecclesiæ adiungit, quasi
inito fœdere spondere Deo et ecclesiæ solenniter debebit, se,
quantum in se est, omnia illa præstiturum et erga Deum et
erga ecclesiam, quæ et ad sui et ad fratrum ædificationem
pertinent. Et hoc proprie in baptismo fieri debuerat; quæ est
15 cuiusque, non infantis, sed adulti introductio in ecclesiam.

Et quia fere fit, ut plerique sedem ac domicilium sæpe
mutent, idcirco toties iteranda hæc sponsio erit, quoties quis
ab una particulari ecclesia in alteram se transfert; nisi erit ab
alia ecclesia orthodoxa testimonio amplissimo commendatus:
20 neque enim aliud videtur posse satis disciplinam stabilire, ne
sensim diffluat et dissolvatur.

Mos cœtuum habendorum, non ex hodierna consuetudine
retinendus, sed ex apostolorum institutis restituendus est.

in the spirit, joying, and beholding your order, and the steadfastness of your faith in Christ."

It is a prudent as well as a pious custom, to solemnize the
formation or re-establishment of a particular church by a
5 public renewal of the covenant; as was frequently done in
the reformations of the Jewish church; Deut. xxix. 1. "these
are the words of the covenant which Jehovah commanded
Moses to make with the children of Israel in the land of
Moab, beside the covenant which he made with them in
10 Horeb." The same took place under Asa, Ezra, Nehemiah,
and others.

So also, when an individual unites himself to a particular
church, it is requisite that he should enter into a solemn covenant with God and the church, to conduct himself in all
15 respects, both towards the one and the other, so as to promote
his own edification and that of his brethren. This covenant
ought properly to take place in baptism, as being the rite appointed for the admission of all persons, that is, of all adults,
into the church. Seeing also that most men are liable to a
20 frequent change of residence, it will be necessary that this
promise should be repeated so often as they pass from one
particular church to another, unless they are provided with
the most satisfactory testimonials from some other orthodox
church; this being apparently the only means by which dis-
25 cipline can be adequately maintained, or prevented from sink-
ing into gradual decline and dissolution.

The custom of holding assemblies is to be maintained, not
after the present mode, but according to the apostolical insti-

Ubi non unus isque mercede conductus, ius omne verba faciendi e superiore loco solus occupabat, sed unusquisque fidelium pro donis sibi concessis, vices obtinebat suas loquendi, prophetandi, docendi, hortandi, et infirmissimus quisque interrogandi et consulendi seniores et doctiores. 1 Cor. xiv. 26, &c. *quoties convenitis, quisque vestrum——*.

Quem morem ab Iudaica synagoga imitati apostoli, in ecclesiis retinuerunt. Luc. ii. 46. *audientem eos, et eos interrogantem.* et iv. 16. *surrexit ut legeret——:* et alibi quoties in synagoga vel etiam in templo Christus docuisse perhibetur; Matt. xxvi. 55. Ioan. vii. 14. facta enim est Christo ista potestas ab Iudæis non ut Christo, sed ut cuilibet donis prædito: sicuti et apostolis; Act. xiii. 5. *annuntiarunt sermonem Dei in synagogis Iudæorum——.* et v. 15. *post lectionem legis et prophetarum miserunt præfecti synagogæ ad eos dicentes, viri fratres, si quis est in vobis sermo exhortationis ad populum dicite:* etenim præfecti synagogæ constituti sunt qui omnia moderarentur; Marc. v. 22. *unus ex archisynagogis;* Luc. viii. 41. *præfectus synagogæ.* et xiii. 14. *archisynagogus indignans, quod——.* Act. xiii. 15. ut supra, et alibi.

tution, which did not ordain that an individual, and he a stipendiary, should have the sole right of speaking from a higher place, but that each believer in turn should be authorized to speak, or prophesy, or teach, or exhort, according to
5 his gifts; insomuch that even the weakest among the brethren had the privilege of asking questions, and consulting the elders and more experienced members of the congregation. 1 Cor. xiv. 26, &c. "when ye come together, every one of you," &c.

10 This custom was derived by the apostles from the synagogue, and transferred by them to the churches. Luke ii. 46. "hearing them, and asking them questions." iv. 16. "he stood up for to read." Compare also other places where Christ is related to have taught in the synagogue, and even in the
15 temple, Matt. xxvi. 55. John vii. 14. a permission which was granted to him not as Christ, but simply as a gifted individual, in the same manner as it was afterwards granted to the apostles, Acts xiii. 5. "they preached the word of God in the synagogues of the Jews." v. 15. "after the reading of the law
20 and the prophets, the rulers of the synagogue sent unto them, saying, Ye men and brethren, if ye have any word of exhortation for the people, say on." These rulers of the synagogue were persons appointed to see that all things were done in order. Mark v. 22. "one of the rulers of the synagogue."
25 Luke viii. 41. "a ruler of the synagogue." xiii. 14. "the ruler of the synagogue answered with indignation, because that Jesus had healed on the sabbath day." Acts xiii. 15. as above, &c.

Mulieres autem tacere in ecclesia iubentur. 1 Cor. xiv. 34, 35. *mulieres vestræ in conventibus sileant; nec enim permissum est iis ut loquantur, sed ut subditæ sint, sicut et lex dicit:* (nempe Gen. iii. 16.) *quod si quid discere volunt, domi suos* 5 *viros interrogent; nam turpe est muileribus in ecclesia loqui.* 1 Tim. ii. 11, 12. *mulier cum silentio discito, cum omni submissione. Mulieri vero docere non permitto, neque auctoritatem usurpare in virum, sed ut sit in silentio.*

Administratio disciplinæ *potestas clavium* dicitur; quæ non 10 Petro soli aut sub eo nomine cuivis pastori mandatur, sed omni ecclesiæ particulari, membrorum quamvis paucorum: Matt. xvi. 19. *tibi dabo claves regni cœlorum; et quicquid ligaveris in terra, erit ligatum in cœlis,* cum cap. xviii. 17, 18, 19, 20. *dic ecclesiæ——. Amen dico vobis, quæcunque ligave-* 15 *ritis in terra, erunt ligata in cœlo; et quæcunque solveritis in terra, erunt soluta in cœlis. Rursum dico vobis, si duo ex vobis consenserint in terra, de omni re quam petierint, fiet iis a patre meo qui in cœlis est: ubi enim sunt duo vel tres congregati in nomine meo, illic sum in medio eorum.* Ioan. xx. 22, 20 23. *quum hoc dixisset, inhalavit et dixit iis accipite spiritum sanctum: si quorum remiseritis peccata, remittuntur iis; si quorum retinueritis, retenta sunt.* 1 Cor. v. 4. *vobis et meo*

Women, however, are enjoined to keep silence in the church. 1 Cor. xiv. 34, 35. "let your women keep silence in the churches, for it is not permitted unto them to speak, but they are commanded to be under obedience, as saith the law"

5 (Gen. iii. 16.); "and if they will learn anything, let them ask their husbands at home; for it is a shame for women to speak in the church." 1 Tim. ii. 11, 12. "let the woman learn in silence in all subjection: but I suffer not a woman to teach, nor to usurp authority over the man, but to be in silence."

10 The administration of discipline is called "the power of the keys"; a power not committed to Peter and his successors exclusively, or to any individual pastor specifically, but to the whole particular church collectively, of whatever number of members composed. Matt. xvi. 19. "I will give unto thee the

15 keys of the kingdom of heaven; and whatsoever thou shalt bind on earth, shall be bound in heaven," compared with xviii. 17–20. "tell it unto the church . . . verily I say unto you, Whatsoever ye shall bind on earth shall be bound in heaven, and whatsoever ye shall loose on earth shall be loosed

20 in heaven: again, I say unto you, that if two of you shall agree on earth, as touching anything that they shall ask, it shall be done for them of my Father which is in heaven: for where two or three are gathered together in my name, there am I in the midst of them." John xx. 22, 23. "when he had said this,

25 he breathed on them, and saith unto them, Receive ye the Holy Ghost: whosesoever sins ye remit, they are remitted unto them; and whosesoever sins ye retain, they are retained." 1 Cor. v. 4. "when ye are gathered together, and my spirit."

spiritu. et 2 Ep. ii. 7, 8. *vos condonetis*—. *quapropter precor vos ut ratam faciatis in illum charitatem.* Apoc. iii. 7, 8. *hæc dicit sanctus et verax ille, qui habet clavem Davidis; qui aperit, et nemo claudit; et claudit, et nemo aperit. ecce posui* 5 *in tuo conspectu ostium apertum; nec quisquam potest illud claudere.*

Versatur autem disciplinæ administratio, primum in suscipiendis leniterque tractandis infirmis aut lapsis. Rom. xiv. 1. *eum qui fide est infirmus assumite; non tamen ad alterca-* 10 *tiones disputationum.* Gal. vi. 1. *fratres, etiamsi præoccupatus fuerit homo in aliqua offensa, vos spirituales reconcinnate huiusmodi hominem cum spiritu lenitatis; considerans unusquisque temetipsum, ne et tu tenteris.* Matt. ix. 16. *nullus indit panniculum novum in vestimentum vetus: illud enim* 15 *ipsius supplementum tollit aliquid ex illo vestimento, et fit peior fissura.* Ioan. xvi. 12. *adhuc multa habeo quæ vobis dicam, sed nunc non potestis portare.* 1 Thess. v. 14. *consolamini eos qui pusillo animo sunt; sublevate infirmos.* Iudæ 22, 23. *alios quidem habito delectu commiseramini*—. 20 Eorum causa facta sunt ab apostolis decreta illa temporaria, Act. xv. et Paulus Timotheum circumcidit, Act. xvi. 3. et purificavit se in templo, cap. xxi. 26.

Tum in componendis fratrum dissidiis. Matt. xviii. 17. *quod si neglexerit te audire, dic ecclesiæ.* 25 In iis qui gravius offendunt monendis vel palam reprehendendis. 1 Tim. v. 20. *eos qui peccant, in conspectu omnium*

2 Cor. ii. 7, 8. "ye ought rather to forgive him . . . wherefore I beseech you that ye would confirm your love toward
him." Rev. iii. 7, 8. "these things saith he that is holy, he that
is true, he that hath the key of David, he that openeth and
5 no man shutteth; and shutteth, and no man openeth . . .
behold, I have set before thee an open door, and no man can
shut it."

The administration of discipline consists, first, in receiving
and treating with gentleness the weak or lapsed members of
10 the church. Rom. xiv. 1. "him that is weak in the faith receive ye, but not to doubtful disputations." Gal. vi. 1. "brethren, if a man be overtaken in a fault, ye which are spiritual
restore such an one in the spirit of meekness, considering
thyself, lest thou also be tempted." Matt. ix. 16. "no man
15 putteth a piece of new cloth unto an old garment; for that
which is put in to fill it up taketh from the garment, and the
rent is made worse." John xvi. 12. "I have yet many things
to say unto you, but ye cannot bear them now." 1 Thess. v.
14. "comfort the feeble-minded, support the weak." Jude 22,
20 23. "of some have compassion, making a difference." It was
for the sake of such that those temporary decrees were made,
Acts xv. For similar reasons Paul circumcised Timothy, xvi.
3. and purified himself in the temple, xxi. 26.

Secondly, in composing differences between the brethren,
25 Matt. xviii. 17. "if he shall neglect to hear them, tell it to
the church."

Thirdly, in admonishing or openly rebuking grievous of-
fenders. 1 Tim. v. 20. "them that sin rebuke before all."

argue—. Tit. iii. 10. *hæreticum hominem post unam et alte-*
ram admonitionem admittere recusa. 1 Cor. iv. 21. *cum virga*
veniam ad vos, an cum charitate, et spiritu lenitatis? et 2 Ep.
ii. 6. *sufficit istiusmodi homini ista increpatio a pluribus illis*
5 *profecta.* 1 Thess. v. 14. *admonete inordinatos.* 1 Tim. v. 1,
&c. *seniorem ne increpato*—. 3 Ioan. 10. *si venero, memo-*
riam renovabo ipsius facinorum quæ facit—.

In immorigeris a communione segregandis. Rom. xvi. 17.
precor vos fratres, ut observetis dissidiorum et offendiculorum
10 *auctores contra doctrinam quam vos didicistis: et declinetis*
ab eis. 1 Cor. v. 11. *cum eiusmodi ne comeditote.* 2 Thess.
iii. 6. *denuntiamus vobis, fratres, in nomine Domini nostri*
Iesu Christi, ut subducatis vos ab omni fratre qui inordinate
ambulat, et non ex tradita doctrina quam accepit a nobis. et
15 v. 14. *si quis non auscultat nostro per epistolam sermoni, hunc*
notate; et ne commercium habete cum eo, ut erubescat. 2 Ioan.
10, 11. *si quis venit ad vos, et hanc doctrinam non adfert,*
ne recipite eum domum, nec Ave ei dicite: qui enim dicit ei
Ave, communicat operibus eius malis. Apoc. ii. 14. *sed habeo*
20 *adversum te pauca, quod habeas istic qui teneant doctrinam*
Balaam—.

Vel etiam eiiciendis; ad conversationem tamen eorum si
resipiscant, non ad interitum: et more quidem synagogæ,
Ioan. ix. 22, 34. et xii. 42. Matt. xviii. 17. *quod si ecclesiam*
25 *audire neglexerit, sit tibi velut qui est ethnicus et publicanus.*

Tit. iii. 10. "a man that is an heretic, after the first and second admonition reject." 1 Cor. iv. 21. "shall I come unto you with a rod, or in love, and in the spirit of meekness?" 2 Cor. ii. 6. "sufficient to such a man is this punishment, which was
5 inflicted of many." 1 Thess. v. 14. "warn them that are unruly." 1 Tim. v. 1. "rebuke not an elder." 3 John 10. "if I come, I will remember his deeds which he doeth."

Fourthly, in separating the disobedient from the communion of the church. Rom. xvi. 17. "I beseech you, brethren,
10 mark them which cause divisions and offences contrary to the doctrine which ye have learned, and avoid them." 1 Cor. v. 11. "with such an one no not to eat." 2 Thess. iii. 6. "we command you, brethren, in the name of our Lord Jesus Christ, that ye withdraw yourselves from every brother that
15 walketh disorderly, and not after the tradition which he received of us." v. 14. "if any man obey not our word by this epistle, note that man, and have no company with him, that he may be ashamed." 2 John 10, 11. "if there come any unto you, and bring not this doctrine, receive him not into your
20 house, neither bid him God speed; for he that biddeth him God speed, is partaker of his evil deeds." Rev. ii. 14. "I have a few things against thee, because thou hast there them that hold the doctrine of Balaam."

Or even, lastly, in ejecting them from the church; not
25 however for their destruction, but rather for their preservation, if so they may be induced to repent; as was done in the ancient synagogue, John ix. 22, 34. xii. 42. Matt. xviii. 17. "if he neglect to hear the church, let him be unto thee as an

1 Cor. v. 5. *huiusmodi homo tradatur Satanæ,* (id est rursus mundo, qui extra ecclesiam cum sit, Satanæ regnum est) *ad exitium carnis, ut spiritus salvus sit die illo Domini Iesu.* 2 Cor. ii. 7, 8. *ut e contrario potius vos condonetis, eumque* consolemini, *ne quo modo redundante tristitia, absorbeatur vir eiusmodi—.* et xiii. 10. *propterea hæc absens scribo, ne præsens præcisa severitate utar ex auctoritate quam dedit mihi Dominus ad ædificationem, ac non ad destructionem.* 2 Thess. iii. 15. *neque ut inimicum ducite, sed admonete ut fratrem.* 1 Tim. i. 20. *quos tradidi Satanæ, ut castigati discant non blasphemare.* Apoc. ii. 2. *novi patientiam, et quod non possis ferre malos.*

Sunt tamen qui insanabiles merito habentur. 1 Cor. xvi. 22. *si quis non amat Dominum Iesum Christum, esto anathema, maran-atha:* qua voce ad iudicium terribile venientis Domini reus insanabilis reiicitur. 1 Ioan. v. 16. *est peccatum ad mortem; non pro illo dico ut roget.*

Inter potestatem civilem et ecclesiasticam hæc intersunt: 1. in ditione civili est quivis homo; in causis nimirum civilibus; Rom. xiii. 1. *omnis anima potestatibus sublimioribus subiecta esto:* in ditione ecclesiastica tantum ecclesiæ membra; idque in causis tantummodo ad religionem spectantibus, pœ-

heathen man and a publican." 1 Cor. v. 5. "deliver such an one unto Satan," that is, give him over again to the world, which, as being out of the pale of the church, is the kingdom of Satan, "for the destruction of the flesh, that the spirit may be saved in the day of the Lord Jesus." 2 Cor. ii. 7, 8. "so that contrariwise ye ought rather to forgive him, and comfort him, lest perhaps such an one should be swallowed up with overmuch sorrow." xiii. 10. "therefore I write these things, being absent, lest being present I should use sharpness, according to the power which the Lord hath given me to edification, and not to destruction." 2 Thess. iii. 15. "yet count him not as an enemy, but admonish him as a brother." 1 Tim. i. 20. "whom I have delivered unto Satan, that they may learn not to blaspheme." Rev. ii. 2. "I know thy patience, and how thou canst not bear them that are evil."

There are some, however, who may justly be considered irrecoverable. 1 Cor. xvi. 22. "if any man love not the Lord Jesus Christ, let him be Anathema, Maran-atha"; by which form of words an incurable sinner is abandoned to the dreadful judgment of the Lord at his final advent. 1 John v. 16. "there is a sin unto death; I do not say that he shall pray for it."

The civil power differs from the ecclesiastical in the following respects. First, every man is subject to the civil power; that is to say, in matters properly civil. Rom. xiii. 1. "let every soul be subject unto the higher powers." On the contrary, none but the members of the church are subject to ecclesiastical power, and that only in religious matters, with

nisque duntaxat ecclesiasticis, id est, duntaxat internis: Matt.
xviii. 15, 16. *si peccaverit in te frater tuus, dic ecclesiæ*—: *si
ecclesiam*—, *sit tibi velut qui est ethnicus et publicanus;* Ioan.
viii. 11. *nec ego te condemno;* 1 Cor. v. 11, 12, 13. *nunc*
5 *scripsi vobis ne commisceamini*—. *Siquis frater nominatus
sit scortator*—; *cum eiusmodi ne comeditote. Quid enim mea
interest de extraneis iudicare?* 2. in illa ditione sunt corpus
et facultates externæ tantum; in hac facultates duntaxat animi,
et in hac quidem sola; Luc. xii. 14. *quis me vobis iudicem*
10 *aut partitorem præfecit?* Act. v. 4. *nonne si servasses*—?
1 Cor. vi. 4. *itaque si iudicia habeatis de iis quæ ad huius vitæ
usum pertinent, eos qui nullo loco habentur in ecclesia, eos,
inquam, in subselliis, collocate.* et 2 Ep. x. 3, 4. *in carne
ambulantes, non secundum carnem militamus: arma enim*
15 *militiæ nostræ non carnalia sunt*—. Iacob. iv. 12. *unus est
legislator qui potest servare et perdere: tu quis est qui damnas
alium?* immo hortatur nos apostolus ne quid in religione
imperari nobis ab hominibus sinamus; 1 Cor. vii. 23. *pretio
empti estis; ne fiatis servi hominum.* 3. in illa resipiscentibus
20 etiam pœna irrogatur; in hac resipiscentibus quibuscunque
gratia conceditur, Ioan. viii. 7. *quum perseverarent eum in-
terrogare, dixit ad eos, qui vestrum immunis est*—.

a liability to ecclesiastical punishment alone, that is, to punishment inflicted by their own body: Matt. xviii. 15, 16. "if thy brother shall trespass against thee . . . tell it unto the church; if he neglect to hear the church, let him be unto thee as an heathen man and a publican." John viii. 11. "neither do I condemn thee." 1 Cor. v. 11–13. "now I have written unto you not to keep company, if any man that is called a brother be a fornicator . . . with such an one no not to eat: for what have I to do to judge also them that are without?" Secondly, the civil power has dominion only over the body and external faculties of man; the ecclesiastical is exercised exclusively on the faculties of the mind, which acknowledge no other jurisdiction. Luke xii. 14. "who made me a judge or a divider over you?" Acts v. 4. "whiles it remained, was it not thine own?" 1 Cor. vi. 4. "if then ye have judgments of things pertaining to this life, set them to judge who are least esteemed in the church." 2 Cor. x. 3, 4. "though we walk in the flesh, we do not war after the flesh; for the weapons of our warfare are not carnal—." James iv. 12. "there is one lawgiver who is able to save and to destroy: who art thou that judgest another?" Nay, we are expressly enjoined not to suffer ourselves to be governed by the commandments of men in matters of religion. 1 Cor. vii. 23. "ye are bought with a price; be not ye the servants of men." Thirdly, the civil power punishes even such as confess their faults; the ecclesiastical, on the contrary, pardons all who are penitent. John viii. 7. "when they continued asking him, he lifted up himself, and said unto them, He that is without sin among you, let him first cast a stone at her."

Potestas ecclesiæ contra disciplinæ contemptores permagna
et potentissima est: 2 Cor. x. 4, &c. *arma militiæ nostræ non
carnalia sunt, sed divinitus valida ad destructionem muni-
tionum; ratiocinationes evertendo, omnemque sublimitatem*
5 *quæ sese extollit adversus cognitionem Dei; et in captivitatem
redigendo omnem cogitationem ad obediendum Christo; et
paratum habendo quo ulciscamur omnem inobedientiam.*

Derogant itaque multum potestati ecclesiæ, atque diffi-
dunt, qui vi et armis magistratuum opus esse ad regendas
10 ecclesias putant.

CAPUT XXXIII.

DE GLORIFICATIONE PERFECTA; UBI DE SECUNDO CHRISTI ADVENTU, ET RESURRECTIONE MORTUORUM, HUIUSQUE MUNDI CONFLAGRATIONE.

DICTUM est supra capite xxv. de GLORIFICATIONE
NOSTRA INCHOATA in hac nempe vita: dicendum
nunc postremo est de GLORIFICATIONE PERFECTA in
sempiterno tandem ævo perficienda.

15   Huius ante legem typus fuit Enochus cœlo receptus, Gen.
v. 24. et Elias, 2 Reg. ii. 11.

Ea perfici demum et consummari incipit ab adventu secundo Christi ad mundum iudicandum et resurrectione mor-

The power of the church against those who despise her discipline is exceedingly great and extensive. 2 Cor. x. 4, &c. "the weapons of our warfare are not carnal, but mighty through God to the pulling down of strong holds; casting 5 down imaginations, and every high thing that exalteth itself against the knowledge of God, and bringing into captivity every thought to the obedience of Christ; and having in a readiness to revenge all disobedience."

It is therefore highly derogatory to the power of the church, 10 as well as an utter want of faith, to suppose that her government cannot be properly administered without the intervention of the civil magistrate.

CHAPTER XXXIII.

OF PERFECT GLORIFICATION, INCLUDING THE SECOND ADVENT OF CHRIST, THE RESURRECTION OF THE DEAD, AND THE GENERAL CONFLAGRATION.

IN THE twenty-fifth chapter I treated of that IMPERFECT GLORIFICATION to which believers attain in this life. I now proceed to consider, lastly, that PERFECT GLORIFICATION which is effected in eternity.

Before the law this was typified by the translation of Enoch, Gen. v. 24. as it was under the law by that of Elijah, 2 Kings ii. 11.

20 Its fulfilment and consummation will commence from the period of Christ's second coming to judgment, and the resur-

tuorum. Luc. xxi. 28. *quum hæc fieri incipient, sursum respicite et attollite capita vestra, quoniam appropinquat redemptio vestra.* 2 Thess. i. 7. *vobis vero qui affligimini, relaxationem nobiscum, in revelatione Domini Iesu de cœlo.*

5 DE ADVENTU DOMINI AD IUDICIUM, quo is cum sanctis angelis suis mundum iudicaturus est, prædictum est, primum ab Enocho et prophetis, deinde ab ipso Christo et apostolis. Iudæ 14, 15. *prophetavit etiam de istis septimus ab Adamo, Enochus; dicens, Ecce venit Dominus cum sanctis millibus*
10 *suis: ut ferat iudicium adversus omnes, et redarguat quicunque ex ipsis sunt impii, de factis omnibus quæ impie patrarint, deque omnibus duris quæ locuti fuerint adversus ipsum peccatores impii.* Dan. vii. 22. *usquedum veniret antiquus dierum, et iudicium daretur sanctis——.* Matt. xxv. 31. *quum*
15 *venerit filius hominis cum gloria sua, et omnes sancti angeli cum eo.* Act. i. 11. *hic Iesus qui——, ita veniet quemadmodum spectastis eum proficiscentem in cœlum.* et x. 42. *eum esse qui definitus sit a Deo iudex vivorum ac mortuorum.* et xvii. 31. *eo quod statuit diem, quo iuste iudicaturus est orbem terrarum*
20 *per eum virum quem definiit——; illo ex mortuis suscitato.* 2 Thess. i. 7, 8. *in revelatione Domini Iesu de cœlo cum angelis suis potentibus.*

Diem et horam adventus Christi solus pater novit; Matt. xxiv. 36. Marc. xiii. 32. *de die illo ac hora nemo novit——.*
25 Act. i. 7. *non est vestrum nosse tempora sive opportunitates*

rection of the dead. Luke xxi. 28. "when these things begin
to come to pass, then look up, and lift up your heads, for your
redemption draweth nigh." 2 Thess. i. 7. "to you who are
troubled rest with us, when the Lord Jesus shall be revealed
5 from heaven."

THE COMING OF THE LORD TO JUDGMENT, when he shall
judge the world with his holy angels, was predicted, first, by
Enoch and the prophets; afterwards by Christ himself and his
apostles. Jude 14, 15. "Enoch also, the seventh from Adam,
10 prophesied of these, saying, Behold, the Lord cometh with
ten thousand of his saints, to execute judgment upon all, and
to convince all that are ungodly among them of all their ungodly deeds which they have ungodly committed, and of
all their hard speeches which ungodly sinners have spoken
15 against him." Dan. vii. 22. "until the Ancient of days came,
and judgment was given to the saints of the most High."
Matt. xxv. 31. "the Son of man shall come in his glory, and
all the holy angels with him." Acts i. 11. "this same Jesus
. . . shall so come in like manner as ye have seen him go
20 into heaven." x. 42. "it is he which was ordained of God to
be the judge of quick and dead." xvii. 31. "he hath appointed
a day in the which he will judge the world in righteousness
by that man whom he hath ordained . . . in that he hath
raised him from the dead." 2 Thess. i. 7, 8. "the Lord Jesus
25 shall be revealed from heaven with his mighty angels."

The day and hour of Christ's coming are known to the
Father only. Matt. xxiv. 36. Mark xiii. 32. "of that day and
that hour knoweth no man." Acts i. 7. "it is not for you to

quas pater in sua ipsius auctoritate statuit. Dan. xii. 8, 9. *dixi, Domine mi, quis finis futurus istorum? Et ille, Abi inquit, Daniel; nam occlusæ sunt et obsignatæ hæ res usque ad tempus determinatum.* Poterit etiam hac de re legi utilissimus
5 liber Zanchii de fine sæculi, tom. vii.

Erit itaque repentinus. Matt. xxv. 6. *media autem nocte clamor ortus est dicentium, ecce, sponsus venit, exite in occursum eius.* Luc. xvii. 26, &c. *prout in diebus Noæ—; et ut in diebus Lot—.* et xxi. 34, 35. *cavete vobis ne quando—;*
10 *et repente vobis superveniat dies ille: nam ut laqueus invadet in omnes qui habitant in superficie totius terræ.* 1 Thess. v. 2, 3. *scitis diem illum Domini, ut fur nocte ita venturum esse: quum enim dicent pax et securitas, tunc repentinum eis imminet exitium—.*

15 Signa tamen quædam a Christo et apostolis sunt tradita, quæ de adventu eius nos admoneant: Matt. xxiv. a v. 3. ad 27. cum Marc. xiii. et Luc. xxi.

Signa autem illa communia sunt vel propria.

Communia sunt quæ excidium Hierosolymitanum veluti
20 typum adventus sui et adventum ipsum communiter prænuntiant: cuiusmodi sunt pseudoprophetæ, pseudochristi, bella, terræ motus, persecutiones, pestis, fames, fidei et charitatis imminutio ad hunc usque diem, Matt. xxiv. a v. 3. ad 27. 2 Tim. iii. 1, &c.

25 Propria sunt securitas atque impietas extrema, et universa

know the times or the seasons which the Father hath put in his own power." Dan. xii. 8, 9. "then said I, O my lord, what shall be the end of these things? and he said, Go thy way, Daniel; for the words are closed up and sealed till the
5 time of the end." The treatise of Zanchius *De fine sæculi,* tom. vii. may be likewise advantageously consulted on this subject.

Hence it will be sudden. Matt. xxv. 6. "at midnight there was a cry made, Behold, the bridegroom cometh; go ye out
10 to meet him." Luke xvii. 26, &c. "as it was in the days of Noe . . . likewise also as it was in the days of Lot." xxi. 34, 35. "take heed to yourselves, lest at any time," &c. "and so that day come upon you unawares; for as a snare shall it come upon all them that dwell on the face of the whole earth."
15 1 Thess. v. 2, 3. "for yourselves know perfectly, that the day of the Lord so cometh as a thief in the night: for when they shall say, Peace and safety, then sudden destruction cometh upon them."

Certain signs however are pointed out by Christ and his
20 apostles as indicative of its approach; Matt. xxiv. 3–27. Mark xiii. Luke xxi. These signs are either general or peculiar.

The general signs are those which relate equally to the destruction of Jerusalem, the type of Christ's advent, and to the advent itself; such as false prophets, false Christs, wars,
25 earthquakes, persecutions, pestilence, famine, and the gradual decay of faith and charity, down to the very day itself. Matt. xxiv. 3–27. 2 Tim. iii. 1, &c.

The peculiar signs are, first, an extreme recklessness and

prope defectio. Luc. xviii. 8. *filius hominis cum venerit, num repturus est fidem in terra?* 2 Thess. ii. 3. *non adveniet dies Christi, quin venerit defectio prius*—. 1 Tim. iv. 1.

Secundo, antichristi revelatio, et per spiritum oris Christi
5 abolitio. 2 Thess. ii. 3. *et revelatus fuerit homo ille peccati, filius ille perditionis*—. et v. 8. *et tum revelabitur exlex ille, quem Dominus absumet spiritu oris sui, et evanescere faciet illo suo illustri adventu.*

Signum aliud huc referunt nonnulli, vocationem univer-
10 sam non Iudæorum solum, sed etiam Israelitarum. Isa. xi. 11, 12. *erit enim tempore illo, ut adhibeat Dominus secundo manum suam*—. et xiv. 1, &c. *miserebitur Iehova Iacobi, et eliget rursus Israelitas, quos reponat*—. et xxvii. 14, 15. *excutiet Iehova inde a fluxu illius fluminis usque ad*—: Ier.
15 iii. 7. *revertere aversa Israel*—. et v. 13. *temporibus illis euntes domus Iehudæ cum domo Israelis*—. et xxx. 3. *reducam captivam multitudinem populi mei Israelis et Iehudæ*—. et xxxi. 5. *adhuc conseras vineas in montibus Samariæ*—. et v. 36, &c. *si amovebuntur statuta ista a conspectu meo*—.
20 et cap. xxxiii. 7. *reducam captivam multitudinem Iehudæ captivamque multitudinem Israelis*—. Ezech. xx. 41, 42. *et experiemini me esse Iehovam, cum reduxero vos*—. et xxxvii. 21, 22. *et efficiam eos gentem unam in illa terra*—. Hos. iii. 5. *postea reversi Israelitæ*—. Amos. ix. 14, 15. *et reducam*

impiety, and an almost universal apostasy. Luke xviii. 8. "when the Son of man cometh, shall he find faith on the earth?" 2 Thess. ii. 3. "that day shall not come, except there come a falling away first." Compare also 1 Tim. iv. 1.

5   Secondly, the revealing of antichrist, and his destruction by the spirit of the mouth of Christ. 2 Thess. ii. 3. "that man of sin shall be revealed, the son of perdition—." v. 8. "and then shall that Wicked be revealed, whom the Lord shall consume with the spirit of his mouth, and shall destroy with the 10 brightness of his coming."

    Some refer to the same event another sign, namely, the calling of the entire nation of the Jews, as well as of the ten dispersed tribes. Isa. xi. 11, 12. "it shall come to pass in that day, that Jehovah shall set his hand again the second time—." 15 xiv. 1. "Jehovah will have mercy on Jacob, and will yet choose Israel, and set them in their own land." xxvii. 12. "Jehovah shall beat off from the channel of the river unto the stream of Egypt." Jer. iii. 12. "return, thou backsliding Israel." v. 18. "in those days the house of Judah shall walk with the house 20 of Israel." xxx. 3. "I will bring again the captivity of my people Israel and Judah." xxxi. 5. "thou shalt yet plant vines upon the mountains of Samaria." v. 36, &c. "if those ordinances depart from before me—." xxxiii. 7. "I will cause the captivity of Judah and the captivity of Israel to return—." 25 Ezek. xx. 42. "ye shall know that I am Jehovah, when I shall bring you into the land of Israel." xxxvii. 21, 22. "I will make them one nation in the land—." Hos. iii. 5. "afterward shall the children of Israel return." Amos ix. 14, 15.

captivam multitudinem populi mei Israelis—. Zech. viii. 23.
erit diebus illis quum prehendent decem homines—. et xii.
4, &c. *die illo, dictum Iehovæ, percutiam omnem equum*—.
Itaque reduces Iudæi, Ezræ vi. 17. *obtulerunt hircos lactentes*
5 *in peccata pro toto Israele duodecim, pro numero tribuum*
Israelis; utpote quas Deus omnes adhuc pro suis habebat; etsi
in hunc usque diem ex captivitate nondum reduces. Luc.
xxi. 24. *Ierusalem conculcata erit a Gentibus, donec implean-*
tur tempora Gentium. Rom. xi. 12, 13. *quod si offensa eorum*
10 *est*—; *quanto magis plenitudo ipsorum?* et v. 15. *nam si*
abiectio eorum—, *quæ erit assumptio?* et v. 25. *nolim enim*
vos ignorare, fratres, mysterium hoc—; *obdurationem ex*
parte Israeli evenisse, tantisper dum—: *et ita totus Israel*
servabitur.
15 Adventus Christi erit tardus. 2 Thess. ii. 1, 2, 3. *rogamus*
autem vos fratres, per adventum Domini nostri Iesu Christi
et nostri ad eum aggregationem, ne cito a mente dimoveamini,
neque per spiritum neque per sermonem neque per epistolam
tanquam per nos scriptam, quasi instet dies ille Christi. ne
20 *quis vos seducat ullo modo. non enim adveniet dies Christi,*
quin venerit—. 2 Pet. iii. 3, 4, &c. *venturos extremis diebus*
irrisores—; *dicentes, ubi est pollicitatio adventus eius*—, ad
finem capitis: ubi et ratio redditur cur diem adventus sui dif-
ferat Dominus.

"I will bring again the captivity of my people of Israel." Zech.
viii. 23. "in those days it shall come to pass that ten men shall
take hold . . . of him that is a Jew," &c. xii. 4, &c. "in
that day, saith Jehovah, I will smite every horse with astonish-
5 ment—." Thus the Jews, on their return from the Babylonish captivity, Ezra vi. 17. "offered for a sin-offering for all
Israel, twelve he-goats, according to the number of the tribes
of Israel," all which God still accounted as his own, though
even to the present day they have not returned out of cap-
10 tivity. Luke xxi. 24. "Jerusalem shall be trodden down of the
Gentiles, until the times of the Gentiles be fulfilled." Rom.
xi. 12, 13. "now if the fall of them be the riches of the world
. . . how much more their fulness?" v. 15. "if the casting
away of them be the reconciling of the world, what shall the
15 receiving of them be?" v. 25. "I would not, brethren, that
ye should be ignorant of this mystery . . . that blindness in
part is happened to Israel until the fulness of the Gentiles be
come in: and so all Israel shall be saved."

Christ will delay his coming. 2 Thess. ii. 1–3. "now we
20 beseech you, brethren, by the coming of our Lord Jesus Christ,
and by our gathering together unto him, that ye be not soon
shaken in mind, or be troubled, neither by spirit, nor by word,
nor by letter as from us, as that the day of Christ is at hand:
let no man seduce you by any means; for that day shall not
25 come, except there come a falling away first—." 2 Pet. iii.
3, 4, &c. "there shall come in the last days scoffers . . . saying, Where is the promise of his coming?" &c. to the end of
the chapter; where the reason of his delay is assigned.

Erit illustris. Matt. xxiv. 27. *sicut fulgur exit ab oriente, et apparet usque ad occidentem, ita etiam erit adventus filii hominis.* et v. 30. *videbunt filium hominis venientem in nubibus cœli cum potentia et gloria multa.* Luc. xxi. 27. 5 idem. Matt. xxv. 31. *quum venerit filius hominis cum gloria sua, et omnes sancti angeli cum eo, tunc sedebit in throno gloriæ—.* 1 Thess. iv. 16. *nam ipse Dominus cum hortationis clamore, cum voce archangeli, et cum Dei tuba descendet e cœlo.* et 2 Thess. i. 10. *quum venerit, ut glorificetur in* 10 *sanctis suis, et admirandus fiat in credentibus omnibus die illo.* Tit. ii. 13. *expectantes beatam illam spem, et illustrem adventum gloriæ magni Dei ac servatoris nostri Iesu Christi.* Iudæ 14. *ecce, venit Dominus cum sanctis millibus suis.*

Erit terribilis. Isa. lxvi. 15, 16. *nam ecce, Iehova cum* 15 *igne venturus est et curribus suis similibus turbini, ad reddendum cum excandescentia iram et increpationem suam cum flammis ardentibus.* et cap. xiii. 9, 10. cum Matt. xxiv. 29, 30. *statim autem post afflictionem dierum illorum, sol obscurabitur, nec edet luna splendorem suum, et stellæ cadent* 20 *de cœlo, et potestates cœlorum concutientur.* Marc. xiii. 24, 25. idem. Luc. xxi. 25, 26. *tunc erunt signa in sole et luna et stellis, et in terra anxietas gentium consilii inopia, resonante mari et salo: exanimatis hominibus præ metu—.* 2 Thess. i. 7, 8. *in revelatione Domini Iesu de cœlo cum angelis suis* 25 *potentibus, cum igne flammante—.* Apoc. vi. a v. 12. ad

His advent will be glorious. Matt. xxiv. 27. "as the light-
ning cometh out of the east, and shineth even unto the west,
so shall also the coming of the Son of man be." v. 30. "they
shall see the Son of man coming in the clouds of heaven with
5 power and great glory." See also Luke xxi. 27. Matt. xxv.
31. "when the Son of man shall come in his glory, and all the
holy angels with him, then shall he sit upon the throne of his
glory." 1 Thess. iv. 16. "the Lord himself shall descend from
heaven with a shout, with the voice of the archangel, and
10 with the trump of God." 2 Thess. i. 10. "when he shall come
to be glorified in his saints, and to be admired in all them that
believe in that day." Tit. ii. 13. "looking for that blessed hope,
and the glorious appearing of the great God and our Savior
Jesus Christ." Jude 14. "behold, the Lord cometh with ten
15 thousand of his saints."

It will be terrible. Isa. lxvi. 15, 16. "behold, Jehovah will
come with fire, and with his chariots like a whirlwind, to
render his anger with fury, and his rebuke with flames of
fire." xiii. 9, 10. compared with Matt. xxiv. 29, 30. "imme-
20 diately after the tribulation of those days shall the sun be
darkened, and the moon shall not give her light, and the stars
shall fall from heaven, and the powers of the heavens shall
be shaken." See also Mark xiii. 24, 25. Luke xxi. 25, 26.
"there shall be signs in the sun and in the moon, and in the
25 stars, and upon the earth distress of nations, with perplexity,
the sea and the waves roaring, men's hearts failing them for
fear." 2 Thess. i. 7, 8. "the Lord Jesus shall be revealed from
heaven with his mighty angels, in flaming fire." Rev. vi. 12.

finem capitis; *et ecce, terræ motus magnus—, et reges terræ, et optimates, et divites, et tribuni— occultarunt se in speluncis et in petris montium—.*

Adventum Christi secundum sequitur mortuorum resurrectio et iudicium extremum.

RESURRECTIO MORTUORUM non sub evangelio primum credita est. Iob. xix. 25, 26, &c. *equidem ego novi redemptorem meum vivere; et posteriorem super pulverem resurrecturum. et postquam vermes confoderint istud evigilante me, tunc carne mea me visurum esse Deum.* Psal. xvi. 10, &c. *non es derelicturus animam meam in sepulchro—.* et xvii. 14, 15. *ab hominibus e mundo, quorum portio est in hac vita—.* et xlix. 15, 16. *tanquam pecudes, in sepulchro dispositos mors depascet eos, donec—.* Isa. li. 6, &c. *cœlos velut fumum—; salus vero mea in sæculum erit.* et xxvi. 19. *reviviscunt tui mortui, cadavera quæque mea resurgunt: expergiscemini, inquis, et cantate qui inhabitatis pulverem—.* Zech. iii. 7. *sic ait Iehova exercituum, si—, utique disponam tibi qui ambulent inter adstantes istos.* Dan. xii. 2. *tandemque multi ex dormientibus in pulverulenta terra expergiscentur: hi ad vitam æternam, illi ad opprobria et contemptum æternum.* Hos. xiii. 14. cum I Cor. xv. 54. *e potestate sepulchri redimam eos, a morte vindicabo eos: ubi sunt pestes tuæ, o mors? ubi exitium tuum o sepulchrum?* Act. xxiv. 15. *et spem habeam in Deo, fore, quam etiam ii ipsi expectant, resurrectionem mortuorum, tum iustorum tum iniustorum.* et xxvi. 6, 7, 8. *ob spem pro-*

to the end of the chapter; "lo, there was a great earthquake
. . . and the kings of the earth, and the great men, and the
rich men, and the chief captains . . . hid themselves in the
dens and in the rocks of the mountains."

5   The second advent of Christ will be followed by the resurrection of the dead and the last judgment.

A belief in the RESURRECTION OF THE DEAD existed even before the time of the gospel. Job xix. 25, 26, &c. "I know that
my Redeemer liveth, and that he shall stand at the latter day
10 upon the earth; and though after my skin worms destroy this
body, yet in my flesh I shall see God." Psal. xvi. 10, &c. "thou
wilt not leave my soul in hell." xvii. 14, 15. "from men of
the world, which have their portion in this life." xlix. 14, 15.
"like sheep they are laid in the grave; death shall feed on
15 them," &c. Isa. li. 6, &c. "the heavens shall vanish away like
smoke . . . but my salvation shall be for ever." xxvi. 19.
"thy dead men shall live, together with my dead body shall
they arise; awake and sing, ye that dwell in dust." Zech. iii.
7. "thus saith Jehovah of hosts; if," &c. "I will give thee
20 places to walk among these that stand by." Dan. xii. 2.
"many of them that sleep in the dust of the earth shall awake;
some to everlasting life, and some to shame and everlasting
contempt." Hos. xiii. 14. compared with 1 Cor. xv. 54. "I
will ransom thee from the power of the grave, I will redeem
25 thee from death: O death, I will be thy plagues; O grave, I
will be thy destruction." Acts xxiv. 15. "have hope toward
God, which they themselves also allow, that there shall be a
resurrection of the dead, both of the just and unjust." xxvi.

missionis factæ patribus nostris a Deo, sto in iudicium vo-
catus—. Quid? incredibile iudicatur apud vos quod Deus
mortuos suscitet? Heb. xi. 10. *expectabat enim civitatem*
illam habentem fundamenta, cuius artifiex et conditor est
5 *Deus.*

Deinde sub evangelio, testante Christo. Matt. xii. 41.
Ninevitæ resurgent in iudicio cum gente ista—. Ioan. v. 28,
29. *veniet hora quum omnes qui in monumentis sunt, audient*
vocem eius. Et prodibunt qui bona fecerint, in resurrecti-
10 *onem vitæ; qui vero mala egerint, in resurrectionem condem-*
nationis. et vi. 39, 40. idem. et 1 Cor. vi. 14. idem. et
xv. 52. *canet tuba, et mortui excitabuntur incorrupti.* et 2
Ep. iv. 14. *scientes fore, ut qui suscitavit Dominum Iesum,*
nos quoque per Iesum suscitet, et sistat vobiscum. 1 Thess. iv.
15 14. idem.

Testimoniis hisce de resurrectione rationes quoque acce-
dunt: 1. quia Dei fœdus morte non dissolvitur. Matt. xxii.
32. *Deus non est Deus mortuorum, sed viventium.* 2. *si*
resurrectio non est futura, ne Christus quidem adhuc resur-
20 *rexit,* 1 Cor. xv. 13, 20. et v. 23. *unusquisque suo ordine;*
primitiæ Christus, postea qui sunt Christi, in adventu ipsius.
Ioan. xi. 25. *dixit ei Iesus, ego sum resurrectio et vita.* 3.
iusti essent omnium miserrimi; impii beatissimi, quorum
portio in hac vita longe opimior est; quod divina providentia

6–8. "I stand and am judged for the hope of the promise made of God unto our fathers . . . why should it be thought a thing incredible with you, that God should raise the dead?" Heb. xi. 10. "he looked for a city which hath foundations, whose builder and maker is God."

This expectation was confirmed under the gospel by the testimony of Christ. Matt. xii. 41. "the men of Nineveh shall rise in judgment with this generation." John v. 28, 29. "the hour is coming, in the which all that are in the graves shall hear his voice, and shall come forth, they that have done good unto the resurrection of life, and they that have done evil unto the resurrection of damnation." See also vi. 39, 40. and 1 Cor. vi. 14. xv. 52. "the trumpet shall sound, and the dead shall be raised incorruptible." 2 Cor. iv. 14. "knowing that he which raised up the Lord Jesus, shall raise up us also by Jesus, and shall present us with you." See also 1 Thess. iv. 14.

To these testimonies from Scripture, may be added several arguments from reason in support of the doctrine. First, the covenant with God is not dissolved by death. Matt. xxii. 32. "God is not the God of the dead, but of the living." Secondly, "if there be no resurrection of the dead, then is Christ not risen," 1 Cor. xv. 13–20. v. 23. "every man in his own order; Christ the first-fruits, afterward they that are Christ's at his coming." John xi. 25. "Jesus said unto her, I am the resurrection and the life." Thirdly, were there no resurrection, the righteous would be of all men most miserable, and the wicked, who have a better portion in this life, most happy; which would be altogether inconsistent with the providence

ac iustitia plane indignum foret? 1 Cor. xv. 19. *si in hac solum vita speramus in Christum*—. et v. 30, 31, 32. *cur etiam nos periclitamur omni momento*—.

Fit autem resurrectio vel mortuorum resuscitatione, vel viventium subita mutatione.

Videtur idem numero quisque homo resurrecturus: Iob. xix. 26, 27. *postquam vermes confoderint istud evigilante me, tunc carne mea me visurum esse Deum. Idem qui sum ac non alienus visurus sum mihi, et oculi mei aspecturi.* 1 Cor. xv. 53. *oportet corruptibile istud induere incorruptibilitatem.* et 2 Ep. v. 4. *in quo constituti non cupimus eo exui, sed superindui; ut absorbeatur mortale a vita.* et v. 10. *ut unusquisque reportet quæ in corpore fecerit congruenter ad id quod fecerit, sive bonum sive malum.* Hoc nisi sit, Christo conformes non erimus; qui et ipse corpore proprio, carne et sanguine proprio, eodem scilicet quo mortuus est et resurrexit, et gloriam est ingressus.

Viventium mutatio docetur, 1 Cor. xv. 51, 52. *ecce mysterium*—; *omnes mutabimur*—. 1 Thess. iv. 15, 17, 18. *hæc enim vobis dicimus verbis Domini, fore ut nos vivi qui reliqui erimus in adventum Domini, non præveniamus eos qui obdormierint: et qui mortui fuerint in Christo, resurgent primum; deinde nos vivi qui reliqui erimus, rapiemur simul cum iis in nubes, in occursum Domini, in aëra; et ita semper cum Domino erimus.*

and justice of God. 1 Cor. xv. 19. "if in this life only we have
hope in Christ—." v. 30–32. "why stand we in jeopardy
every hour?"

This resurrection will take place partly through the resus-
citation of the dead, and partly through a sudden change
operated upon the living.

It appears indicated in Scripture that every man will rise
numerically one and the same person. Job xix. 26, 27.
"though after my skin worms destroy this body, yet in my
flesh shall I see God: whom I shall see for myself, and mine
eyes shall behold, and not another." 1 Cor. xv. 53. "this cor-
ruptible must put on incorruption." 2 Cor. v. 4. "not for that
we would be unclothed, but clothed upon, that mortality
might be swallowed up of life." v. 10. "that every one may
receive the things done in his body, according to that he hath
done, whether it be good or bad." Otherwise we should not
be conformed to Christ, who entered into glory with that
identical body of flesh and blood, wherewith he had died and
risen again.

The change to be undergone by the living is predicted 1
Cor. xv. 51. "behold, I show you a mystery . . . we shall
all be changed." 1 Thess. iv. 15–18. "this we say unto you
by the word of the Lord, that we which are alive and remain
unto the coming of the Lord shall not prevent them which
are asleep . . . and the dead in Christ shall rise first: then
we which are alive and remain shall be caught up together
with them in the clouds, to meet the Lord in the air, and so
shall we ever be with the Lord."

IUDICIUM EXTREMUM est quo CHRISTUS CUM SANCTIS, GLORIA ATQUE POTENTIA PATRIS INSTRUCTUS MALOS ANGELOS, HOMINUMQUE GENUS UNIVERSUM IUDICABIT.

GLORIA ET POTENTIA PATRIS INSTRUCTUS. Ioan. v. 22. *nec pater*
5 *iudicat quenquam, sed omne iudicium dedit filio.* et v. 27.
auctoritatem ei dedit iudicium exercendi, quatenus filius ho
minis est: id est, quatenus etiam homo est; ut Act. xvii. 31.
iudicaturus est orbem terrarum per eum virum——. Rom. ii.
16. *in die quo iudicabit Dominus de occultis hominum ex*
10 *evangelio meo, per Iesum Christum.*

CUM SANCTIS. Matt. xix. 28. *vos qui secuti estis me in re*
generatione, quum sederit filius hominis in throno gloriæ suæ,
sedebitis vos etiam in thronis duodecim, iudicantes duodecim
tribus Israel. Luc. xxii. 30. idem. 1 Cor. vi. 2, 3. *an ignoratis*
15 *sanctos mundi iudices futuros? An ignoratis fore ut ange*
lorum iudices simus?

ANGELOS MALOS. 1 Cor. vi. 2, 3. ut supra.

HOMINUM GENUS UNIVERSUM. Matt. xxiv. 31. *mittet angelos*
suos cum tubæ voce magna, et congregabunt electos eius a
20 *quatuor ventis, a cœlorum extremo ad eorum extremum.* et
xxv. 32, &c. *congregabuntur coram eo omnes gentes, et*
separabit eos alios ab aliis, ut pastor separat oves ab hœdis——.
Rom. xiv. 10. *omnes sistemur apud tribunal Christi.* 2 Cor.
v. 10. *omnes nos comparere oportet coram tribunali Christi.*
25 Apoc. xx. 12, 13. *vidi mortuos parvos et magnos stantes in*
conspectu Dei. et reddidit mare &c. mors quoque et Infernus
reddiderunt mortuos quos habebant.

IUDICABIT. Eccles. xii. 16. *omne opus Deus ipse adducet in*

The LAST JUDGMENT is that wherein CHRIST WITH THE SAINTS, ARRAYED IN THE GLORY AND POWER OF THE FATHER, SHALL JUDGE THE EVIL ANGELS, AND THE WHOLE RACE OF MANKIND.

5   ARRAYED IN THE GLORY AND POWER OF THE FATHER. John v. 22. "the Father judgeth no man, but hath committed all judgment unto the Son." v. 27. "he hath given him authority to execute judgment also, because he is the Son of man"; that is, because he is himself man. So Acts xvii. 31. "he will

10 judge the world in righteousness by that man—." Rom. ii. 16. "in the day when God shall judge the secrets of men by Jesus Christ, according to my gospel."

WITH THE SAINTS. Matt. xix. 28. "ye which have followed me in the regeneration, when the Son of man shall sit in the

15 throne of his glory, ye also shall sit upon twelve thrones, judging the twelve tribes of Israel." See also Luke xxii. 30. 1 Cor. vi. 2, 3. "do ye not know that the saints shall judge the world? . . . know ye not that we shall judge angels?"

SHALL JUDGE. Eccles. xii. 14. "God shall bring every work

20 into judgment, with every secret thing, whether it be good, or whether it be evil." Matt. xii. 36, 37. "every idle word that men shall speak, they shall give account thereof in the day of judgment; for by thy words thou shalt be justified, and by thy words thou shalt be condemned"; that is to say, where

25 our actions do not correspond with our words. Rom. xiv. 12. "so then every one of us shall give account of himself to God." 1 Cor. iv. 5. "until the Lord come, who both will bring to light the hidden things of darkness, and will make manifest

iudicium cum omni re occulta, sive bonum sive malum. Matt.
xii. 36, 37. *quodcunque verbum futile locuti fuerint homi-*
nes, de eo reddituros rationem in die iudicii: ex sermonibus
enim tuis iustificaberis, et ex sermonibus tuis condemnaberis:
5 nempe si probi cum fuerint, facta non respondeant. Rom.
xiv. 12. *unusquisque vestrum de seipso rationem reddet Deo.*
1 Cor. iv. 5. *usquedum venerit Dominus; qui et illustraturus*
est res tenebris occultatas, et manifesta faciet consilia cor-
dium: ac tunc laus erit unicuique a Deo. et 2 Ep. v. 10. *ut*
10 *unusquisque reportet quæ in corpore fecerit, congruenter ad*
id quod fecerit, sive bonum sive malum.

　　Norma iudicii erit ipsa conscientia, ex illa luce quam quisque accepit. Ioan. xii. 48. *qui dedignatur, nec recipit verba*
mea, habet qui condemnet ipsum: sermo quem locutus sum,
15 *ille condemnabit eum ultimo die.* Rom. ii. 12. *quicunque*
absque lege peccaverunt, absque lege quoque peribunt: et
quicunque cum lege peccaverunt, per legem damnabuntur.
et v. 14. *nam quum gentes quæ legem non habent natura*
quæ legis sunt faciunt; istæ legem non habentes, sibi ipsis
20 *sunt lex: ut qui ostendant opus legis scriptum in cordibus*
suis; una testimonium reddente ipsorum conscientia, et cogi-

the counsels of the hearts; and then shall every man have praise of God." 2 Cor. v. 10. "that every one may receive the things done in his body, according to that he hath done, whether it be good or bad."

5 THE EVIL ANGELS. 1 Cor. vi. 2, 3, as above.

THE WHOLE RACE OF MANKIND. Matt. xxiv. 31. "he shall send his angels with a great shout of a trumpet, and they shall gather together his elect from the four winds, from one end of heaven to the other." xxv. 32, &c. "before him shall be
10 gathered all nations; and he shall separate them one from another, as a shepherd divideth his sheep from the goats." Rom. xiv. 10. "we shall all stand before the judgment-seat of Christ." 2 Cor. v. 10. "we must all appear before the judgment-seat of Christ." Rev. xx. 12, 13. "I saw the dead, small
15 and great, stand before God . . . and the sea gave up the dead which were in it, and death and hell delivered up the dead which were in them."

The rule of judgment will be the conscience of each individual, according to the measure of light which he has en-
20 joyed. John xii. 48. "he that rejecteth me, and receiveth not my words, hath one that judgeth him; the word that I have spoken, the same shall judge him at the last day." Rom. ii. 12. "as many as have sinned without law, shall also perish without law; and as many as have sinned in the law shall be
25 judged by the law." v. 14. "when the Gentiles, which have not the law, do by nature the things contained in the law, these having not the law, are a law unto themselves: which show the work of the law written in their hearts, their con-

tationibus se mutuo accusantibus aut excusantibus; in die quo
iudicabit Dominus de occultis hominum ex evangelio meo,
per Iesum Christum. Iacob. ii. 12. *ut per legem libertatis*
iudicandi. Apoc. xx. 12. *et libri aperti sunt: et alius liber*
5 *apertus est qui est liber vitæ; iudicatique sunt mortui ex iis*
quæ scripta erant in libris, secundum opera ipsorum.

Iudicii huius extremi tempore (neque enim unius diei
spatio tot angelorum hominumque myriades sisti et iudicari
posse verisimile est, et dies pro quovis tempore sæpe intelligi-
10 tur) ab initio inquam huius iudicii ad finem usque et aliquanto post finem, promissum illud toties Christi cum sanctis
suis regnum in terris gloriosum videtur futurum; quoad hostes
eius omnes debellati erunt. Nam ab adventu eius primo regnum quidem gratiæ, quod et *regnum cœlorum* dicitur, et
15 promulgatum fuisse ab Ioanne baptista et initium habuisse
constat; regnum autem gloriæ non nisi ab adventu eius secundo, Dan. vii. 13, 14. *ecce cum nubibus cœli similis filio*
hominis veniebat—: et huic datus est dominatus, gloriaque
ac regnum—; nempe ex quo cum nubibus veniebat, quo
20 modo semper alias describitur adventus eius, non in carnem,
ut vult Iunius, (etenim tum similis filio hominis fuisset ante-

sciences also bearing witness, and their thoughts the mean-
while accusing or else excusing one another; in the day when
God shall judge the secrets of men by Jesus Christ according
to my gospel." James ii. 12. "as they that shall be judged by
5 the law of liberty." Rev. xx. 12. "the books were opened; and
another book was opened, which is the book of life; and the
dead were judged out of those things which were written in
the books, according to their works."

Coincident, as appears, with the time of this last judgment
10 —I use the indefinite expression time, as the word day is
often employed to denote any given period, and as it is not
easily imaginable that so many myriads of men and angels
should be assembled and sentenced within a single day—
beginning with its commencement, and extending a little
15 beyond its conclusion, will take place that glorious reign of
Christ on earth with his saints, so often promised in Scripture, even until all his enemies shall be subdued. His kingdom of grace, indeed, which is also called "the kingdom of
heaven," began with his first advent, when its beginning was
20 proclaimed by John the Baptist, as appears from testimony
of Scripture; but his kingdom of glory will not commence
till his second advent. Dan. vii. 13, 14. "behold, one like the
Son of man came with the clouds of heaven . . . and there
was given him dominion and glory, and a kingdom"; "given
25 him," that is, from the time when he came with the clouds
of heaven (in which manner his final advent is uniformly
described) not to assume our nature, as Junius interprets it,
(for then he would have been like the Son of man before he

quam homo erat, quod certe minus conveniebat) sed ad iudicium; ad id usque tempus quo regnum depositurus est, 1 Cor.
xv. 24. *deinde erit finis*—: de quo infra dicetur. In terris
autem futurum illud regnum testimonia quam plurima de-
5 monstrant. Psal. ii. 8, 9. cum Apoc. ii. 25, 26, 27. *donabo*
gentes in possessionem tuam; et fines terræ ius possessionis
tuæ: confringes eos virga ferrea; ut vas figlinum dissipabis eos.
et cx. 5, 6. *Dominus ad dexteram tuam, frangens die iræ suæ*
reges: iudicium exercebit in gentes, complens corporibus,
10 *frangens caput in regionibus plurimis.* Isa. ix. 7. *amplitudini*
illius principatus et pacis nullus erit finis, in solio Davidis et
in regno eius—. Dan. vii. 22. *usquedum veniret antiquus*
dierum, et iudicium daretur sanctis excelsorum, et tempus
perveniret quo regnum illud possiderent sancti. et v. 27.
15 *regnum dominatusque et amplitudo regnorum sub toto cœlo*
dabitur populo sanctorum excelsorum—. Luc. i. 32, 33.
dabit ei Dominus Deus sedem Davidis patris sui: regnabitque
in domo Iacobi in æternum, et regni eius non erit finis. Matt.
xix. 28. *vos qui secuti estis me, in regeneratione, quum sederit*
20 *filius hominis in throno gloriæ suæ, sedebitis vos etiam in*
thronis duodecim, iudicantes duodecim tribus Israelis. Luc.
xxii. 29, 30. *ego vero dispono vobis, sicut disposuit mihi pater,*
regnum: ut edatis et bibatis in mensa mea in regno meo; et

became man, which would be an incongruity) but to execute
judgment; from the period so indicated, to the time when he
should lay down the kingdom, 1 Cor. xv. 24. "then cometh
the end," of which more shortly. That this reign will be on
5 earth, is evident from many passages. Psal. ii. 8, 9. compared
with Rev. ii. 25–27. "I shall give thee the heathen for thine
inheritance, and the uttermost parts of the earth for thy possession; thou shalt break them with a rod of iron; thou shalt
dash them in pieces like a potter's vessel." cx. 5, 6. "Jehovah
10 at thy right hand shall strike through kings in the day of his
wrath: he shall judge among the heathen, he shall fill the
places with the dead bodies, he shall wound the heads over
many countries." Isa. ix. 7. "of the increase of his government and peace there shall be no end, upon the throne of
15 David and upon his kingdom." Dan. vii. 22. "until the
Ancient of days came, and judgment was given to the saints
of the most High, and the time came that the saints possessed
the kingdom." v. 27. "the kingdom, and dominion, and the
greatness of the kingdom under the whole heaven, shall be
20 given to the people of the saints of the most High—." Luke
i. 32, 33. "the Lord God shall give unto him the throne of his
father David; and he shall reign over the house of Jacob for
ever, and of his kingdom there shall be no end." Matt. xix.
28. "ye which have followed me, in the regeneration, when
25 the Son of man shall sit in the throne of his glory, ye also shall
sit upon twelve thrones, judging the twelve tribes of Israel."
Luke xxii. 29, 30. "I appoint unto you a kingdom, as my
Father hath appointed unto me; that ye may eat and drink

sedeatis super thronos, iudicium ferentes de duodecim tri-
bubus Israelis: Videtur hoc iudicium non diurnum sed diu-
turnum, non tam iudiciarium quam moderatorium; quo
sensu Gedeon, Iephtes et reliqui iudices per multos annos
5 iudicasse dicuntur. 1 Cor. xv. 23, 24, 25, 26. *unusquisque*
suo ordine: primitiæ Christus; postea qui sunt Christi, in
adventu ipsius: deinde erit finis—. Apoc. v. 10. *fecisti nos*
Deo nostro reges et sacerdotes, et regnabimus in terra. et xi.
15. *mundi regna facta sunt Domini nostri et Christi eius, qui*
10 *regnabit in sæcula sæculorum.* et 20. a v. 1. ad. v. 7. *deinde*
vidi thronos, et sederunt super eos, et iudicium datum est
iis—; viventque et regnabunt cum Christo mille annos. Re-
liqui vero ex mortuis non reviviscent donec consummati fue-
rint anni mille. hæc est resurrectio prima. beatus et sanctus
15 *qui habet partem in resurrectione prima: in hos secunda mors*
non habet potestatem; sed erunt sacerdotes Dei et Christi, et
regnabunt cum eo mille annis.

Post mille annos rursus furit Satanas et obsidet ecclesiam
collectis hostium maximis copiis: sed igne cœlitus misso fun-
20 ditur et ad sempiternum supplicium damnatur. Apoc. xx.
7, 8, 9. *postquam vero consummati fuerint anni mille, sol-*
vetur Satanas e carcere suo; et exibit ut seducat gentes quæ
sunt in quatuor angulis terræ, Gogum et Magogum; ut con-

at my table in my kingdom, and sit on thrones judging the twelve tribes of Israel." It appears that the "judgment" here spoken of will not be confined to a single day, but will extend through a great space of time; and that the word is used to
5 denote, not so much a judicial inquiry properly so called, as an exercise of dominion; in which sense Gideon, Jephthah, and the other judges are said to have judged Israel during many years. 1 Cor. xv. 23–26. "every man in his own order; Christ the first-fruits, afterward they that are Christ's at his coming:
10 then cometh the end—." Rev. v. 10. "thou hast made us unto our God kings and priests, and we shall reign on the earth." xi. 15. "the kingdoms of this world are become the kingdoms of our Lord, and of his Christ; and he shall reign for ever and ever." xx. 1–7. "I saw thrones, and they sat upon
15 them, and judgment was given unto them . . . and they lived and reigned with Christ a thousand years: but the rest of the dead lived not again until the thousand years were finished: this is the first resurrection: blessed and holy is he that hath part in the first resurrection; on such the second death
20 hath no power, but they shall be priests of God and of Christ, and shall reign with him a thousand years."

After the expiration of the thousand years Satan will rage again, and assail the church at the head of an immense confederacy of its enemies; but will be overthrown by fire from
25 heaven, and condemned to everlasting punishment. Rev. xx. 7–9. "when the thousand years are expired, Satan shall be loosed out of his prison, and shall go out to deceive the nations which are in the four quarters of the earth, Gog and Magog,

*greget eos ad prælium—: et circumierunt castra sanctorum
et urbem illam dilectam: sed descendit ignis a Deo de cœlo,
qui devoravit eos—.* 2 Thess. ii. 8. *et tunc revelabitur exlex
ille, quem Dominus absumet spiritu oris sui, et evanescere*
5 *faciet illo suo illustri adventu.*

Malorum angelorum hostiumque maximorum iudicium
sequitur omnium hominum. Apoc. xx. 11. ad finem capitis:
*tum vidi thronum magnum candidum, et quendam ei insi-
dentem—: et vidi mortuos parvos et magnos stantes in con-*
10 *spectu Dei, et libri aperti sunt: et alius liber apertus est, qui
est liber vitæ: iudicatique sunt mortui ex iis quæ scripta erant
in libris, secundum opera ipsorum. Et reddidit mare mortuos
quos habebat; mors quoque et sepulchrum reddiderunt mortuos quos habebant; et iudicatum est de singulis secundum*
15 *opera ipsorum.*

Tunc illa sententia pronuntiatum iri videtur. Matt. xxv.
34. *adeste benedicti patris mei, possidete regnum paratum
vobis a iacto mundi fundamento.* et v. 41. *execrandi, abite a
me in ignem illum æternum, paratum diabolo et angelis eius.*
20 Sententiam sequitur sententiæ executio: improborum
nempe supplicium, et iustorum perfecta glorificatio. Matt.
xxv. 46. *et abibunt isti ad supplicium æternum: iusti vero ad
vitam æternam.* Apoc. xx. 14, 15. *sepulchrum autem et mors
coniecta sunt in stagnum ignis: quæ est mors secunda. Et qui*

to gather them together to battle . . . and they compassed
the camp of the saints about, and the beloved city; and fire
came down from God out of heaven, and devoured them."
2 Thess. ii. 8. "then shall that Wicked be revealed, whom the
5 Lord shall consume with the spirit of his mouth, and shall
destroy with the brightness of his coming."

After the evil angels and chief enemies of God have been
sentenced, judgment will be passed upon the whole race of
mankind. Rev. xx. 11–15. "I saw a great white throne, and
10 him that sat on it . . . and I saw the dead, small and great,
stand before God; and the books were opened; and another
book was opened, which is the book of life; and the dead were
judged out of those things which were written in the books,
according to their works: and the sea gave up the dead which
15 was in it, and death and hell delivered up the dead which
were in them; and they were judged every man according to
their works."

Then, as appears, will be pronounced that sentence, Matt.
XXV. 34. "COME, YE BLESSED OF MY FATHER, INHERIT THE KING-
20 DOM PREPARED FOR YOU FROM THE FOUNDATION OF THE WORLD."
V. 41. "DEPART FROM ME, YE CURSED, INTO EVERLASTING FIRE,
PREPARED FOR THE DEVIL AND HIS ANGELS."

The passing of the sentence will be followed by its execu-
tion; that is to say, by the punishment of the wicked, and the
25 perfect glorification of the righteous. Matt. xxv. 46. "these
shall go away into everlasting punishment, but the righteous
into life eternal." Rev. xx. 14, 15. "death and hell were cast
into the lake of fire: this is the second death: and whosoever

inventus non est in libro vitæ scriptus, coniectus est in stagnum ignis.

Tum demum erit finis ille, de quo 1 Cor. xv. 24, 25, 26, 27, 28. *deinde erit finis quum tradiderit regnum Deo ac* 5 *patri; quum evanescere fecerit omne imperium et omnem potentiam et virtutem: nam oportet eum regnare usquequo omnes inimicos supposuerit pedibus eius. ultimus autem hostis evanescet mors: nam omnia subiecit sub pedibus eius. Quum autem dicit omnia esse ei subiecta; palam est hoc dici* 10 *excepto eo qui subiecit ei omnia. Postquam vero subiecta fuerint ei omnia, tunc et ipse filius subiicietur ei qui subiecerit ipsi omnia, ut Deus sit omnia in omnibus.*

At inquies, si Christus traditurus est regnum Deo ac patri, quo pacto erunt vera illa, Heb. i. 8. *ad filium autem, thronus* 15 *tuus, Deus, in sæculum sæculi;* Dan. vii. 14. *cuius dominatus, dominatus est perpetuus qui non præterit; et regnum eius regnum quod non corrumpitur;* Luc. i. 33. *regni eius non erit finis.* Respondeo, regni eius non fore finem in sæculum sæculi, id est, dum mundi sæcula durabunt, donec *tempus* 20 *non erit amplius,* Apoc. x. 6. donec omnia implebuntur quorum causa regnum accepit: non itaque præteribit regnum illud quasi irritum, non corrumpetur; neque erit finis ille dissolutionis sed perfectionis potius et impletionis, ut finis

was not found written in the book of life, was cast into the lake of fire."

Then will be the end, spoken of 1 Cor. xv. 24–28. "then cometh the end, when he shall have delivered up the king-
5 dom to God, even the Father, when he shall have put down all rule, and all authority, and power; for he must reign till he hath put all enemies under his feet: the last enemy that shall be destroyed is death; for he hath put all things under his feet: but when he saith, all things are put under him, it
10 is manifest that he is excepted which did put all things under him: and when all things shall be subdued unto him, then shall the Son also himself be subject unto him that put all things under him, that God may be all in all."

It may be asked, if Christ is to deliver up the kingdom to
15 God and the Father, what becomes of the declarations, Heb. i. 8. "unto the Son he saith, Thy throne, O God, is for ever and ever (*in sæculum sæculi*, for ages of ages)," and Dan. vii. 14. "his dominion is an everlasting dominion, which shall not pass away, and his kingdom that which shall not
20 be destroyed"; Luke i. 33. "of his kingdom there shall be no end." I reply, there shall be no end of his kingdom "for ages of ages," that is, so long as the ages of the world endure, until "time" itself "shall be no longer," Rev. x. 6. until every thing which his kingdom was intended to effect shall have been
25 accomplished; insomuch that his kingdom will not "pass away" as insufficient for its purpose; it will not be "destroyed," nor will its period be a period of dissolution, but rather of perfection and consummation, like the end of the

ille legis, Matt. v. 18. Quo sensu alia quoque multa dicuntur nunquam præteritura, sed perpetua atque æterna fore; ut circumcisio, Gen. xvii. 13. et lex ipsa cæremonialis, Lev. iii. 17. et xxiv. 8. et terra Canaan, Gen. xiii. 15. Ier. vii. 7.
5 et xxv. 5. et sabbathum, Exod. xxxi. 16. et sacerdotium Aaronis, Num. xviii. 8. et monumentum illud lapideum ad Iardenem, Ios. iv. 7. et signa cœlestia, Psal. cxlviii. 6. et terra, Eccles. i. 4. hæc tamen omnia finem aut habuerunt aut habitura sunt.

10 Mors autem secunda mortis primæ ratione, quæ corporalis dicta est, secunda nominatur: estque ex tribus illis gradibus, de quibus cap. xiii. ubi de pœna peccati; quartus atque ultimus mortis gradus, mors nempe æterna, damnatorum pœna.

Ad hanc referri potest mors mundi ipsius immundi atque
15 polluti, id est, finis et conflagratio. De huius mundi fine et conflagratione (quæ utrum ad substantiæ abolitionem an ad qualitatum duntaxat immutationem futura sit, incertum est et nostra parum refert) quantum scire nobis expedit, docemur, Iob. xiv. 13. *usquedum non erunt cœli.* Psal. cii. 27.
20 *ista peritura sunt—.* Isa. xxxiv. 4. *convolventurque tanquam liber cœli, et totus exercitus eorum decidet—.* et li. 6. *cœlos velut fumum evanituros esse—.* Matt. xxiv. 35. *cœlum et terra præteribunt—.* 1 Cor. vii. 31. *præterit species huius mundi.* 2 Pet. iii. 7. *qui nunc sunt cœli—, asservantur igni*

law, Matt. v. 18. In the same manner many other things are spoken of as never to pass away, but to remain eternally; as circumcision, Gen. xvii. 13. the ceremonial law in general, Lev. iii. 17. xxiv. 8. the land of Canaan, Gen. xiii. 15. Jer.
5 vii. 7. xxv. 5. the sabbath, Exod. xxxi. 16. the priesthood of Aaron, Num. xviii. 8. the memorial of stones at the river Jordan, Josh. iv. 7. the signs of heaven, Psal. cxlviii. 6. the earth, Eccles. i. 4. although every one of these has either already come to an end, or will eventually be terminated.

10   The second death is so termed with reference to the first, or death of the body. For the three other, or preparatory degrees of death, see chap. xiii. on the punishment of sin. The fourth and last gradation is that of which we are now speaking, namely, eternal death, or the punishment of the damned.
15   Under this death may be included the destruction of the present unclean and polluted world itself, namely, its FINAL CONFLAGRATION. Whether by this is meant the destruction of the substance of the world itself, or only a change in the nature of its constituent parts, is uncertain, and of no impor-
20 tance to determine; respecting the event itself, we are informed, so far as it concerns us to know, Job xiv. 12. "till the heavens be no more." Psal. cii. 26. "they shall perish." Isa. xxxiv. 4. "the heavens shall be rolled together as a scroll, and all their host shall fall down." li. 6. "the heavens shall van-
25 ish away like smoke." Matt. xxiv. 35. "heaven and earth shall pass away." 1 Cor. vii. 31. "the fashion of this world passeth away." 2 Pet. iii. 7. "the heavens and the earth, which are now . . . reserved unto fire against the day of judg-

in diem damnationis et exitii impiorum hominum. et v. 10.
quo die cœli cum stridore præteribunt—. et 12. *in quo cœli*
conflagrantes—. Apoc. x. 6. *iuravit per eum qui—, tempus*
non fore amplius. et xxi. 1. *primum enim cœlum et prima*
terra abierat et mare non amplius extabat.

Mors secunda, damnatorum pœna, in amissione summi
boni, id est, gratiæ atque tutelæ divinæ visionisque beatificæ,
quæ vulgo pœna damni vocatur, et in cruciatu æterno, quæ
vocatur pœna sensus, videtur esse posita. Matt. xxv. 41. *male-*
dicti abite a me in ignem æternum paratum diabolo et angelis
eius. Luc. xiii. 27, 28. *nescio unde vos sitis: abscedite a me*
omnes qui datis operam iniustitiæ. Illic erit fletus et stridor
dentium, quum videritis Abrahamum et Isaacum et Iacobum
et omnes prophetas in regno Dei, vos autem eiici foras. et xvi.
23. *quum esset in tormentis, vidit Abrahamum e longin-*
quo—. 2 Thess. i. 9. *expulsi a facie Domini, et a gloria roboris*
ipsius.

Pœnarum gravitas et duratio varie describitur. Isa. xxx. 33.
paratus est iam ante exitii locus, hic etiam ipsi regi constitutus
est, profundissimum, latissimum fecit Iehova, pyræ eius ignis,
et lignorum multum est; flatus Iehovæ quasi torrente sul-
phuris incendit eam. et lxvi. 24. cum Marc. ix. 44. *ubi vermis*
eorum non moritur, et ignis non extinguitur. Dan. xii. 2. *ad*

ment and perdition of ungodly men." v. 10. "in the which the heavens shall pass away with a great noise." v. 12. "wherein the heavens being on fire—." Rev. x. 6. "he sware by him that liveth for ever and ever . . . that there should
5 be time no longer." xxi. 1. "the first heaven and the first earth were passed away, and there was no more sea."

The second death, or the punishment of the damned, seems to consist partly in the loss of the chief good, namely, the favor and protection of God, and the beatific vision of his
10 presence, which is commonly called the punishment of loss; and partly in eternal torment, which is called the punishment of sense. Matt. xxv. 41. "depart from me, ye cursed, into everlasting fire, prepared for the devil and his angels." Luke xiii. 27, 28. "I know you not whence ye are; depart from me,
15 all ye workers of iniquity: there shall be weeping and gnashing of teeth, when ye shall see Abraham and Isaac and Jacob, and all the prophets, in the kingdom of God, and you yourselves thrust out." xvi. 23. "being in torments, he seeth Abraham afar off." 2 Thess. i. 9. "who shall be punished
20 with everlasting destruction from the presence of the Lord, and from the glory of his power."

The intensity and duration of these punishments are variously intimated. Isa. xxx. 33. "Tophet is ordained of old; yea, for the king it is prepared: he hath made it deep and
25 large; the pile thereof is fire and much wood; the breath of Jehovah, like a stream of brimstone, doth kindle it." lxvi. 24. compared with Mark ix. 44. "where their worm dieth not, and the fire is not quenched." Dan. xii. 2. "to shame and

opprobria et contemptum æternum. Matt. viii. 12. *tenebræ
exteriores, ubi erit fletus et stridor dentium;* et xiii. 42. et
alibi. Marc. ix. 43. *ignis inextinguibilis.* Rom. ii. 8, 9. *ira,
excandescentia, afflictio, angustia.* 2 Thess. i. 9. *qui pœnam*
5 *pendent æterni exitii.* Apoc. xiv. 11. *fumus tormenti ipsorum
ascendet in sæcula sæculorum; nec habebunt requiem die ac
nocte.* et xix. 3. idem. et xxi. 8. *portio assignata est in stagno,
ubi ardet ignis et sulphur.*

Gradus tamen pœnarum sunt pro ratione peccatorum.
10 Matt. xi. 22. *Tyri et Sidonis tolerabilior erit conditio in die
iudicii, quam vestra.* Luc. xii. 47, 48. *cædetur multis plagis.
cædetur paucis.*

Locus pœnæ INFERNUS vocatur: *Topheth,* Isa. xxx. 33. *ge-
henna ignis,* Matt. v. 22. sed clarius Matt. x. 28. *tenebræ*
15 *exteriores,* cap. viii. 12. et xxii. 13. et xxv. 30. *fornax ignis,*
cap. xiii. 42. ᾅδης, Luc. xvi. 23. et alibi. *locus tormenti,* v. 28.
puteus abyssi, Apoc. ix. 1. *lacus ignis,* cap. xx. 15. *ardens
igne et sulphure,* cap. xxi. 8.

Locus inferni videtur esse extra hunc mundum. Luc. xvi.
20 26. *inter nos et vos ingens hiatus constitutus est, ut ii qui
volunt—. Tenebræ exteriores,* ut supra. Apoc. xxii. 14, 15.
ingrediantur in civitatem: foris autem erunt canes—.

Nec rationes desunt; siquidem infernus damnatorum idem
est qui diabolo angelisque eius erat paratus, ut supra Matt. xxv.
25 41. et diaboli defectio ante lapsum hominis fuit, verisimile non

everlasting contempt." Matt. viii. 12. "outer darkness, there shall be weeping and gnashing of teeth." See also xiii. 42, &c. Mark ix. 43. "fire that never shall be quenched." Rom. ii. 8, 9. "indignation and wrath, tribulation and anguish." 2 Thess.

5 i. 9. "who shall be punished with everlasting destruction." Rev. xiv. 11. "the smoke of their torment ascendeth up for ever and ever, and they have no rest day nor night." See also xix. 3. xxi. 8. "they shall have their part in the lake which burneth with fire and brimstone."

10 Punishment, however, varies according to the degree of guilt. Matt. xi. 22. "it shall be more tolerable for Tyre and Sidon at the day of judgment, than for you." Luke xii. 47, 48. "he shall be beaten with many stripes . . . he shall be beaten with few stripes."

15 The place of punishment is called HELL; "Tophet," Isa. xxx. 33. "hell fire," Matt. v. 22. and still more distinctly x. 28. "outer darkness," viii. 12. xxii. 13. xxv. 30. "a furnace of fire," xiii. 42. "Hades," Luke xvi. 23; and elsewhere: "a place of torment," v. 28. "the bottomless pit," Rev. ix. 1. "the

20 lake of fire," xx. 15. "the lake which burneth with fire and brimstone," xxi. 8. Hell appears to be situated beyond the limits of this universe. Luke xvi. 26. "between us and you there is a great gulf fixed, so that they which would pass from hence to you cannot." Matt. viii. 12. "outer darkness." Rev.

25 xxii. 14, 15. "they may enter in through the gates into the city; for without are dogs." Nor are reasons wanting for this locality; for as the place of the damned is the same as that prepared for the devil and his angels, Matt. xxv. 41. in pun-

est, ut infernus intra mundum, et visceribus terræ nondum maledictæ pararetur. Eadem sententia Chrysostomi et Lutheri aliorumque recentiorum esse fertur. Quod si totus mundus demum conflagrabit, ut aliquot ex locis evangelii iam de-
5 monstratum est, quid fiet inferno, si in terræ meditullio est situs? certe conflagret una necesse erit, et eandem cum terra sortem subeat. Quod si fieret, præclare sane cum damnatis actum esset.

Hactenus de improborum supplicio: restat iustorum per-
10 fecta glorificatio.

Glorificatio perfecta est in vita æterna ac beatissima, quæ oritur potissimum ex visione Dei: describiturque Psal. xvi. 11. *notam facis mihi semitam vitæ; satietatem gaudiorum in conspectu tuo amœnissimorum; dextera tua in æternitatem.* et xvii.
15 15. *ego in iustitia videbo vultum tuum; satiabor quum expergiscar similitudine tua.* Dan. xii. 3. *erudientes splendebunt quasi splendore expansi; et iustificantes multos, ut stellæ, in sempiterna sæcula.* Matt. xiii. 43. *tunc iusti fulgebunt ut sol, in regno patris sui.* et xxii. 30. *sunt ut angeli Dei in cœlo.* et
20 cap. v. 8. *beati qui sunt mundi corde; quoniam ipsi Deum videbunt.* 1 Cor. ii. 9. *prædicamus, sicut scriptum est, quæ oculus non vidit, nec auris audivit, nec subierunt cor hominis quæ præparavit Deus iis a quibus ipse diligitur.* et xiii. 12.

ishment of their apostasy, which occurred before the fall of
man, it does not seem probable that hell should have been
prepared within the limits of this world, in the bowels of the
earth, on which the curse had not as yet passed. This is said
5 to have been the opinion of Chrysostom, as likewise of Luther
and some later divines. Besides, if, as has been shown from
various passages of the New Testament, the whole world is
to be finally consumed by fire, it follows that hell, being situated in the center of the earth, must share the fate of the
10 surrounding universe, and perish likewise; a consummation
more to be desired than expected by the souls in perdition.

Thus far of the punishment of the wicked; it remains to
speak of the perfect glorification of the righteous.

Perfect glorification consists in eternal life and perfect
15 happiness, arising chiefly from the divine vision. It is described Psal. xvi. 11. "thou wilt show me the path of life;
in thy presence is fulness of joy; at thy right hand there are
pleasures for evermore." xvii. 15. "I will behold thy face in
righteousness; I shall be satisfied, when I awake, with thy
20 likeness." Dan. xii. 3. "they that be wise shall shine as the
brightness of the firmament, and they that turn many to righteousness as the stars for ever and ever." Matt. xiii. 43. "then
shall the righteous shine forth as the sun in the kingdom of
their Father." xxii. 30. "they are as the angels of God in
25 heaven." v. 8. "blessed are the pure in heart, for they shall
see God." 1 Cor. ii. 9. "as it is written, Eye hath not seen,
nor ear heard, neither have entered into the heart of man, the
things which God hath prepared for them that love him."

videmus enim nunc per speculum et per ænigma; tunc autem coram cernemus; nunc aliquatenus, tunc vero amplius cognoscam prout amplius edoctus fuero. et xv. 42, 43. *ita erit et resurrectio mortuorum. Seritur corpus cum corruptione,*
5 *suscitatur cum incorruptione. Seritur fœdum, suscitatur cum gloria: seritur viribus cassum, suscitatur potens: seritur corpus animale, suscitatur corpus spirituale.* 2 Cor. iv. 16, 17. *excellenter excellentis gloriæ pondus æternum.* et v. 1. *scimus enim nos, si terrestris huius domus nostræ tabernaculum dis-*
10 *solutum fuerit, ædificium ex Deo habituros, domicilium non manu factum, æternum in cœlis—.* Eph. ii. 6. *unaque suscitavit, unaque collocavit in cœlis in Christo Iesu.* Philipp. iii. 21. *qui transfigurabit corpus nostrum humile, ut conforme fiat corpori eius glorioso—.* 1 Thess. iv. 17. *rapiemur simul*
15 *cum iis in nubes, in occursum Domini in aëra; et ita semper cum Domino erimus.* 2 Tim. iv. 8. *reposita est mihi iustitiæ corona, quam reddet mihi Dominus in illo die iustus iudex: non solum autem mihi, sed et omnibus qui expetiverint illustrem illum ipsius adventum.* 1 Pet. i. 4. *ad hæreditatem quæ*
20 *nec corrumpi potest, nec contaminari, nec marcescere: vobis in cœlis asservatam.* et v. 4. *quum conspicuus factus fuerit ille pastorum princeps, reportetis amarantinam illam gloriæ coronam.* et v. 10. *qui vocavit vos ad æternam suam gloriam in Christo Iesu.* 1 Ioan. iii. 2. *scimus autem fore, ut quum*
25 *ipse manifestus factus fuerit, similes ei simus, quoniam videbimus eum sicuti est.* Apoc. vii. 14, 15, 16, 17. *hi sunt qui—: ideo sunt ante thronum illum Dei; et colunt eum die*

xiii. 12. "now we see through a glass, darkly, but then face to
face; now I know in part, but then shall I know even as also
I am known." xv. 42, 43. "so also is the resurrection of the
dead: it is sown in corruption, it is raised in incorruption; it
5 is sown in dishonor, it is raised in glory; it is sown in weakness, it is raised in power; it is sown a natural body, it is
raised a spiritual body." 2 Cor. iv. 17. "a far more exceeding
and eternal weight of glory." v. 1. "we know that if our
earthly house of this tabernacle were dissolved, we have a
10 building of God, a house not made with hands, eternal in
the heavens." Eph. ii. 6. "hath raised us up together, and
made us sit together in heavenly places in Christ Jesus."
Philipp. iii. 21. "who shall change our vile body, that it
may be fashioned like unto his glorious body." 1 Thess.
15 iv. 17. "we shall be caught up together with them into the
clouds, to meet the Lord in the air, and so shall we ever be
with the Lord." 2 Tim. iv. 8. "henceforth there is laid up
for me a crown of righteousness, which the Lord, the righteous Judge, shall give me at that day, and not to me only, but
20 to all them also that love his appearing." 1 Pet. i. 4. "an
inheritance incorruptible, and undefiled, and that fadeth not
away, reserved in heaven for you." v. 4. "when the chief
shepherd shall appear, ye shall receive a crown of glory that
fadeth not away." v. 10. "who hath called us unto his eternal
25 glory by Christ Jesus." 1 John iii. 2. "we know that when he
shall appear we shall be like him, for we shall see him as he
is." Rev. vii. 14–17. "these are they . . . therefore are they
before the throne of God, and serve him day and night in his

ac nocte in templo eius; et is qui insidet illi throno, proteget
eos umbraculo. non esurient amplius, neque—. et xxi. 4.
abstersurus est Deus omnem lacrymam ab oculis eorum: et
mors amplius non extabit; neque luctus, neque clamor; neque
5 *labor extabit amplius.* et xxii. a v. 1. ad 5. *deinde ostendit*
mihi purum fluvium aquæ vivæ, splendidum tanquam cry-
stallum, procedentem ex throno Dei et agni—.

Sanctorum omnium parem fore in cœlo statum gloriæ non
videtur. Dan. xii. 3. *erudientes splendebunt quasi splendore*
10 *expansi, et iustificantes multos, ut stellæ, in sempiterna sæcula.*
Matt. xx. 23. *sedere ad dexteram meam et sinistram meam,*
non est meum dare, sed quibus paratum est a patre meo. 1
Cor. xv. 41, 42. *alius decor solis, et alius decor lunæ, et alius*
decor stellarum; stella enim stellæ præstat decore. Ita et resur-
15 *rectio mortuorum.*

IN CŒLIS. Matt. v. 12. *merces vestra multa est in cœlis.* Luc.
xii. 33. *parate vobis—thesaurum in cœlis qui nunquam de-*
ficiat. Philipp. iii. 20. *nostra civitas in cœlis est.* Heb. x. 34.
ut qui sciretis vos habere apud vos potiorem substantiam in
20 *cœlis et permanentem.*

Glorificationis nostræ comes erit cœli et terræ rerumque in
iis creatarum, quæ quidem nobis usui aut oblectationi esse
possint, renovatio et possessio. Isa. lxv. 17. *nam ecce, ego*
creaturus sum cœlos novos et terram novam, neque commem-
25 *orabuntur hæc priora, neque venient in animum.* et lxvi. 22.

temple; and he that sitteth on the throne shall dwell among them; they shall hunger no more, neither thirst—." xxi. 4. "God shall wipe away all tears from their eyes, and there shall be no more death, neither sorrow, nor crying, neither
5 shall there be any more pain." xxii. 1–5. "he showed me a pure river of water of life, clear as crystal, proceeding out of the throne of God and of the Lamb—."

It appears that all the saints will not attain to an equal state of glory. Dan. xii. 3. "they that be wise shall shine as the
10 brightness of the firmament, and they that turn many to righteousness as the stars for ever and ever." Matt. xx. 23. "to sit on my right hand and on my left is not mine to give, but it shall be given to them for whom it is prepared of my Father." 1 Cor. xv. 41, 42. "there is one glory of the sun,
15 and another glory of the moon, and another glory of the stars; for one star differeth from another star in glory: so also is the resurrection of the dead."

In heaven. Matt. v. 12. "great is your reward in heaven." Luke xii. 33. "provide yourselves . . . a treasure in the
20 heavens that faileth not." Philipp. iii. 20. "our conversation is in heaven." Heb. x. 34. "knowing in yourselves that ye have a better and an enduring substance."

Our glorification will be accompanied by the renovation of heaven and earth, and of all things therein adapted to our
25 service or delight, to be possessed by us in perpetuity. Isa. lxv. 17. "behold, I create new heavens and a new earth, and the former shall not be remembered, nor come into mind." lxvi. 22. "as the new heavens and the new earth, which I

*nam quemadmodum cœli illi novi et terra ipsa nova quam
ego facturus sum, constituta sunt coram me, dictum Iehovæ,
ita constitutum est semen vestrum et nomen vestrum.* Act. iii.
21. *quem oportet quidem cœli capiant, usque ad tempora*
5 *restitutionis omnium, de quibus locutus est Deus a sæculo per
os omnium sanctorum suorum prophetarum.* Matt. xix. 29.
*quisquis reliquerit domos aut fratres aut sorores, aut patrem
aut matrem aut uxorem aut liberos aut agros causa nominis
mei, centuplicia accipiet, et vitam æternam hæreditario iure*
10 *possidebit.* et xxvi. 29. *non bibam ab hoc tempore ex hoc
fructu vitis usque ad diem illum quum ipsum bibam vobiscum
in regno patris mei.* Luc. xiv. 15. *quidam ex iis qui simul
discumbebant dixit ei, Beatus qui edit panem in regno Dei:*
nec reprehenditur a Christo. et xxii. 30. *ut edatis ac bibatis in*
15 *mensa mea in regno meo.* Rom. viii. a v. 19 ad v. 24. *nam
expectatio creaturæ, revelationem filiorum Dei expectat—sub
spe quod et ipse conditus mundus liberabitur ex servitute cor-
ruptionis in libertatem filiorum Dei—.* 2 Pet. iii. 13. *cœlos
novos ac terram novam secundum promissum eius expecta-*
20 *mus, in quibus iustitia inhabitat.* Apoc. v. 10. *fecisti nos Deo
nostro reges et sacerdotes, et regnabimus in terra.* Et xxi. 1,
&c. *deinde vidi cœlum novum et terram novam: primum
enim cœlum et prima terra abierat, et mare non amplius extabat. Et ego Ioannes vidi sanctam illam civitatem Hierusalem*
25 *novam, descendentem a Deo e cœlo, paratam, ut sponsam or-
natam viro suo.*

Finis libri Primi

will make, shall remain before me, saith Jehovah, so shall your seed and your name remain." Acts iii. 21. "whom the heavens must receive until the times of restitution of all things, which God hath spoken by the mouth of all his holy prophets since the world began." Matt. xix. 29. "every one that hath forsaken houses, or brethren, or sisters, or father, or mother, or wife, or children, or lands, for my name's sake, shall receive an hundredfold, and shall inherit everlasting life." xxvi. 29. "I will not drink henceforth of this fruit of the vine, until that day when I drink it new with you in my Father's kingdom." Luke xiv. 15. "one of them that sat at meat with him . . . said unto him, Blessed is he that shall eat bread in the kingdom of God"; nor is he reproved by Christ for this saying. xxii. 30. "that ye may eat and drink at my table in my kingdom." Rom. viii. 19–24. "the earnest expectation of the creature waiteth for the manifestation of the sons of God . . . in hope, because the creature itself also shall be delivered from the bondage of corruption, into the glorious liberty of the children of God." 2 Pet. iii. 13. "we according to his promise look for new heavens and a new earth, wherein dwelleth righteousness." Rev. v. 10. "thou hast made us unto our God kings and priests, and we shall reign on the earth." xxi. 1, &c. "I saw a new heaven and a new earth; for the first heaven and the first earth were passed away; and there was no more sea: and I John saw the holy city, new Jerusalem, coming down from God out of heaven, prepared as a bride adorned for her husband."

COLUMBIA UNIVERSITY PRESS
Columbia University
New York

———

FOREIGN AGENT
OXFORD UNIVERSITY PRESS
Humphrey Milford
Amen House, London, E.C. 4